PLAYING THROUGH

Also by William Wartman

Life Without Father

PLAYING THROUGH

Behind the Scenes on the American PGA Tour

William Wartman

MAINSTREAM
PUBLISHING

First published in the United States of America by William Morrow and Company Inc.

First published in the United Kingdom by
MAINSTREAM PUBLISHING COMPANY (EDINBURGH) LTD.
7 Albany Street, Edinburgh EH1 3UG

British Library Cataloguing in Publication Data
Wartman, William
   Playing through: behind the scenes on the P.G.A. tour.
   I. United States, Professional golf
   I. Title
   796 . 352640973

ISBN 1-85158-381-5

Printed in Great Britain by Collins, Glasgow.

FOR JOE AND OUR GOLF

Acknowledgments

I would like to thank the friends from the golf world, whom I met while I was on the road with the PGA Tour, for sharing their companionship and information. I will not mention these people by name, for they remain behind in a place I have left, but they know who they are, and they made my life more enjoyable and my work less difficult.

A large number of people provided invaluable assistance in gathering the great amount of research materials this book required. They included Gary Hayden, Ullik Rouk, Emanuel Schwager, and the members of my family, Helen Wartman, Anne Mandell, and Helen Marie Durso.

Sheila Weinstein handled my travel arrangements with skill and warmth, and Jeannette Karaska was my splendid and vital link to my life at home while I was on the road. While I was at home, Anthony DeCrosta and Michael Schwager shared my enthusiasm for my work and adventures, and offered important suggestions on my manuscript.

I would also like to thank my editor, Adrian Zackheim, for his always insightful readings of various drafts of the manuscripts, his helpful advice on bringing the project to realization, and for his enthusiastic support of the book. My agent, Alice Fried Martell, was a wonder of professional and moral support throughout the project.

Contents

THE BEST GOLFER IN THE WORLD

PART ONE

Roots

Curtis Strange didn't come to the Masters tournament alone anymore. He might travel to the match each April without family or friends, but, since 1985, he always had company. It was the sound of a fairway wood cracking sharply against a golf ball, followed by the soft plunking of that sphere into the shallows of a creek that passed just short of the 13th green. Before Strange's ball took to the waters of Augusta National Golf Club, he had held a two-stroke lead in the final round of one of golf's premier events. After he made a similar deposit in a pond on the 15th hole thirty minutes later, he was an also-ran. Another one of the PGA Tour's cash cows. Men who could wail the windings out of balls on the practice range, who could pile up money like a farmer stacking hay but who, when it really counted, shattered under the monstrous pressure of a major tournament.

Strange saw more of that water when he stepped to the tee of the par-three 12th hole in April of 1988 with a seven-iron in his hand. A creek snaked in from his left and flowed quietly before a tiny green that looked deceptively distant, while remaining 155 yards from where he stood. Strange ignored the water and the thousands of spectators at his back and the memory of being branded a man who couldn't win the big ones, then lofted his ball toward its fate. The ball crested over the creek, bounced on the green three times, and disappeared into the hole.

It was a historic moment at a tournament where the past is sanctified and the future profaned. Strange had scored the first Masters tournament hole in one in sixteen years, and only the third ever on the treacherous 12th hole. There might be a place for this ball in the Trophy Room, where the members of the host club supped amidst the Chippendales and good rugs.

The multitudes adjoining the hole roared their earnest approval, following the dictates of the tournament's founder, amateur golfing immortal Bobby Jones, whose quoted instructions were printed on their pairings sheets: "It is appropriate for spectators to applaud successful strokes in proportion to difficulty." And so they did, for these were not common fans, these possessors of Masters tournament admission badges, which sold for ninety dollars on the week to the select on the A lists, but brought eight hundred dollars amongst the riffraff on the street. They donned their golf cleats to show they played as well as watched, and their good clothes to demonstrate their worth. Then they clapped appropriately to salute Strange's impeccable execution and their own good sense at having been there to witness the event.

Strange acknowledged the reception as he walked from the tee, grinning rather than smiling. Ever since that watery day in 1985, Strange had needed to show the golfing world his grit. The golf public and the media never forgot a closing-hole crash at the Masters, and it could haunt a golfer for life. Curtis Strange, however, resolved that he was not going to be devastated by that loss, and he wanted everyone to know that was the case. But if a man can't be devastated he can't be elated, and there was no mirth in Strange's step as he arrived at the green.

Strange approached the flag and raised his pant legs by pinching them delicately between his thumbs and forefingers as he bent toward the hole. He fished the ball from the cup with two fingers of his right hand, examined it briefly, glanced silently at his caddie and turned to face the creek. Without further hesitation, Strange reared back and threw that goddamn ball into the middle of the water like it was a rock he had found on his lawn while cutting the grass.

The gallery gasped collectively at the sacrilege. Strange stood to observe the splash, then walked away with the first smile on his lips.

Lee Trevino, having been eliminated from the 1988 Masters field during the Friday cut, was heading for his private locker room at Augusta—the trunk of his car—when he stopped to fume at reporters who were standing near the course. Trevino, who had shot twenty over par during the last two days—barely lining up his shots before whacking the ball on the final holes—was displeased with the ultrafast greens, a condition he believed was created to amuse the spectators at the golfers' expense as they struggled to break par, and with the club itself.

"They've done five hundred dollars worth of renovations on the greens," Trevino accused, "but I'll bet in the books it's seven hundred thousand dollars. A good husband on a weekend could have done it. Naw, they don't make any money here. They damn sure don't give anything to charity."

Trevino was of Mexican heritage and had been raised in the 1940s by his mother, a maid, and his grandfather, a grave digger, in a farmhouse without plumbing or electricity that bordered a country club in Texas. Trevino quit school in the eighth grade and went to work at the country club cutting fairways, while flirting with golf on public courses in his spare time. After a stint in the Marines, Trevino returned home and spent seven years pounding millions of golf balls on a driving range to refine his public-course swing into a game he could make a living with.

Trevino joined the PGA Tour, of which the Masters was not a part, in 1967. Over the next twenty years he won twenty-seven tournaments and over three million dollars. Now, at forty-eight, Trevino was waiting for the day he turned fifty so he could play the Senior PGA Tour, passing his time with the occasional tournament and with lucrative deals as an NBC golf analyst and as a spokesman for various goods.

Trevino was in fat city. He had risen from a shanty to become a respected member of the golf establishment. Yet every time Trevino passed through the restricted gates of Augusta National, he was reminded that if he weren't a professional golfer, he'd be arrested if he tried to set foot in the place.

Trevino's outburst at the 1988 Masters was the latest act in a tragicomedy he had been performing in at Augusta for twenty years. The plantation heritage was still discernible at Augusta, and every time Trevino was one of the select ninety or so players whose past performance earned them coveted spots in the tournament, he was torn with ambivalence. He didn't know whether to graciously accept or rudely decline the invitations when they arrived. Three times he said no, only to later call those decisions the greatest mistakes in his career. He came for years and played dismally, until, in 1986, he brought one of his sons to the tournament as a guest and officials told Trevino it would cost eighty-five dollars for the young man's pass. Trevino ranted that no other tournament charged players' family members, and swore he'd never return. Then Augusta grudgingly allowed the boy a freebie and Trevino relented and came back.

Now Trevino was storming off the course to drive down Augusta's famous Magnolia Lane in a fury, while on his way to milk cows at a dairy he owned in nearby Hephzibah. This was it, Trevino told the reporters. It was over for him and the Masters—sort of.

"I hope to God they don't send me another invitation," he said. "I don't want to be here. I'm going to pray they don't. If they send me one, I'll have to come."

Fuzzy Zoeller is known as the Dean Martin of golf: an affable, humorous man who was thought to enjoy a taste now and then, and who played professional golf because it suited his lifestyle—fast and easy. Zoeller did little to discourage these notions—he brought champagne for all who attended his press conference after he won the 1984 U.S. Open—even if a bad back caused him to spend far more of his evenings in bed than on bar stools. Zoeller genuinely loved the crowds that came to see him, and he was fond of saying that without the galleries he would be playing before squirrels and deer, who didn't pay very well.

When Zoeller would arrive at the mishit ball during a tournament and discover a tree blocking his line to the green, he would drop his ever-present cigarette onto the grass, smirk at the challenge that faced him—one he, but not the spectators, knew was relatively minor—then turn to the gallery gathered at his side. "Christ," he'd say, "whose idea was it to plant a goddamn tree there?"

The fans would laugh and say, "That Fuzzy, he's something, isn't he?" By the time they grew quiet, Zoeller would have blocked them from his mind, grabbed a club from his bag, and curved the ball easily around the tree. Now happy-go-lucky Zoeller, who had shot the day's low round of six-under-par 66, was in the press-room ventilating *his* wrath about course conditions at the 1988 Masters.

"It's like war out there. I'm as competitive as they come, but it's not fun when the greens are as hard and as fast as they are. If you've got a downhill putt, you're just touching the ball and praying to God you can make the ten-footer coming back," Zoeller said, referring to the difficulty of stopping missed putts close to the hole. "If that's golf, I'm in the wrong damn league. Golf is supposed to be fun. This wasn't fun."

Zoeller argued that, since Johnny Miller had shot a record low score of 63 at the 1973 U.S. Open, organizers of the four major tournaments—the Masters, the U.S. Open, the British Open, and the PGA Championship—had moved to prevent scores from reaching that level again by tricking up their courses. The U.S. Open had become infamous for its tall rough, the Masters had replaced the Bermuda grass on its greens with slicker bent grass in 1981, and scores in majors had been rising ever since.

"They're making the greens as hard as marble," Zoeller said, "and whoever gets the lucky bounces wins that week. Why do egos have to get in the way of great golf courses? Somebody's got to speak up or it is going to be a total joke in ten years. A number of the other guys feel the same way but they're afraid of the press, afraid to speak their mind. If I've got to be the guinea pig and speak up, okay, I'll be the guinea pig."

Horn Hardin, the seventy-six-year-old retired lawyer and banker from St. Louis who served as the chairman of the Masters tournament and Augusta National Golf Club, could dismiss the antics of Curtis Strange and Lee Trevino easily enough. They were simply PGA Tour golfers with bad manners and, if the truth be told, he would just as soon not have Trevino back anyway. Hardin had had enough of Trevino's "minority" act. But Fuzzy Zoeller, well, that was a tricky one, for Zoeller had won the Augusta tournament in 1979, and that made him a Masters champion—a station in life that was viewed by members of Augusta National as approaching the value of knighthood to a citizen of the United Kingdom.

Past winners of the Masters were the only players in golfdom who had lifetime invitations to the tournament, who could change in the Champions' Room in the clubhouse, and who could attend the annual Champions' Dinner during Masters week. Even more exclusively, the reigning Masters champion was the only mortal in the world who could wear his Masters green coat—a two-hundred-dollar blazer that had the club emblem stitched on the breast pocket in Ohio—outside the confines of Augusta National Golf Club. Club members were compelled to leave their green coats behind when they left the grounds.

Hardin should have had an inkling that Zoeller was going to be trouble when he won during his rookie year at the tournament. Augusta, as it is set up for the Masters, prides itself on being a thinking golfer's course where every shot requires careful attention to club selection. But when Zoeller earned his green coat he told reporters that, being unfamiliar with the course, he simply asked his local caddie prior to each shot which club he should use and how hard he should swing it, and that approach had been good enough to win.

Nonetheless, Hardin was dismayed when reporters told him of Zoeller's attack on the course. "It's disappointing to hear this from one of our champions. I can't believe that Byron Nelson, Ben Hogan, Sam Snead, or Gene Sarazen," Hardin said, referring to winners from the 1930s, '40s, and '50s, "would have the same reaction that Fuzzy has to our present conditions."

For some time now, Hardin had been lamenting the passing of those simpler days when the boys from the pro tour would enter Augusta National genuflecting to all that was good and pure in golf. The club went to elaborate lengths to cultivate its image as the cathedral of the game. They employed a grounds crew of twenty-eight to keep the fairways plush and the greens—when the pros arrived—lightning fast. The nursery staff of fifteen ensured that the flowers that punctuated the course were always in bloom. They banned tournament commercialism to the extent that the brand names on the soda dispensers in the refreshment stands were covered with tape. And they always included a good number of top amateurs on the invitation list to honor the game's nonprofessional heritage.

By most counts, the formula was still working. The waiting list for tickets was cut off when it reached fifty years. Arnold Palmer still circled the course twice in his private jet, and buzzed the fairways that were as thick and green as the members' wallets, upon his arrival at and departure from Augusta. Television coverage of the tournament was now beamed to twenty-five nations. But Hardin and his colleagues were still deeply concerned about the new boys in the pro game.

Hardin told the press before the start of the 1988 Masters that he was worried that golfers would stop coming to his tournament because of that most vile of topics: money. The 1988 purse at the Masters, although Hardin preferred not to discuss exact figures, was one million dollars, an amount equaled at many tournaments, but exceeded at only a few. Nonetheless, purse inflation was epidemic on the PGA Tour, and Hardin was troubled that his tournament was going to have to perpetually cough up more lucre for the pot.

"I may be alone in this thinking," Hardin said, "but I know the fellows pretty good and the new breed, you're not talking about the Arnold Palmers and the Gene Sarazens. Those fellows would have played even if there wasn't any money. There is a new breed of golfers, and I don't know if they think of the Masters the same way we do."

Hardin allowed his imagination to wander to a mythical time when the Masters was preceded and followed by five-million-dollar tournaments, and envisioned a day when players yawned when they received Masters invitations in the mail. "You have a whole bunch of new fellows coming along, and they are money oriented," complained the chairman of a club whose ten wealthiest members had an estimated combined worth of six billion dollars.

"Maybe I'm in dreamland or something, and I will never say never, but I just don't think the members of this club would want to continue if the only alternative was to get as much out of television as we could, or to sandbag our patrons for every nickel, or to have hospitality houses all over the place."

Hardin's qualified threat that increased purse demands might lead to a discontinuation of the tournament was the same pose—albeit in gentler language—that he had taken recently when a reporter from *Golf* magazine asked how the club might respond to legislative or judicial action against Augusta National's male-only membership policy.

"We feel," Hardin said, "that the State of Georgia, the County of Richmond, and the City of Augusta view the National as an asset, existing for the good of golf and for the enjoyment of its members. If anything happened that would drastically alter our policies, I think there would be a very good chance the club would close up and the Masters would be no more."

If observers found Hardin's responses to these challenges to be reactionary, they were at least in character. Hardin treated his affluent and powerful members in precisely the same way, and they seemed to love it.

One did not apply for membership at Augusta National. One crept, palms coated with perspiration, through a labyrinth of trials of one's acceptability. A nominee for membership could be brought to the club as a guest from mid-October to mid-May, the only time the place was open. If the nominee-guest was found to be a fun guy and a golf guy—and if Hardin's discreet background checks revealed no evidence of indecorous behavior—membership would be tendered—once and only once—at such time during the ensuing years that one of the existing three hundred members had the good manners to vanish. Living a considerable distance from the club improved one's chances for acceptance, since it established that one would not have the poor taste to use the facilities too often.

During a member's anticipated two to three visits a year, he would have to be on best behavior at all times, lest he fail to receive a dues bill in late summer, and thus learn that he had lost his membership. Expulsion-provoking acts included using the club for business purposes, complaining, or failing to be a fun guy. In return for enduring this flagellation and paying a twenty-thousand-dollar initiation fee plus annual dues, members were entitled to play one of the best golf courses in the country, to be served by the staff without having to tip, to have their hair cut in the barber shop for eight dollars, and to refer to Kathryn Murphy, a married woman with three grandchildren who had been club secretary for twenty-seven years, as "Miss Murphy."

Horn Hardin kept to his office, working at the desk President Eisenhower had used when he was a member of the club, while the players were creating their maelstrom on Friday. Fuzzy Zoeller suggested Hardin was hiding, but perhaps he was quietly giving thanks for one modern enterprise that appreciated the need for rules and order, no matter how autocratic: television.

On Saturday and Sunday afternoons, CBS, having paid one million dollars for the right, would broadcast the tournament to one of the largest golf audiences of the year, and they would do it Hardin's way. There would be no mention of prize money, there would be little talk of grievances about the course, and there would be no more than four minutes of commercials per hour, rather than the standard thirteen. There would be, in essence, nothing that Hardin could possibly object to, or there would be no contract for CBS next year.

The air was thick with smoke and noise in Adam's lounge in the Augusta Holiday Inn on Friday evening as a congestion of tourists and natives jockeyed to get to the bar. One local man of middle years, sporting an oversized buckle on the belt that secured his jeans, tired of the jostling and stepped out into the entryway to get some air, and to appraise the young ladies who were arriving in substantial numbers. Men and women were still sorting out their differences in Georgia, and while there was a billboard on a road into Augusta that proclaimed "Real Men Don't Hit Women," there was also a restaurant chain in town called "Wife Saver."

The man at the door knew what he liked in both women and transportation, and when a sleek stretch limousine rolled to a halt before him and a striking young woman emerged from the rear, the man stepped forward to exchange pleasantries.

"I've always wanted to ride in one of those stretch things," the man said, grinning ingratiatingly.

"Well," the woman replied with a smile, "you've already got your hands in your pockets, so why don't you just stretch that little dick of yours instead?"

Masters week in Augusta was a time of such celebrations for the folks at Adam's lounge—an occasion for rejoicing over the annual deliverance of manna that was the Masters—and a time of resentment for others. Few of the town's fifty thousand residents would ever get to attend the tournament, and clerks who were stuffing money into cash registers were inclined to say to patrons whose accents differed from their own, "My, my, isn't it interesting that folks from so far away can get tickets to the Masters, and folks who have lived here their whole lives can't?" before giving them their change.

Many residents avoided the entire affair by renting out their homes for thousands of dollars and then going on vacation with the take. Those who remained made out the best they could. On Thursday, two gentlemen walked into a snack bar at a country club neighboring Augusta National, blew away a TV with a shotgun to capture everyone's attention, then turned their firearms on the waitress and demanded money.

More than thirty million dollars would stream into the normally quiet town during the week, an input equivalent to the arrival of a new business employing one thousand people. Hotels doubled their rates at the minimum, restaurants with waiting lines added premium entrées to their menus and rushed people out without mention of dessert. People who lived near the course turned their yards, driveways, and sidewalks into parking lots, accommodating those who didn't have tournament parking stickers at five dollars a pop.

The name Masters was plastered everywhere—Welcome Masters golfers and fans; Masters happy hour 5–7 P.M.; Master the art of buying for less—except in the southern part of town where black families lived in dilapidated boxlike houses resembling sharecropper shacks. Some of the men from the south of town used to work as caddies at the Masters, but that ended in 1983 when, after years of resistance, the tournament bowed to pressure from the golfers, who wanted to use their regular caddies, and rescinded its rule requiring contestants to use Augusta National caddies during the tournament. The club had opposed the change because, by teasing caddies, who traditionally get 3 to 10 percent of their golfer's winnings, with the possibility of earning a few thousand dollars by carrying the winner's bag during the Masters, they could underpay them the rest of the year.

Should the people in the south of town somehow benefit from the Masters prosperity today, and then wish to rent a room in a more pleasant neighborhood, the *Augusta Chronicle-Herald* classified ads hinted at which vacant rooms they shouldn't consider, noting that some were with "white families," or in "private white homes."

Australian golfer Greg Norman came to the practice field at Augusta National before his final round on Sunday morning and said to his caddie, "God, I feel so loose this morning I'll hit ten or fifteen balls and that will do me." Norman was well back in the field at the Masters, at eleven shots behind the leader, but Norman didn't believe for a moment that he was out of contention. Norman liked to say that he had an almost perverse love of being down, even being defeated, because it spurred him on to greater things.

Norman left the practice field after hitting a few balls and walked over to the putting green, and a huge gallery followed him. The thirty-three-year-old Norman was one of the most popular golfers in the world. Whenever Norman appeared on the course, a crowd would bunch at the ropes, mesmerized, absorbing his bleached-straw blond hair, his strong jaw, his ample shoulders, and his model-slim hips in clingy polyester slacks. Norman saw golfer Ray Floyd, who was also preparing to begin his round, at the putting green and walked over to him. "If someone shoots a sixty-four or sixty-five today," Norman said to Floyd, "he would be in it."

Norman's scores had been improving since his disastrous opening round of five over par on Thursday but, even if he shot a 64 on Sunday, the nine golfers who currently had subpar scores in the tournament would all have to fold in the closing round for Norman to emerge the victor. Having a potential win in a major be contingent upon the collapse of other players was a relatively new position for Norman to be in.

Norman had held the final-round lead in each of the four major tournaments in 1986 but, when the last ball was holed, he surrendered three out of the four matches. Norman lost the Masters by one shot on the 18th hole that year to Jack Nicklaus who, at forty-six and with an abating career, seemed to have risen from the dead. Norman had felt predestined to win that tournament with his Sunday morning lead, and he was badly shaken by the loss. He became obsessed with winning the Masters, thinking about his defeat constantly.

After losing the 1986 U.S. Open two months later, Norman rebounded to take the British Open, only to blow a four-stroke margin in the PGA Championship a month after that. When Norman returned to the Masters—the tournament he wanted to win more than any other in the world—in April of 1987, he lost the match in the second hole of a playoff to Larry Mize, a little-known player whom Norman had previously belittled to the press.

The 1987 Masters loss was the worst jolt Norman had suffered in his life. He went to the pressroom and made jokes about his defeat, but he was devastated. He finished fifty-first, thirty-fifth, and seventieth in the remaining 1987 majors and, coming into the 1988 Masters, he had not won a tournament in the United States since June of 1986.

Norman was currently identified as the best golfer in the world by the Sony World Rankings, a rating system administered by the International Management Group (IMG), a monolithic player management agency headquartered in Cleveland which also runs overseas tournaments, produces sports television programming, markets overseas television rights for tournaments and, overall, rivals the PGA Tour office as the most powerful entity in golf. The Sony rankings consider a player's performance over the last three years, weighted for the perceived competitiveness of the field in various tournaments in which he has played.

A growing number of golf journalists and tour observers were beginning to question Norman's status. Some objected to his Sony rating simply because the IMG both represented Norman and administered the ratings. Others thought overseas tournaments, where Norman had won forty-three times, but which are generally acknowledged to be less competitive than their American counterparts, were considered too heavily in the computations.

IMG distinguished among six different grades of tournaments in the calculations that yielded the Sony rankings. The number of ranking points a golfer earned for a good finish in a tournament was highest for a Grade 1 tournament and lowest for a Grade 6 tournament. The major tournaments were rated Grade 1, with six U.S. tournaments that usually attracted strong fields rated Grade 2. Most regular American tournaments were rated as Grade 3, as were about half of those on the European tour, a fifth of the Japanese tour, and a tenth of the Australian tour. The bulk of the overseas tournaments were rated Grade 4 or below.

Under a bonus system IMG employed, however, when one or more golfers from the top of the Sony rankings participated in a tournament, the value of the tournament was inflated. This means that when top players competed in one of the Grade 4 tournaments that were most prevalent overseas, the value of that tournament would be raised so that it would be worth more Sony points than a Grade 3 tournament.

IMG represented half of the players in the top fifteen of the Sony rankings, and a major source of income for the agency came from placing their top golfers in low-ranked overseas tournaments, where the golfers received appearance fees and, hopefully, sold more tickets to the match. In addition, IMG owned and operated fifteen golf tournaments in Europe, Japan, and Australia as profit-making enterprises.

The upshot of this incestuousness was that every time an IMG golfer like Greg Norman won a Grade 4 tournament, some of which were also run by IMG, it became possible for Norman to earn more IMG-administered Sony points than if he had won a Grade 3 tournament in the States—against a presumably stronger field overall—simply because a highly ranked golfer like Norman elevated the points value of the tournament just by being in it.

There was a self-serving and self-perpetuating quality to the calculations that had kept Norman at the top of the heap since shortly after the ranking system was instituted in 1986. Norman also took a personal hand in maintaining his spot at the top. When golfer Paul Azinger spoke disparagingly of Norman's abilities to reporters, and Azinger's words appeared in print, Norman challenged Azinger to a fight.

Norman was as macho an Australian as ever carried a kangaroo-skin golf bag. At the 1986 U.S. Open, a gallery heckler had called Norman a choker—the most grievous invective that can be hurled at a golfer because the prospect for self-immolation is native to the game—and Norman stormed the ropes and informed the taunter he could meet him after the match if he wanted to say that, but until then he should shut his mouth.

The most damning evidence against Norman was his paucity of victories on the highly competitive American circuit. Although he had played well and earned almost two million dollars in the States in five years, Norman had won only four times. And in sudden death playoffs, where the match effectively rides on every shot, his record was one win versus four losses. None of this fazed the people who paid the charismatic Norman over five million dollars a year for product endorsements and personal appearances, nor did it deter legions of fans from flocking to golf courses to be in his presence.

Norman proved true to his word on Sunday at the Masters, picking up six strokes on par on the front nine and two on the back to finish at 64 for the day and two strokes off the lead. But twenty golfers who had started the day with better scores than Norman were still on the course, and he could only wait to have them determine the finale.

It was an ironic plight for a man whose favorite word was "aggressive," but Norman's appearance at the top of the leaderboard going into the final round had become rarer since his crashes of 1986. It was as if he had adopted a perhaps unconscious strategy of positioning himself in the middle of the field at the beginning of a tournament, only to come charging into contention in the final moments. Sunday morning's leader was subjected to a four-hour endurance test as he walked from shot to shot with the onus of preserving his margin always weighing upon him. Those long afternoons in the sun gave a man abundant opportunity to concoct new ways to sabotage his swing and, if he faltered, the television lights at his postround press conferences would seem to make his throat more constricted than it had felt on the course.

Conversely, golfers who started slowly but dove for the finish line were spoken of positively. They were thought to be the personification of determination—never-say-die types who might be on the verge of a comeback. Norman had won a lot of points with the press with his genial public behavior in the aftermath of his 1986 losses in the majors, but a golfer could only give a limited number of those performances before the media people stopped praising him for his sportsmanship and began questioning his mettle.

Norman was buoyant and proud when he left the course on Sunday, telling reporters, "I think everyone should have learned something today—don't give up," and insisting that it was only a minor flaw in his putting stroke, which he had corrected after his Saturday round, that had accounted for his high scores earlier in the week. Norman remained in theoretical contention for an hour, until a golfer completed the tournament with a lower score, and Norman dropped into what would eventually be a tie for fifth place in the final standings.

When Scottish golfer Sandy Lyle woke up at two A.M. on Sunday, he had a two-shot lead going into the final round of the Masters and a stuffed-up head from a cold. It was twelve hours until his tee time, so he couldn't do anything about winning the tournament, but he had to clear his sinuses if he was going to be properly rested to accomplish that task later in the day. Lyle nudged his girlfriend, Jolande Huurman, and asked if she wouldn't tickle his feet.

The thirty-year-old Lyle had been traveling with Huurman, a sports masseuse and physiotherapist, in the months since his wife had left him and taken the children. Lyle, like Huurman, was just over six feet, but Huurman's larger bone structure made her appear the more powerful of the two, and Lyle found that her touch had been most beneficial in keeping his head clear and his body relaxed. Lyle had been highly successful on the European PGA Tour in the early 1980s, but had achieved little in America until he won once in 1986 and 1987. Now, with the 1988 season only four months old, he had already won two U.S. tournaments and $408,000.

A Scotsman had never won the Masters, and a pre-Masters poll of 172 sportswriters by a golf magazine had not produced a single call for Lyle to finish among the top three in the tournament. But Lyle was a talented player who was on a roll, something that occasionally happens with golfers when their concentration is keen and their swing is easy and the putts always seem to break their way. Streaks forsake golfers as spontaneously as they arrive, but Lyle could rest easily after Huurman had rubbed his feet to clear his nasal passages, for he had the added advantage of being an overseas visitor to the States, and foreign golfers were coming to be known as the best golfers in the world.

The waters of Augusta National got Lyle on Sunday afternoon when he arrived at the 12th hole, the same hole Curtis Strange had scored an ace on two days earlier. Lyle hit his tee shot short of the green, and the ball rolled through a bunker, down a bank and into the creek. Lyle's two-shot lead in the tournament vanished when he walked off the 12th green having carded a five on the par-three hole.

Lyle's somewhat shy and soft-spoken manner, and his subdued behavior on the course, had earned him a reputation for being even tempered, but Lyle was badly shaken by the events of the 12th hole. Lyle missed a chip for an eagle on the 15th hole that would have restored his lead, and he yanked off his visor and flung it to the ground in disgust. Lyle regained a tie for the lead with a birdie on the 16th, and when he came to the 18th, a long, uphill par-four with huge bunkers guarding the left perimeter of the fairway at the midpoint, he needed a birdie to win the tournament, after having been in or near the lead since the first round.

Lyle put his tee shot into a bunker 143 yards from the pin, and he thought he was done for. He stood over the ball in the glaring white sand for a long time, stopping twice to steady his nerves, then picked his ball clean from the sand with a brilliant shot that left his ball thirty yards above the flag, until gravity and the absence of grass Fuzzy Zoeller had screamed about caused the ball to roll twenty feet toward the hole. Lyle dropped the ball from there in one stroke, and he was the new Masters champion. Lyle acknowledged the tremendous applause from the people packed around the green, and went off to the televised awards ceremony, where he would receive his green coat and be interviewed and accepted into Augusta National as an honorary member by Horn Hardin.

Although Lyle was the man who had battled off his competitors to win the match, tournament chairman Horn Hardin had had the tougher day. Lyle had been absorbed by his chores on the course, while Hardin had to sit in his office and fret over how badly he would bungle this year's TV interview with the winner.

Hardin was a lawyer by training, someone who never asked a question before a courtroom audience without having first studied reams of background material, having talked informally with some of the people involved, and having written the query out in longhand on a legal pad so his secretary could type it up. He lived his professional life by the lawyer's dictate of never asking a question he didn't know the answer to beforehand. Then, once a year, he had to go on national television before an audience of millions and have a spontaneous conversation with a professional athlete who, although no doubt quite a fine fellow in his own right, was nothing at all like the carefully homogenized members of Augusta National. Why, most of these golfers had not even graduated from college, let alone attended an acceptable one. What did one say to such people? The anxiety was enough to lock up Hardin's sphincter for a week!

Hardin fumbled through his introductory chitchat with CBS's Brent Musburger without snafu, then Musburger smiled one of his best television smiles and congratulated Hardin on having conducted another successful tournament.

Musburger paused for a second to allow Hardin to mumble "Thank you, the members are very proud . . ." But that's not what Hardin said. After CBS had painstakingly downplayed the players' complaints about the g-r-e-e-n-s all weekend, Hardin blurted out in a wounded little boy's voice: "Sometimes we make the course too hard, and sometimes we make it too easy. One of these days we'll get it right."

Musburger forced a nervous laughlike sound from his mouth, and hurried Hardin on to his chat with Lyle. Hardin attempted to speak to his new Masters champion—and then stopped. Hardin couldn't remember the name of the only man in the world who got to wear his green coat outside the gates of Augusta National. Then it came to Hardin and they chatted and soon the red light went off on the camera and everyone could relax.

Lyle left to talk to the rest of the media. When he was finished with them, he would join Hardin and seventy members of Augusta National for dinner and convivial conversation, although one can only wonder what the wives of Augusta National found to say to Lyle's foot-rubbing girlfriend, Jolande.

On Monday morning Lyle would travel the 125 miles to Hilton Head, South Carolina, and the next stop on the PGA Tour. The tour had been conducting weekly matches since January, as they did each year, but the real core of the season began with the Masters, and Lyle was coming into it with three victories and $591,821 to his credit. He would be deluged with lucrative endorsement and personal appearance opportunities as a result of adding the Masters title to his 1985 British Open win, and pleasant, unexpected things would come his way. One of them would be a story in Tuesday's *New York Times* by golf writer Gordon White.

"With the [Masters] victory, Lyle suddenly stood alone as the premier golfer in the world," it would read. "Seve Ballesteros of Spain and Greg Norman of Australia may still have their champions, but, at this moment, Alexander Walter Barr Lyle, a 30-year-old who was born in England of Scottish parents and now lives in England, is simply the best there is. . . . No American golfer is at the same level."

The remainder of the season seemed limitless for Lyle, as long as he didn't have a sudden desire, as an honorary member, to drop by Augusta National with a few friends and play a round of golf. That could lead to a most embarrassing moment, for although Lyle might be able to wear his green coat anywhere he wanted, Masters champion or no Masters champion, he wouldn't be permitted on the course again until next April unless he came as a guest of a real member. Only real members of Augusta National, ones Horn Hardin understood how to talk to, could play the course at times other than tournament week, and Sandy Lyle would never be one of them.

THE BEST GOLFER IN THE WORLD

PART TWO

Business as Usual

HILTON HEAD, SOUTH CAROLINA.
The early months of the 1988 tour had not gone well for young
Davis Love III. After two top-twenty finishes in January tournaments, he came into the final round of the Phoenix Open at the end
of the month with a two-shot lead that he quickly transformed
into a four-shot deficit, and his game disintegrated in the weeks
that followed. Love started missing Friday cuts, where half the
golfers in the field are dismissed without earnings, and at a Florida
tournament in March he stood on the 7th tee and hit four consecutive balls into a pond before he got one into play.

Love took a week off at the end of March to practice and
prepare for the Masters—to the considerable consternation of the
people in his native North Carolina who were staging the one-
million-dollar Kmart Greensboro Open that week—only to miss
the cut at Augusta. Now he was back on the regular PGA Tour, at
the MCI Heritage Classic, site of his sole tournament victory.

Monday through Wednesday are supposed to be practice days
for the tournaments that run from Thursday to Sunday on the
tour, but they are usually extracurricular activities days for golfers.
Sometimes they fly off to play in corporate outings or small local
tournaments for guarantees that range from $1,500 a day for a
rookie to $50,000 a day for an Arnold Palmer or Greg Norman,
plus expenses. Other times they participate in events at the location where the week's tournament will commence on Thursday.

At the Heritage in Hilton Head, Love and the other golfers
who were invited to do so had a wealth of corporate-sponsored
enterprises to select from. There were pro-ams on Monday—the

Gulfstream Aerospace Harbour Town Cup Pro-Am—and on Wednesday—the MCI Heritage Classic Pro-Am—in which amateur golfers who had paid entry fees of up to $2,250, or who were favored clients of corporate sponsors of the tournament, got to play a round of golf in a fivesome with one pro and three other amateurs. Tuesday was reserved for the MCI Pro-Celebrity Long Distance Competition, and the Merrill Lynch Shoot-Out.

It was unseasonably cold mid-April Tuesday when Love, nine other pros, and six celebrity golfers gathered at the first tee shortly after noon for the long distance competition. It was raining steadily, as it had been since late morning, and the people in the gallery huddled under expansive, brightly colored golf umbrellas and pulled their spring coats taut against their necks to ward off the chill as they waited for the contest to begin. The spectators at the pretournament event were affluent-looking senior citizens who had retired to one of the planned communities that housed the twenty thousand permanent residents of the barrier island in South Carolina's lowlands.

An effervescent, velvet-voiced announcer who had been retained by MCI explained that each of the pros would blast two drives down the rain-soaked fairways, the distances would be measured, and MCI would distribute $10,000 in prize money among the pros, ranging from $3,500 for the longest drive to $200 for the shortest.

Big, booming tee shots, Davis Love's specialty, are the sexiest part of the game of golf. They are the only time raw power is displayed in a sport that is otherwise dominated by finesse, and the crowds respond to smashed drives accordingly. Galleries cheer shots from the fairway that land near the flag, and applaud long putts that find the cup, but they shout and whoop at arching three-hundred-yard drives the way football fans respond to the sacking of an opponent's quarterback.

The crowd's reaction at Hilton Head was subdued, however, for the rain and soggy turf scrubbed fifty yards off the distance the pros normally drive the ball, and the winning distance for the pros was only 257 yards—a length within the range of many amateurs. When the six celebrities stepped to the tee, they were not Bob Hope and Dinah Shore, but a former tennis champion, a football player, three reporters from local TV stations, and an editor from a local newspaper. The amateurs hit drives that averaged two hundred yards, and the winner was the tennis player, with a Channel 3 reporter in second, and a Channel 11 reporter edging out a Channel 11 anchor for third.

As Love and the other washed-out golfers crowded into an open-sided tent to avoid the rain, the camera operators for the local TV stations focused their plastic-shrouded Minicams on the Southeast regional president of MCI as he awarded an oversized first-place check for $3,500 to pro Bill Sanders, which was more money for hitting two drives than Sanders had won during his entire first year on the tour in 1978, and trophies to the amateurs. "Well," the MCI man said, shaking hands with the television reporters, "given who the celebrity winners are, there's sure to be coverage of the competition on the news this evening."

The Merrill Lynch Shoot-Out followed the driving contest and, as defending tournament champion, Love was expected to participate in that match as well. The Shoot-Out involved ten players competing over nine holes. One player was eliminated each hole—Love lasted for four—until Bernhard Langer, a German golfer who won $366,430 in the fifteen tournaments he played in the United States during 1987, emerged victorious. As Langer walked off the sopping course to collect *his* oversized $3,000 check, two workmen who had been sitting idly on the sidelines sprang into action. They hustled over to the area where the TV camera operators stood waiting for the award ceremony. As Langer and a Merrill Lynch official faced the cameras six feet apart, the workmen sprinted behind the two figures, dropped to their knees, and quickly filled the distance between the men with a banner that read "Merrill Lynch Shoot-Out" at chest height, just as the cameras began recording.

As spectators walked over to the harbor bordering the course for the opening ceremony of the tournament, they saw the MCI logo everywhere: on three large orange and white signs on the corporate hospitality tent, on the flags on the greens, on the overblouses caddies wore, and on the windbreakers that corporate employees sported. Everywhere, in fact, except for those spaces occupied by the Nabisco scoreboards, although the electronic board did flash the MCI logo periodically.

Tournament officials weren't troubled by the rampant commercialism. Far from it. They had brought the governor of the state in to thank the communications company for the support in person. As alligators swam through the ponds of the vacation and retirement community that had been carved out of swamp, marsh, and subtropical forests, the governor joined a parade of bagpipes and men in Scottish garb, then climbed to the lectern at the harbor and offered his hosannas to MCI, the company that had made South Carolinia, where tourism is the second-largest employer, safe for the PGA tour.

In 1986 Hilton Head almost lost the tournament that had been staged there since 1969. Hilton Head Holdings Corporation, the third company to have control of the financially troubled Sea Pines resort and the tournament in three years, was forced into involuntary bankruptcy in November of 1986. Although the 1987 match was already scheduled, Deane Beman, commissioner of the PGA Tour and a man who always played hardball, informed Hilton Holdings he would not allow a bankrupt corporation to present a tournament.

Local officials scrambled to form a freestanding nonprofit organization, Hilton Classic Corporation, to conduct the tournament, negotiated with MCI to become the title sponsor, arranged TV coverage with CBS, and then, having done all the ground work to conduct a tournament—as all local organizers are required to do if they wanted a PGA Tour event—they went to Beman and told him they were ready to go.

While Hilton Classic Corporation was hustling, however, Avron Fogelman, part owner of the Kansas City Royals, was entertaining thoughts of buying Sea Pines resort, and the developer decided he would like to have a tournament of his own. Fogelman had been speaking with Beman privately, and he told the commissioner he would swell the purse and improve the course if he were awarded the Heritage. Fogelman subsequently backed out of the deal, but when Hilton Classic Corporation officials went to Beman, Beman recognized that, as was customary, he had the upper hand. Sure, Beman told the people from Hilton Classic, they could keep the tournament people from Hilton Head had been conducting for seventeen years, but they would now have to match the terms that Fogelman had offered speculatively.

Hilton Classic had no choice but to scramble to meet Beman's demands. The bulk of the two million dollars they needed—the tournament was an inexpensive one to conduct by PGA Tour standards—came from title sponsor MCI ($450,000), secondary sponsors ($220,000), television ($280,000), pro-am entry fees ($270,000), and ticket sales ($600,000). The nonprofit estimated it would contribute $200,000, or 10 percent of operating revenues, to Children's Hospital, its designated charity.

Expenses would consume 90 percent of revenues, and the tournament would require tens of thousands of volunteer hours to stage, but no one in Hilton Head complained about expending all that effort in order to make a relatively small charitable contribution. The panache a PGA Tour event bestowed on a resort location—and particularly one with financial difficulty—would sell a lot of building plots, condominiums, and time-shares, and both Hilton Classic and Deane Beman knew that if Hilton Classic didn't meet Beman's demands, someone else would.

Beman's filing cabinets were bloated with letters and proposals from people begging for a tour slot and, since the PGA Tour was actually a trade association owned by the golfers themselves, Beman was the only man who could deliver a sanctioned event. Beman was in some ways a union boss. Without his okay, his boys didn't report to the job site.

It was late in the afternoon at the 1988 Heritage when the pretournament activities at the course drew to a close, and Davis Love was tired and discouraged. When he came out on the tour he thought it was to play golf. Then, suddenly, he had to keep sponsors happy, worry about making all of this money and wonder what he was going to do with it. He couldn't even think in terms of the size of the purses they were playing for each week, much less the several hundred thousand dollars a year he was earning at twenty-three. His dad was his financial advisor and coach, so he had help, but he still wondered if this was what he left college for.

Love had already participated in one pro-am, the long distance contest, and the shoot-out that week. Tomorrow there was to be another pro-am. He knew this was expected of the defending champion—he had, after all, won $117,000 here last year—but he wondered when he was going to be able to practice and get his game back. The money was nice, but he wanted to win again.

Love had one more official duty for the day. He had to drive a golf ball into Calibogue Sound, adjacent to the 18th green, as a nine-pound cannon was fired, signifying the beginning of the Heritage. Old-timers at the tournament watched the man who would ignite the cannon carefully, for during the opening of the first tournament in 1969 the cannon had gone off in the middle of Jack Nicklaus's backswing, causing Nicklaus to leap right off the ground and then miss the damn golf ball entirely when he swung at it.

But Love put the ball into the sound, the local TV folks got their video, and the governor shook a lot of hands. Love could go back to his room with his pregnant wife and compel himself to think positive thoughts about his game on the eve of his twenty-fourth birthday. Love would not be attending the Davis Love Look-Alike contest being held at the White Parrot Lounge at the Hilton Head Holiday Inn that evening.

CBS Sports, which would be broadcasting the tournament on Saturday and Sunday, was headquartered at the Holiday Inn for the week, and the hotel bar had planned a party for the crew. The affair featured a jiggly, sweaty exhibition by the Spandex-clad ladies from the Reebok Workout Team, and the Love contest. The caddie of golfer John Mahaffey, who resembled Love only in that he was tall and had blond hair, narrowly won the competition over the second-place finisher, who was strongly promoted for the award by the emcee.

The runner-up was a short, brunette nurse whose shapely breasts had been threatening to escape into the room from the low-cut sides of her sleeveless black top all evening. "Don't you think," the emcee had argued, pulling back his arms and thrusting his chest into the spotlight of the crowded bar, "that if Davis Love had been a girl and he spent all the time swinging golf clubs, his chest would look like that?"

Greg Norman was pounding balls on the driving range at one o'clock on Friday, loosening up for his early afternoon second round of the Hilton Head tournament. There were two sacks of gleaming white balls at his feet—part of the five hundred dozen new balls tournaments provide for golfers to pummel on the practice range before and after each round. Norman would fish a ball from the pile with a nine-iron, carefully position it, in keeping with practice-range etiquette, on the grass edge of the large spot of earth his divots were exposing, crack the ball at one of the faux flags that dotted the range, then, freezing at the top of his follow-through, squint into the sun to follow the flight of the ball. He, like most pros on the tour, would repeat this act as many as three hundred times each day. He'd start with his wedges, then work up to the woods, all the while moving a storm of balls closer to the fence that defined the far edge of the range.

What distinguished Norman from the other golfers on the practice field was the mob of people who materialized behind him the moment his spikes pierced the surface of the range. Passersby would see the commotion, spot Norman, and call out to their friends, "Hey, the Shark is hitting balls, come on." The gallery would study Norman and pass remarks quietly among themselves. The women would roll their eyes and, depending on their age, say either, "He's gorgeous," or, "What a nice-looking fellow." If they wanted to rile their husbands, they'd add, "If I were a single woman, boy, could I keep him up at night."

The husbands would snap back, "Well, you're not single," and tighten their jaws. After the husbands watched Norman sail more balls through the air, they'd shake their heads in amazement and turn to their buddies. "Look how far that son of a bitch hits a golf ball," they'd say. Few of them would notice that there wasn't a golfer on the range who couldn't do amazing things with a golf ball, or that there would be several other golfers on the range who could routinely send a ball as far, or farther, than the Shark.

Tournament officials brought a young boy behind the ropes and introduced him to Norman as he hit balls. The boy had a cute, freckle-faced, midwestern look, and appeared to be nine or ten. Norman chatted and joked with the boy and, on their way to the first tee, sprayed the lad's bare arms with insecticide the tournament provided in defense against the no-see-ums—nearly invisible, but bitey, gnats that surfaced and disappeared according to vagaries in the weather. The boy walked along the gallery ropes with Lawrence Levy, an English photographer who is a close friend of Norman's, as the Shark made his way down the first hole.

Norman's traveling gallery had quadrupled by the second hole, where his tee shot sliced off the fairway and came to rest with a row of seventy-foot trees blocking the line to the green. Course marshals hustled over to protect the ball, while a circle of people ten deep strained to glimpse it. Norman was known for his aggressive play and, after quickly surveying his lie, he didn't disappoint his fans. Rather than bumping his ball back into the fairway, he yanked a lofted club decisively from his bag and went for the top of the trees. As soon as the trajectory showed the ball was going to clear the uppermost limb, the crowd became ecstatic. They were still cheering while observers closer to the green began moaning as the projectile fell from the sky and plopped into a sand trap.

Norman had played unusually well—for a first round—on Thursday, shooting six under par to share the lead with two other golfers. Norman continued playing well on Friday, scoring the occasional birdie while avoiding bogeys, when, after his second shot on the 13th hole, he abruptly ducked under the gallery rope and walked from the fairway. Spectators heading to the 13th green were startled to see Norman outside the ropes. They halted to follow him with their eyes, then laughed when they saw his destination was a courseside men's room.

Two men in their early twenties who had been touring the course with the accompaniment of a large cooler of beer were at the head of the line inside the latrine when they heard the clomp, clomp, clomp of golf cleats on the concrete walkway outside. They turned to challenge whoever was trying to jump into the queue and were confronted by Norman.

"Hi, guys," Norman called out, "mind if I get ahead of you?"

The point man, who was wearing a sleeveless T-shirt, ratty cut-off jeans, and high-top sneakers without socks, staggered backward from the impact of the beer and his vision. "You can't just walk off the course and come in here, can you?" he asked incredulously.

"Hey," Norman called out over his shoulder from the urinal, "a guy has to piss sometime, doesn't he?"

"You see that shit," the first man said to the second as they relieved themselves after Norman had returned to the course. "I told you we shouldn't go to work today. Wait till those guys hear that we watched Greg Norman drain his lizard."

The men paused outside the rest room to pop the tabs on some fresh brews, and to survey the passing scene. With their long hair, thick southern accents and shabby clothes, they were anomalies on a course where it costs ten dollars for breakfast and a hundred dollars for a round of golf. They watched as striking yet prim southern women with precisely fixed hair and delicate jewelry passed by, their perfume hanging in the air, their men ever attentive—holding their hands or waists, directing them with a careful touch to the shoulder. After the point man had stared after one carefully fixed woman too long, he grabbed the beer cooler and headed down the course. "Let's go," he called back to his buddy. "When that stuff starts looking good I know I'm drunk."

Norman came off the 18th hole two under for the day and eight under for the tournament, and there were a multitude of contingents waiting for him. Immediately outside the scorer's tent was a flock of television and radio reporters who needed some quick quotes for their reports, at the end of a roped-off walkway was a tournament volunteer in a golf cart who would ferry Nor-

man to the press tent for a more in-depth group interview with
other reporters, and just outside the ropes was a cluster of fans
who wanted Norman's autograph on anything they could find.

Overlooking the scene was a collection of young men who, by
virtue of employment or connections, had gained access to a plat-
form at the top of the sponsors' grandstand, where an open bar
dispensed libations and waitresses circulated with trays of hors
d'oeuvres.

Norman, who always had time to speak with reporters, was
detained longer than normal by the electronic media. He was as
big an attraction for the reporters as he was for the fans, and his
being one shot off the lead only intensified that appeal. The assembly of autograph hounds built as Norman's interviews dragged
out, and the woman driving the cart nervously inched closer to her
quarry until, by the time Norman was free, he only had to walk a
few feet and fall into the seat beside her.

The guys in the grandstands had been growing rowdy with
drink, tossing cans of beers to the lesser lights who had to observe
the activities from the ground and calling out noisy greetings to the
golfers as they left the course. When they saw Norman was about
to be whisked away, one of the men called out over the din of the
crowd, "Greg, why do you have time to talk to the reporters and
you don't have time for the kids? Come on, you horse's ass, sign
a couple of autographs."

In another time Norman would have jumped from the cart and
demanded the man come down from the stands so he could bloody
his face. But this day Norman signaled his driver to halt the cart,
while he affixed his name to some of the programs and hats that
were thrust his way.

Norman later appeared in the interview room of the press tent
with the young boy he had been introduced to on the driving
range. The boy stood in the back of the small area as Norman took
a seat on the stage, next to the tour's public relations director, Sid
Wilson. Postround interviews of leaders were a fixture on the tour.
Players would be brought in to recount their rounds, specifying the
holes they had birdies and bogeys on, how far they had been from
the hole on various shots and what clubs they had used, and to
answer general questions that came from the floor.

Norman went over his round quickly, then Wilson asked for
questions from the reporters. As there had been nothing especially
notable about Norman's play, and as Norman had been in the

pressroom the previous day, the questions were dull, the pauses in between long.

"Is that all?" Wilson asked when silence settled over the room. Reporters answered this question by not answering it, and Norman bounded from the room, headed for the practice range, with the young boy following close behind. Norman was stopped outside the press room by a squad of reporters who had missed the conference, and he halted to talk some more, as the boy stood four steps back with his hands buried deeply in his pockets.

Norman then went to the raised putting green in front of the clubhouse to putt some balls, where he was accosted by photographers. Word had begun to filter through the media room that the boy who appeared to be so young was actually a seriously ill seventeen-year-old named Jamie Hutton. Jamie had come to the tournament with his mother, and he was said to be from a one-parent family. Jamie's visit with Norman had been arranged by an organization that grants wishes for gravely sick children, and the photographers wanted pictures of Norman and Jamie for their papers, which had sensed a story.

Norman posed with his arm around Jamie's shoulder, then, as the day continued to grow older, he hurried to the driving range with Jamie running to keep up. Norman hit balls as another crowd watched, then he stopped to holler a greeting to Bernhard Langer as Langer left the range with wife and young daughter. "Jackie," Norman called to the two-year-old with a sly grin, as spectators hung on every word, "ask your mother and father when you're going to get a little brother to play with."

As the crowd laughed and the Langers headed out for dinner, Davis Love III was in the clubhouse emptying his locker. He had missed another cut.

Golfers call Saturday moving day. It's when they try to break out of the pack of seventy-some players who survive the cut, and advance to the upper reaches of the leaderboard. They are looking for an edge they can maintain until the time the tournament really begins—during the final nine holes on Sunday. Fred Couples had just such an edge going for him at Hilton Head. He came into Saturday tied for the lead at nine under with David Frost, his playing partner for the day. Couples quickly pulled away from Frost, birdieing half of the first eight holes, and bringing a four-shot lead over him to the 17th tee.

Couples was trying to alter his image, and he was badly in need of the positive exposure a winning performance would bring. He was widely regarded as a classic American golf-tour bum—a highly talented but unmotivated golfer, one who disdained the rigors of the practice tee while affecting stylish clothing and a distracted demeanor on the course. The twenty-eight-year-old Couples had won only three times in seven years, but he managed to live comfortably on the $1.5 million plus he had earned while not breaking a sweat.

Couples's image problems had intensified when he was singled out the previous August by Jack Nicklaus, the most unanimously respected golfer in the world, as a model of everything wrong with the PGA Tour. Reporters had asked Nicklaus why American golfers no longer dominated the sport, and Nicklaus had replied that the PGA Tour had become so fat and comfortable—ninety-seven players having won over $100,000 during 1987, many without coming close to winning a tournament—that young Americans had lost the desire and ability to win. Nicklaus cited Couples to the reporters as the premier example of sloth on the homefront, but it was golf commissioner Deane Beman whom Nicklaus thought was responsible for the apathy having infected Couples and the other young golfers on the tour in the first place.

When Beman and Nicklaus—a golf prodigy—were adversaries on the amateur golf circuit in the late 1950s, Nicklaus thought Beman was a wonderful little golfer. Nicklaus, at five feet eleven inches and well over two hundred pounds at the time—his Ohio State University chums called him Blob-O—was substantially larger than the diminutive Beman. But physical differences weren't the essence of Nicklaus's characterization of the man, whom Nicklaus considered to be his friend. What Nicklaus meant was that Beman managed to wring every ounce of performance possible out of a finite amount of talent, and Nicklaus admired that the way Norman Mailer might regard the work of a good science fiction writer. It was a way for Nicklaus to say that Beman was a notable golfer, but of course he's no Jack Nicklaus, without using those words.

Nicklaus and Beman met for the final time as amateur opponents at the 1961 U.S. Amateur championship at Pebble Beach, California. Each of the young men—Beman was twenty-three to Nicklaus's twenty-one—had already won the title once, and both were ferocious competitors. But Beman took time during a practice round before that match to show Nicklaus a new strategy he had added to the repertoire that had allowed him to tweak an ungainly swing into a game that won championships. Beman told Nicklaus he had begun walking fairways before a match to measure the exact distances from landmarks on each hole to the center of the green. Beman then compiled yardage charts, which he consulted before choosing the club he would use for each shot.

The ideas was to remove the guesswork from club selection and make it a science; to standardize what had previously been a subjective and intuitive process. Nicklaus adopted the Beman approach so readily that he won the tournament that week, and he took the method with him when he joined the professional tour at the beginning of the next year. Within a few years, every pro in the game was walking off yardage, until a caddie made a cottage industry out of measuring fairways and publishing annotated diagrams of each hole at tournament courses.

While Nicklaus went off to the tour, Beman remained behind as an insurance salesman who played golf. Beman won the 1963 U.S. Amateur, and eventually turned pro in 1967 at the relatively advanced age of twenty-nine. Beman won four tournaments during six years on the tour, before retiring to become commissioner. When Beman assumed his new job, he was every bit as methodical as he had been as a golfer, and as security-minded as he had been as an insurance broker.

Beman came to the tour office with a different perspective from the golf pros of the fifties and before. They had lived to play golf, regardless of how much they earned, while allowing the other responsibilities of their lives to fall into place as they might. Beman entered professional golf with the beginnings of a family that would grow to include five children, after having spent years convincing people of the need to be prepared for the unexpected. The roustabout golfers of the early days of the tour couldn't get their cars headed toward Route 66 quickly enough when the winter tournaments in the Sunbelt approached. But if one of them had informed Deane Beman he was about to depart on such an adventure, Beman would have advised him to first increase his auto coverage, and supplement his whole-life policy because golf courses were dangerous places to be during electrical storms.

When Beman was appointed commissioner in 1974, the top sixty money winners on the tour each year were granted what is known as exempt status for the following year. The sixty exempt players could enter whatever PGA Tour events they chose, while anyone else who wished to enter a tournament was required to survive a Monday qualifying tournament for that match. The non-exempt players were called rabbits—men of thin finances who hopped around the country generating expenses while trying to survive a Monday qualifying tournament and, if they made that, the Friday cut, before they earned a cent.

In 1983, Deane Beman and his policy board, out of concern for the financial precariousness of the golfer's lot, increased the number of exempt players to 125, and created the all-exempt tour. The vast majority of players in any tournament were now exempt players and, with Beman managing to persuade tournament sponsors to constantly increase tour purses, everybody in the top 125 was making, at the minimum, a decent living, and many were wealthier than they had ever dreamed possible.

To Jack Nicklaus, the all-exempt tour was the death of competition and, as a man who lived for athletic combat, it troubled him greatly. He believed the all-exempt tour allowed golfers to go on extended vacations once they had earned enough money to guarantee their exempt status for the following year. Most troubling of all to him, however, was his perception that, since so many American golfers no longer had to win tournaments in order to eat, they had lost the ability to dominate on the course, while their hungry European and Australian counterparts came over and took many of the most important matches.

Fred Couples had refused to comment on Nicklaus's remarks after Nicklaus made them in 1987, and the issue began to fade. Then, as if to confirm Nicklaus's words, Couples came to the final hole of the Phoenix Open in January of 1988 needing only a par to defeat Scotsman Sandy Lyle. Couples hooked his tee shot over the fairway and across a pond on the par-four hole, where the errant ball bounced off spectators and into the water. Couples bogeyed the hole, forcing himself into a sudden death playoff with Lyle. Lyle and Couples each scored par on the first two holes before coming to the 18th, the third hold of the playoff. Lyle bogeyed the 18th, but Couples managed to hit into the water without the gallery's help this time, double-bogeying the hole and losing the match, and the heat was back on Couples.

Now the CBS cameras were focused tightly on the boyishly handsome Couples as he stepped to the 17th tee at the Heritage on Saturday afternoon. Tee times and pairings were somewhat random on Thursday and Friday, but they were carefully scheduled on the weekend in reverse order of the previous day's standings so the leaders would be playing the back nine while the telecast was on the air. Couples was about to suffer the consequences of being an early-round leader.

The CBS announcers grew quiet as his tee shot on the 169-yard par-three sailed past the green and came to rest in a bunker. The silence was short-lived, however, for Couples's shot out of the sand was too strong and, although it stopped four feet past the pin, it was not at all to the liking of CBS's properly acerbic English announcer, Ben Wright, who compared Couples's diligence in making the shot to what would be expected in a pocket-change bet between friends. "He played that chip," squawked Wright, "with all the nonchalance of a one-dollar Nassau [wager]."

Couples eyed his third shot for par, addressed the ball and left it a foot short of the hole. He had a tap-in left for bogey to surrender one shot of his lead to Frost. Couples hit his final shot of the hole quickly, with the sedateness that was his trademark, and the ball skirted the perimeter of the cup without falling. He would shoot a double-bogey five on the hole. CBS's Wright was beside himself with indignation. "That's plum madness, Freddie," Wright exclaimed, as Couples walked impassively off the green, his role as flak catcher secure.

Greg Norman had told reporters at the Masters tournament that he felt the time was coming when he would kick the door in on the U.S. tour. One week later, it looked as if his prophecy was beginning to unfold. Norman came into Sunday at the Heritage four shots off the lead. By the 15th hole, he held a one-stroke advantage over the rest of the field.

Norman was in classic "let it rip, mate" form, walloping balls off the tees and charging down the fairways like a man who had already won. The spectators loved it, and as the afternoon progressed they were stampeding from one hole to the next to position themselves for an unimpeded view of his unfolding attack on the course. "Go, Shark," people yelled as they waved Australian flags from the yards of courseside houses. It was theater-in-the-oblong on every hole and Norman, with the sun as his klieg light, was the star.

The throng fell silent as Norman, with his thin, one-shot lead, readied his tee shot on the 18th hole. The harbor that bordered the left side of the hole was filled with pleasure boats that bobbed silently in the water. In the parking lot of a condominium complex to the right, an intoxicated middle-aged man was punching his wife for refusing to get into their car, as she screamed that he was too drunk to drive. "Shhhh!" the gallery hissed, concerned that they would distract the Shark.

Norman drove the ball well, but his second shot dropped short and he missed another green. Norman chipped up to two feet from the pin, and the CBS cameras cut to a close-up of young Jamie Hutton sitting near the green with his fingers crossed under his chin as Norman attempted the par putt that would save his lead. When the putt fell, CBS announcer Steve Melnyk and a sound man moved in on Jamie.

CBS had introduced its viewers to Jamie on Saturday when Melnyk had snagged Norman for an interview as he left the 18th green. Melnyk hadn't wanted to talk to Norman about his round, but about his young companion. Melnyk asked Jamie how he came to be with Norman, and the boy replied that he had been granted a wish because he was "going to be in the hospital for a while."

Norman told Melnyk and the television audience, without being asked, that Jamie's stay at the tournament was going to be longer than Jamie had expected because Norman had arranged to have the youngster flown home on a chartered plane at the end of the tournament.

Norman acknowledged the applause of the crowd on Sunday, then walked around the camera operator who was standing in front of him on the green to shake hands with Jamie who was waiting nearby. Norman sat on his golf bag on the fringe of the green next to Jamie and waited to see if his comeback would be realized. Fred Couples, who was two shots back, was again in the sand trap on 17, and David Frost, who was one shot off the lead, had a birdie putt on the 17th.

Couples bogeyed 17 to drop from contention, and as Frost missed the birdie putt that would have tied him with Norman, CBS's Ben Wright, being considerably kinder to Frost, a native of South Africa, than he had been to Couples on Saturday, said, "Pulled it, absolutely pulled that putt. Of course, that's what pressure can do to even the best in the game," as the cameras jumped back and forth from the action on the course to Norman and Jamie maintaining their vigil.

Frost hit the tee shot on 18 and, as he walked to his second shot, CBS cut to a replay of Jamie with his fingers crossed, then a live picture of Norman and Jamie on the bag. Frost hit his second shot, and Norman leaned around the camera operator in front of him to see where it had landed. The ball was twenty-five feet from the pin. Frost would have to sink the putt to force a playoff with Norman.

As Frost bent over the ball, the cameras cut to a tight shot of Jamie biting a fingernail. When Frost missed the putt, the cameras cut to Jamie smiling a nonmalicious grin that was happiness, but not at Frost's expense. The victorious Norman put his arm around Jamie and rubbed his head as the cameras rolled.

The network went to a commercial break, and tournament officials gave Jamie a red tartan blazer that was the hallmark of the tournament and its Gentleman Golfers Club, and Jamie slipped it on. Melnyk positioned Norman and Jamie before the camera, and they were back on the air.

"In all the years we have been doing golf," Melnyk said, "we have perhaps done tournaments that have been more exciting, but I don't think we've ever been part of one that was more emotional than this here at the twentieth annual MCI Heritage Classic. Greg Norman, congratulations on your win, but this has been a very special one, has it not?"

Norman slid his arm around Jamie's shoulder. "Most definitely, Steve. I could just thank little Jamie here. He shows inspiration and courage that everybody out there should see."

As Melnyk talked with Norman and his young friend, Joe Fraser, the chairman of Heritage Classic Corporation, stepped into the picture to present the winner's trophy to Norman.

Norman held the trophy in front of himself and said, "What I'd like to do with the trophy, Jamie, is I'd like you to take it and put it in your hospital and think how the last four days went. This is your trophy."

Pat Summerall and Ken Venturi made concluding remarks from the control booth, and the cameras cut back to yet more shots of the freckle-faced Jamie before going to credits for the show's production staff, then concluded with a final freeze-frame of Norman shaking hands with Jamie.

When Norman appeared in the pressroom, with Jamie in tow, there was no pretense of objectivity among the press corps—the pressroom broke into thunderous applause. Norman took his chair

next to the tour's PR man Sid Wilson as Jamie settled on the edge
of the stage at their feet.

"How do you think the public will react to this?" a reporter
asked Norman.

"I'm not out here to be a hero. What we tried to come out here
and do was give Jamie a good weekend. What he thought was
going to be half a day turned out to be four days," Norman said,
starting to overstate the length of Jamie's visit before correcting
himself, ". . . or three days of fabulous good time."

"Greg, you've been close to winning a number of times, but
you haven't won in two years . . ."

Norman cut the reporter off testily. "I have won a number of
times, but I haven't won here . . ."

"Will this win give you more confidence about winning on the
American tour?" the reporter continued.

"No, I knew I could win here. You see I don't play here as
much as the other players do, and that never gets mentioned. I only
play fifteen or sixteen tournaments a year here compared to the
twenty-seven to thirty-one the other players do," Norman said,
apparently not knowing that the average tour golfer played
twenty-six events in the States.

"When you don't win in a fifteen-tournament stretch it's not to
say that you're playing bad, it's just that you've come close but the
breaks didn't come your way." Although Norman had pro-
pounded his bad-breaks theory before, there was considerable
emotion in his voice as he spoke.

There was tension in the air, and a reporter broke it by changing the subject. "Why did you do this, Greg?" a reporter asked
Norman about his involvement with Jamie.

"I think that everybody should sit up and look at Jamie for
inspiration and courage. It's very difficult to put it into words. It's
more of an emotional thing. I've had a great life and you want to
give the opportunity for other children to have a taste of that."
Although Norman had been publicity-conscious during his time
with Jamie, his affection for the boy seemed genuine. It was as
though Norman had somehow identified with the seriously ill
young man for their bond to have fused so quickly. Norman had
not suffered from bad health during adolescence, yet he used the
words "other children" when talking of helping Jamie, as if Norman were still a child himself.

When there were no more questions from the media people,

Norman left the pressroom to another round of applause. Most of the reporters had deadlines that were near, and they hurried to their portable computers, but some stayed behind to talk with Jamie before he left. Jamie stood at the back of the room shifting from foot to foot. It was the first time he had been alone with the reporters.

"Greg said that you were a great inspiration to him on the course when he looked over," someone said to Jamie. "Did he talk to you a lot?"

"No, I wanted him to concentrate on his game. If he walked by, I purposely stepped over to where other people were standing so I wasn't in his line of sight. One time he did look over and smile at me, and on one birdie hole he came over and rubbed my head."

"Was that the hole where he kissed the little girl?"

"Yeah, he did that before on the course, but it's not like he's doing it for the publicity. He does it when the cameras aren't around too."

"What is the name of your leukemia, Jamie?"

"I don't know. It's the adult form," Jamie said and called the question over to his mother who was standing back in the corner. But Jamie's mother just shook her head from side to side without saying anything.

Jamie then attempted to leave the pressroom, but he was detained for a time by photographers as they passed their cameras to other photographers, and asked to have their picture taken with their arms around the shoulders of the new young celebrity. When Jamie finally left, he walked past tables of reporters intently writing stories that would prominently mention his name. The stories would not, however, contain the name of a leukemia patient who had spent time at the tournament with Curtis Strange, who finished in seventh place. Strange had not told reporters what he had done.

Cojones

THE WOODLANDS, TEXAS.
Ten days after his triumph in Hilton Head, the gloss of victory
on Greg Norman was still as discernible as the Reebok and Mc-
Donald's logos on his golf shirt. It was Wednesday, and Norman
was playing in a pro-am at the Independent Insurance Agent
Open, north of Houston. His partners were four Texas amateurs, including a man named Boots Kaiser, who had won their
berths with the Aussie during a drawing at the pro-am dinner
earlier in the week.

Norman's galleries had grown exponentially since the televised
drama of his win and, this being pro-am day, the only time spectators are allowed to take photographs and ask for autographs on
the course, Norman was busy. He had perfected the walk-and-
sign, the process by which a golfer wades through a crowd, grabs
pens and writing surfaces at random, and affixes his name while
moving forward to his destination. Today, however, Norman's
fans wanted something more from him.

Spectators, like golfers, often speak softly to themselves to
direct a golf ball's flight during a tournament. "Get up," they urge
fairway shots by their favorite player that appear to be falling
short of the green. "Drop," they wish at balls that seem destined
to fly over the putting surface. But by the second hole at The
Woodlands, the galleries weren't keeping their thoughts to themselves. They were distinctly vocal participants in Norman's game.

"Come back, come back," a man hooted as Norman's drive on
the 2nd hole began slicing off the fairway.

"Come back!" Norman called out increduously to the man. "I

want it to go forward, not come back. The hole's down there, not back here."

The crowd laughed in appreciation, and Norman delivered a second line. "You see," he said, "that's why I'm on this side of the ropes and you're out there."

The group in front of Norman and his partners was still on the green when they arrived at the par-three 8th, so Norman and his caddie sat on Norman's bag near the championship tee, while the amateurs gathered at the members' tee, which is closer to the pin. Norman's galleries had always included some youngsters, but, since the publicity about Jamie, parents flocked to him with their kids as though he were the tour's patron saint of children. Norman and his caddie had barely settled on the bag when a man with a camera ducked under the ropes that skirted the tee, pushing his four-year-old toward Norman.

The caddie hopped off the bag as the boy came to stand next to the golfer, and the father dropped to one knee to get a picture of his son with the Shark. Norman nodded to his caddie when the shutter clicked, and the man went to the back of Norman's bag, unzipped a compartment, and pulled out one of the balls that manufacturers provide to the players. The caddie flipped the ball to Norman as the father got back to his feet.

"Here you go," Norman said, handing the ball to the boy. "This is for you."

The boy grasped at the ball that filled his hand, smiled a bewildered smile and turned to leave, when Norman called after him. "Just a minute, son," he said.

The little boy's eyes expanded as the six-foot golfer rose from his bag and crouched in front of him. "What do you say when someone gives you something?" Norman asked.

The little boy tried to move his jaw to speak, but his lips only quivered, so he shrugged his shoulders instead. "Always say 'Please' when you ask for something, and 'Thank you' when someone gives you something," Norman said in an instructional tone.

The boy nodded quickly. Norman rubbed his head before allowing him to scurry back to his father.

The ice having been broken, a man with five children was next under the ropes. "My God," Norman said, looking at the clan, "you've been a busy man."

A pretty fourteen-year-old with the physical maturity of a high school senior was standing near the tee waiting for her chance to approach Norman. She had come to the course in a new pink outfit with a short skirt, her blond hair carefully folded into a bun, and she had been stalking Norman since the 1st hole. She finally darted onto the tee at the 12th hole, handed her camera to Norman's caddie, then stood next to the golfer. "My," Norman said, "you're shy, aren't you?"

Norman turned away to sign an autograph before the girl could say a word, so she stood on the tee and talked animatedly to the caddie until Norman signaled the man to bring his bag over. The caddie looked back at the girl and whispered in Norman's ear as he removed a club. Norman pushed his caddie away with a wicked laugh.

Norman's disposition was as bright as his hair. The golf course was his kingdom, and his subjects seemed unable to get enough of his presence. They clamored after him constantly, and at the 18th tee the last two in a seemingly endless procession of attractive women were next to him for a photo. The women flanked Norman, ran their arms across his back, then rubbed against him provocatively.

"Whoa!" the crowd roared at the display.

"Tough life isn't it, Greg?" a man called out, and everyone boomed with laughter.

Norman was unnerved, and he looked to the gallery to see who was getting a laugh at what Norman thought was his expense. "Yeah," he called back in a sharp voice, "you never know what you'll catch."

The crowd laughed, but not as long or as loudly this time. Norman started to put his tee in the ground then, sensing he needed to atone for his last remark, stopped to address the man who had called out to him. "Somebody has to do it," Norman said. "Besides, you could be out here if you practiced more."

One hundred and nine professional golfers and four hundred and thirty-six amateurs participated in the three pro-ams that were staged on Wednesday, and as the pros who had played on the two auxiliary courses finished their rounds, they returned to the practice range at the main course to hit balls. They found Jim Van Vleck waiting for them when they arrived there.

Van Vleck was a self-styled forty-two-year-old California inventor with a vague background that varied markedly from recounting to recounting. He had assembled a video camera, recorder, and playback monitor into a portable device he called Swing Check. Golfers could record their practice-range swings on the machine, and then study themselves in blur-free slow motion to detect swing flaws—something golfers were constantly in search of.

The idea had occurred to Van Vleck while he was on a practice range at home, whacking balls that didn't follow his intended trajectory. Van Vleck, like millions of golfers before him, knew that if he could identify his single flaw—amongst the complex combination of motions that comprise the golf swing—he would be shooting close to par. Then it hit him, he liked to say to indicate that he would be retiring early and rich, "like a diamond bullet between the eyes."

Video. Instant playbacks. In color, with sound. Coin-operated video machines leased to driving ranges and country clubs across the land. A fifty-fifty split on the coin box take. A little concession on the side to supply blank tapes that hackers could purchase to ponder their flailings in the privacy of their homes. Eureka! Van Vleck hadn't had an idea like this since he created Astro Deck, a nonskid mat for the tops of surfboards. He had been so pleased with that product he had had its logo tattooed on his chest.

Van Vleck worked out the electronics and found a financial backer to subsidize the construction of several pilot models. He puzzled over promotion, and inspiration came a second time. He got a friend to let him smuggle his machine onto the practice range at the Los Angeles Open and, sure enough, a couple of the pros liked watching themselves on the screen.

Six weeks later, Van Vleck had an official PGA Tour admission badge; a leased Chevy El Camino outfitted to the max with a car phone, a radar detector, and a Swing Check trailer; a pocketful of hundred-dollar bills; and he was on his way across America to the Heritage Classic at Hilton Head. Get out there and find somebody to buy a license for this thing, his backer told him, and we'll sit home counting royalties.

The plan was to get publicity, and to see if a prosperous entrepreneur who had paid ten thousand dollars to enter his three best clients and himself in a pro-am wouldn't wander over to the practice range and be stunned by the possibilities. Van Vleck scored on the first count right off. Two local newspapers ran short items on the newest member of the tour caravan at Hilton Head, a local TV station did a piece at the New Orleans tournament the following week, and here in Houston there was a story in the paper on Tuesday.

It was the Houston story that brought two mean-looking

middle-aged men out to the course on Wednesday. The first was a stout guy with a shaved head and a serious paunch. His companion had long greasy black hair and a soiled T-shirt with the sleeves rolled up. They paid their ten-dollar admission at the gate, walked right to the driving range, talked their way around the marshal at the rope and stomped over to the Swing Check machine. They stared at the device silently, circling it and scrutinizing it like they meant to blow out the circuits with their eyes.

Van Vleck returned from lunch, found the men standing at the machine, and asked if he could help them. The men asked if the device was his, and when Van Vleck said "Yes," the bald guy pulled a color photograph from his pocket and handed it to Van Vleck. Van Vleck carefully examined the shot of the men's brainchild: Insta-view.

Swing Check was a slick, high-tech-appearing machine with graceful lines and a professional finish suitable for the poshest country club. Insta-view looked like its inbred cousin from Appalachia. Its controls, screen, and camera were scattered around the four sides of the head; its bulbous midsection rivaled the bodily disproportions of its skin-headed creator; and, its tiny wheels looked like they were borrowed from a grocery store cart.

Van Vleck laughed contemptuously, slipped the picture into his pocket and lit an unfiltered Camel. "You might as well stop working on this thing," he said. "You've been beaten and outdone."

The men started to argue with him, but Van Vleck pointed to the imprimatur of his gold PGA Tour pin. "Forget it," he said, and wheeled his machine away. "I have the support of the power structure here. You don't have a chance."

Van Vleck parked Swing Check next to a bench behind the golfers on the practice range, watched out of the corner of his eyes until the Insta-view men left, and sat down to study their photograph while awaiting a summons for a taping from a golfer on the firing line. He wasn't idle long, for golfers who hadn't played as well as they thought they should have were streaming in from the courses after the pro-ams, and they needed an immediate solution to their hypothesized swing inadequacies before the tournament started tomorrow.

Van Vleck wasn't winning quick acceptance by the more established golfers on the tour, the very ones who might provide an endorsement or a key introduction, but the younger players, who usually came from the college circuit where they had received intensive coaching, took to his machine quickly. And the caddies, who had long hours to kill while their employers banged balls on the range, were fascinated by it.

On this day a fiftyish caddie whose years on the road at poverty wages were etched into his face like reverse Braille asked Van Vleck to tape his swing. Van Vleck was annoyed by the request. The caddie was not one who regularly worked for a name player, and he certainly was not a potential licensee himself. Van Vleck brushed him off, but when the man persisted he complied. The meter was running on Van Vleck's expenses every moment he spent on the road, and perhaps the caddie would speak favorably about the machine to somebody who knew someone.

The caddie watched the playback of his swing transfixed, before bursting into self-praise. "Look at that shoulder turn, look at that weight transfer, look at that follow-through," he said. "That does it, I'm coming out on the tour next year."

The caddie subjected every other caddie within thirty yards of the machine to an encore of his monologue before attempting to lure a young pro over to appraise his performance. "I don't need to see that," the pro said. "My swing is already in check."

Van Vleck, who had been involved in another conversation, only half-heard the golfer's remark and he panicked that someone might have said something derogatory about his machine. He grabbed the caddie by the back of the shirt and demanded, "What did he say?"

The caddie looked at Van Vleck distractedly. "What do you want?" he asked.

"What did that guy just say?"

"Oh, I don't know," the caddie said with the frown of a man who had been posed a question that did not interest him, before he turned his attention back to the screen. "Don't bother me."

"It doesn't matter what he said anyway," Van Vleck said about the golfer. "Who's he? When was the last time you saw his name on the leaderboard?"

One of the featured guests that week on *Hometown Happenings,* a suburban Houston cable TV show presented by The Woodlands Corporation, owner of the planned community and golf courses of the same name, was Duke Butler, director of golf at The Woodlands and executive director of the Houston Golf Association, the nonprofit administrator of the tournament.

The purpose of Butler's appearance was twofold: to promote the 1988 tournament, and to prepare Houstonites for the changes that would be coming with the 1989 tournament. Houston, with its $700,000 purse, had just lost its late-April time slot on the tour schedule to Greensboro, North Carolina. The Greater Greensboro Open had been rehabilitated into the Kmart Greater Greensboro Open, upping its purse from $600,000 to $1 million and picking up a network TV deal when Kmart agreed to buy sufficient commercial time.

With its new affluence, Greensboro wanted to lose its late March, week-before-the-Masters status, a date when the most prominent American golfers—golfers are only required to play fifteen tournaments of their choosing annually to maintain their voting and pension rights—shunned competition to practice for the Masters.

Houston, the PGA Tour decided, would become the pre-Masters tournament on the 1989 schedule. That left Butler with the task of persuading the top overseas players, who sometimes came to the States a week before the Masters to acclimate themselves, that they should make their adjustments in the hushed, low-crime, always-green preserve of The Woodlands. When Butler appeared on the program, his interviewer noted that Butler was excited about getting some good foreign players for this year's tournament.

"I am," Butler said. "Greg Norman has been a regular participant with us since 1984. He's the number-one-ranked player in the world and he's Australian. We are lucky that we have Ian Woosnam of Wales with us. He was the player of the year in the world last year, and won more money than anybody. He is not a regular PGA Tour player; he is only playing seven or eight American events. We have Tommy Nakajima, the top player in Japan; we have several players from Canada, and Mexico's best player; and South Africans Nick Price and Fulton Allem."

"A lot of people don't understand how difficult it is to get a field like that," the announcer said. "How do you do it?"

"The event gets them here and I'm the mouthpiece for the event. I go to six or eight other events and try to get to know the players on a friendly basis, and tell them about the attributes of the Independent Insurance Agent Open and the golf course we have. I like to think we don't promote the players to play in our event, but that I discuss with them the opportunity they have to play with us. I feel they enjoy playing here and come of their own volition."

Butler didn't say that his staff, like that of most tournaments, would book housing for the players, provide transportation, distribute three hundred tickets to Houston Astros baseball games, find places for them to go fishing, arrange day care for their children, furnish many of their meals, and fix up one of them with a young woman who came by to say she wanted a date with one of the rare single golfers on the tour. Two weeks after his tournament, Butler would travel to a tournament in Dallas to ask the golfers if there had been anything about their stay in Houston they hadn't enjoyed, or if there was anything he could do to make them feel more welcome next year.

Duke Butler's personality always started to improve on Thursday morning of tournament week. The pro-ams were over, the $763,000 in entry fees they brought in was in the bank, and the amateurs were back outside the ropes. Butler could douse sun block on the fair, freckled skin that came with his red hair, and get out into the Texas sun to watch golf being played at its highest, most intensely competitive level. Observing wasn't the same as playing; Butler knew that better than anyone. But to his mind it was much preferable than not being there at all.

Butler had played in fifty tournaments on the tour from 1975 to 1977, while discovering he wasn't going to be the next Arnold Palmer. Butler loved golf and wanted to be around people who felt as he did about the game. He always said golf lovers were the best people in the world, and he could always find a way to get along with them. Butler semiretired his clubs and made golf his life by working his way up through the nonplaying ranks.

Butler's life now sometimes seemed to revolve around the one week each year the PGA express blew through Houston. He had to oversee the twelve-month activities of a paid staff of six, and the 120 volunteer members of the Houston Golf Association—men who, after paying a $300 initiation fee and $125 in annual dues, were required to sell $5,000 worth of sponsorships or ads for the tournament, attend at least ten meetings a year, serve on a committee and work five full days a year. The Golf Association ran seventy-five tournaments a year for junior and senior golfers, and for golf instructors from area courses, but this was the tournament that counted. It was the only one that, if Butler worked it right, made money and helped fund other events and charitable contributions during the year.

Butler was at the course on Thursday before the first of the day's fifty-two threesomes teed off at 7:30, making sure the daily roster from the 1,200 volunteers who were needed for the tournament and the pro-ams were all assigned, and that the golfers' manifold needs were provided for. His two-way radio with the short, stubby antenna crackled ceaselessly as he toured the course, resolving crises ad hoc. There was confusion, but none of it stopped Butler from meeting Justin White, the president of the Houston Golf Association, so they could watch Greg Norman score some birdies.

Butler and White were a study in physical contrast. At thirty-nine, Butler's five-foot-ten-inch frame was still as square as a college wrestler's, while White, a sixtyish beer distributor, had a build that resembled a keg. Despite their external differences, White was as devoted to golf as Butler, having served as a volunteer for the golf association for the last fifteen years.

Butler was happy in Houston, but he had received a nice job offer from the folks at Hilton Head in 1984, and it had weighed heavily on his mind for some time. He finally sat down and figured out the only thing Hilton Head had over Houston was an ocean, and they didn't have Texas A&M football games seventy-five miles away. Butler loved golf, but, my God, he loved Texas Aggie football too.

The only time Butler had questioned that decision was in 1985 when the oil wells stopped pumping money in Houston, and the tournament lost its sponsor. He could pick up the paper any day and see where some corporation had laid off two hundred, three hundred, four hundred or more employees. Butler worked 340 days that year, and the relentless pressure ground on his nerves until his health faltered. But when Butler saw all those people without jobs, he was thankful for what he had. So what if he got a little tired, and so what if he couldn't play the tour? He could be around golf as much as he wanted, and he couldn't think of anything better in life than that.

Butler and White caught up with Norman at the 1st hole, which was Norman's tenth hole of the day. Tournament fields comprise over 150 golfers on Thursday and Friday, before the cut, and officials have to start golfers from the 1st and 10th tees simultaneously to conclude the rounds in eleven hours. Norman had begun his day at the 10th, and he was already four under par and making another run at an early-round lead when he arrived at the 1st tee.

Butler and White slipped inside the ropes, then dropped to one knee to avoid blocking the spectators' view as the golfers hit their shots. "How is the withdrawal situation?" White asked.

"Four have withdrawn so far," Butler said, "and one of them is Tommy Nakajima."

White raised his eyebrows in concern. One of the key foreign players, who were going to be so critical to the tournament next year, had removed himself from the field. "It's okay," Butler said. "He left a note saying that he would like very much to play next year. But you want to know the kicker? I drew him in the pool this morning."

The conversation reminded Butler of another possible withdrawal, and he contacted his office on the radio. "Will you keep me posted on the Lenny Clements situation? I've told an alternate to get a meal in and be on the practice tee for a possible 12:09 starting time."

Norman was shooting par golf, and he remained at four under through the first three holes of the front side. As Norman left the 3rd green, he walked over to Butler. "Is that thing going to be there all weekend?" Norman asked, pointing to the sky. "It's casting a moving shadow on the 17th green."

"The TV people have to have it, Greg," Butler said, "but I'll see if they can move it if it's interfering." Butler tried to raise someone from ABC on his radio without success, and left word for the producer to contact him when he arrived at the network's trailer. The offending object was a miniature red blimp, nicknamed Silvia, that looked toylike and fragile as it floated low over the course on a tether. Rather than being something a child would purchase at Woolworth's, however, the balloon was actually a reflecting antenna that would be used to relay signals from the announcers during the broadcast of the tournament.

"Something else to take care of," Butler said to White after Norman had left. "Oh, by the way, a couple of players want to go skeet shooting. Do you know anybody we can call about that?"

Butler and White stayed with Norman until he went to five under on the 4th hole, then jumped ahead a hole to watch Ray Floyd, a former Houston tournament winner, who was tied with Norman for the first-round lead. Floyd was a twenty-six-year tour journeyman, and, at forty-five, one of its older active members. Floyd was well known on the tour, but he had come to be thought of more as an icon than a contender.

Floyd finished the day tied with Norman, earning a trip to the pressroom, a place he hadn't been in two years. "I haven't played a round like this in a long time," Floyd said as he settled his beefy two-hundred-pound frame into a chair at the front of the interview room. "It was a lot of fun for me."

Floyd talked about his round, then the reporters asked the golfer what had happened to his game since he won the U.S. Open in 1986, when he became the oldest player ever to capture that title. "I was inundated with commitments, charities, and dinners," Floyd said. "I started going through the motions with my golf."

Floyd spent so much time on the banquet circuit that he seldom saw his wife and three children. His bank account grew in inverse proportion to his contentment until, last fall, he went home to Florida, put his clubs in the basement, and removed himself from the golf world for a month—something he hadn't done in fifteen years. The longer the clubs sat there, the heavier Floyd imagined they would be when he thought about picking them up and getting on an airplane. Floyd realized there was little he could do on a course that would affect his stature in the golf world one way or the other, and he could make more money performing other golf-related tasks. That made it even more difficult to get himself motivated for the grind.

Floyd resolved to play a limited schedule and see if that would improve his demeanor and competitiveness on the tour. Now he was tied for the first-round lead with Greg Norman, who had entered the rear of the interview room as Floyd was concluding his session.

"Greg," a reporter asked Norman after he had gone over his round, "you seem to be on a roll here for last few weeks. Is there anything that started you on this hot streak?"

"No, I think I've been playing well for a couple of years," Norman said, implying again that there hadn't been anything wrong with his game during his long American dry spell. "There's nothing different."

"Do you feel like you could win five or six in a row?"

"Every time I play, I play to win," Norman declared. "My game is very strong at the moment, and obviously I'm popular at the same time."

"When did you win six tournaments in a row?" someone asked.

"It was in 1986, and in four different countries too," Norman said, referring to string of victories that included the prestigious British Open—the only major tournament win of his career—and tournaments in Europe and Australia.

"How much does it help to have a guy like Raymond Floyd knocking down birdie after birdie in front of you so that you have something to look at?"

"The only thing I was looking at," Norman concluded, "was Ray Floyd's butt going up in the air while he was picking the ball out of the hole."

While Greg Norman spent Friday afternoon in the clubhouse at The Woodlands, talking hunting and fishing with three other golfers, Rich Luikens, the course superintendent, was out sloshing around in his rain gear, vainly trying to do something about his dearest friend and worst enemy, Mother Nature. Luikens, a handsome young man with sun-blond hair and sun-softened skin around his eyes, had taken a degree in agronomy at Texas A&M recently enough so the shine was still on his class ring. He came to The Woodlands because he wanted to be outside, and because he wanted the people who came to play golf and the people who lived near the course to enjoy the serenity of what he maintained. That he did this at a course that got all the attention the boys from the PGA Tour brought with them was a mixed blessing.

The bad part was having to constantly make excuses to the players as to why things were as they were. Every day they came to the course they expected perfect conditions, not caring that it had rained five inches yesterday, or that it had been 15 degrees the last two weeks. Grass was not healthy and thriving twelve months of the year. It had good times and bad times, and Luikens got tired of having to explain why this or that area of the golf course was not exactly perfect.

Houston had a late cold spell just before the 1987 tournament. It had been nice the previous two months and a lot of the warm-climate Bermuda grass had come back through, pushing out the rye grass that Luikens overseeded into the course to keep it green in winter. Then when it got cold again the Bermuda decided it wasn't time for it to grow, so Luikens was stuck with not a whole lot happening on the ground. The pros howled about the greens and the press said they were dried out, sparse, ultrafirm, patchy and hard to read, while to Luikens's mind they were only a little bit thin and bumpy.

There was a warm spring this year, and the twenty-eight members of The Woodlands grounds crew—people who didn't mind getting up at four o'clock in the morning to earn small salaries—

were out there putting the course perfect for the boys. They let the rough grow a bit taller, but cut in an intermediate rough that the tour office requires so players who hit a little off the fairway won't be penalized as heavily as someone who slices way off. They had the fairways cut to a half-inch, and did some verticutting—nicking the surface of the grass with fine-tooth blades in the mower to thin it out, promote straight grass growth, and control the dead plant material that falls off the grass and causes problems with drainage and diseases.

They cut the greens back from their normal three-sixteenths of an inch to below one-eighth of an inch to speed them up, and that wasn't easy. "I don't care what kind of grass it is," Luikens always said, "grass doesn't like to be one-eighth of an inch. It would much rather be one-half of an inch."

That was just getting ready for the tournament. Once the boys arrived, Luikens's crew double-cut the greens three times a day, whereas normally they would mow them once a day. The fairways were cut twice a day instead of three times a week to make the grass stand up straight. And for the first four days of the week it was nirvana. Golfers came in from the course singing its praises, and Richard Luikens was vindicated. Then on Friday the skies opened and began dumping what seemed to be every droplet of water that had evaporated from the Mississippi River during the drought of 1988 onto Richard Luikens's meticulously, fastidiously, painstakingly prepared course, and play was suspended before a third of the field had completed the second round.

Duke Butler hoped to play a little more on Friday, and then finish the second round on Saturday morning, before having the entire field play their third round Saturday afternoon. The key was to guarantee that the fourth round of the tournament reached its televised conclusion at three o'clock on Sunday. That was where the big television money had been spent by the tournament's sponsor, the Independent Insurance Agents of America, and that was where ABC expected them to be. Everything that was possible would be done to guarantee that ABC and the insurance agents got what they had paid for.

While officials were conferring, Richard Luikens and his crew were out raking the bunkers and doing their best to squeegee the greens of standing water until the continued downpour made that futile, and play was canceled. The grounds crew picked up the trash in the rain until seven o'clock before calling it a day. They were due back at the course on Saturday morning before first light to mow the grass, rake the bunkers, set the tees, and cut the holes at daybreak.

As all this activity was taking place around the course, Greg Norman's confabulation in the clubhouse was breaking up. Norman hadn't played a shot on Friday, and he was scheduled to tee off at 7:42 A.M. on Saturday on the first of the thirty-six holes he would play that day. One member of his discussion group, J. C. Snead, a nephew of Sam Snead, would be in for a surprise when he arrived the next morning. Snead had been on his seventeenth hole of the day when the siren sounded to clear the course on Friday. Snead decided he didn't want to have to return to the course later to play one hole, so he played his eighteenth hole before coming to the clubhouse. When officials learned of Snead's disregarding the siren, a violation of tournament rules, they disqualified him from the tournament.

It rained again in Houston on Saturday morning, slowing down the fairways even further, much to the gratification of Greg Norman. The soggy turf meant that tournament co-leader Norman could slam the bejesus out of the golf ball and not fret that it would roll into a trouble spot as long as it landed close to the fairway. Norman busted balls in a fury during his first round on Saturday, and by the time he birdied the 12th hole he was five under for the day, twelve under for the thirty holes he had played in the tournament, and holding a three-shot lead over Ray Floyd.

Norman was smiling broadly to acknowledge the cheers of his fans, and amusing himself with the idea that he would finish his morning round at fourteen under—an astounding score for two rounds—as he walked to the 13th tee. Norman liked to prognosticate, to stroll over the lush grounds of the more difficult golf courses in the world and let his mind rush ahead of his game, as the applause of his legions poured over the gallery ropes.

Norman ripped a drive off the 13th tee and stood watching in shock as it sailed over the right side of the fairway and bounced out of bounds. He would have to take a penalty stroke, hit a new ball, and shoot carefully to save par on the par-five hole. Rather than making par, however, the Shark took a double-bogey seven on the hole, and lost another stroke and his solo hold on the lead on the next hole.

Norman regained his composure, finished his round with pars

to maintain a tie with Ray Floyd, and went back to his room to nap the tumult out of his head before the 3:39 starting time of his second round of the day.

The rest didn't appear to be the hoped-for balm when Norman came back inside the ropes. He bogeyed the 2nd hole right off, and then three-putted the 4th to lose another stroke and the lead. Spectators were starting to look at each other and wonder aloud about what was transpiring. Men were grabbing at their necks and extending their tongues in pantomimes of a person with a hunk of meat caught in his throat.

Then the Shark was back, and Norman went on a birdie spree, picking up a stroke on four out of the five holes that lead up to the 13th, the locus of the morning's psychological booby trap. Returning to the 13th didn't mean anything, Norman knew that. It was just another hole, and a par-five at that, where the long-hitting pros routinely reach the green in two, and lift their balls from the cup two putts later.

Norman kept the ball on the course this time, but it came to rest in the white sand of a bunker rather than the fairway, and he had no chance of making the green in two. Norman made par, then went to the 14th and hit it over the green again. He salvaged par on 14, and reached the green on 15, a par-five, in two. With skillful putting he could be off the hole with an eagle three, or, at worst, a birdie four. Norman shot a five. He put his tee shot on the par-three 16th twelve feet from the hole, then missed a birdie putt there.

If Norman's game was wavering, he was still in the hunt at three shots under for the day and twelve under for the tournament—the same composite score he had taken to his first visit to the 13th that morning. Without anyone seeming to notice, however, Norman had been quietly displaced from the top of the leaderboard by Curtis Strange, who was playing two groups in front of the center of attention.

Norman and Strange were as dissimilar as two handsome and successful thirty-three-year-old professional golfers could be. Norman was a blond performer and conspicuous consumer who was having a home with lots of glass built on the waterfront in Florida, and who owned a stable of exotic cars. Strange was a prematurely graying, red-meat-and-potatoes man who lived in a colonial-style home near Williamsburg, Virginia. Strange had once owned a Ferrari but, with an income of several million dollars a year, he sold it to buy a pickup truck because that made more sense.

Norman was brash on the course: whaling at the ball, shooting for the flag, waving to the crowd, whose applause nourished him, at every turn. Strange was a methodical player: swinging rhythmically, playing the percentage shot, focusing single-mindedly on the task at hand. He was a perfectionist who was driven to conquer ever-escalating goals, and if the public couldn't appreciate the self-absorption that required, that was their problem.

Strange trudged wearily into the press room at 8:00 P.M., thirteen hours after play had begun that morning. "That was a long haul out there today," he said to the local newspaper writers, a few of whom he knew on a first-name basis as a result of his two previous victories—both in playoffs—in Houston.

Strange recounted his six-under round, then a reporter who had been following him on the course said, "You looked angry about your second shot on the 4th hole." Strange lurched forward in his chair. "What? What?" he sputtered.

Strange was another golfer with an image problem, this one a holdover from his early years on the tour. Strange had had a great deal of difficulty establishing himself on the tour in the late 1970s. During 1978, his second year out, he entered twenty-nine events, missed the cut in fourteen and earned $29,346, out of which came all of his and his young wife's travel expenses. Strange was trying so hard and punishing himself so fiercely that his nights were often plagued by insomnia and his hair was graying at twenty-two.

Strange refashioned his game by working with an instructor to recast his long but erratic shots into shorter but more precise ones, while grinding away in tournament after tournament until, slowly, a life in golf began to appear possible. In 1980, he earned over $271,000 and was third on the year's money list. Strange thought that was better, but not good enough. He wanted to be the best. Expectations came more easily than perfection, however, and Strange was again haunted by frustration, which led to recurrent outbursts of anger on the course.

After missing a shot at a 1982 tournament, Strange kicked the bottom of his golf bag as his caddie was carrying it. The caddie fell to the ground, and later sued Strange for a back injury he claimed resulted from the incident. One week later at a tournament hosted by Arnold Palmer—an important man in Strange's life—Strange cursed a sixty-five-year-old volunteer scorer who got in his way, and a photographer whose camera made noise as Strange was shooting. Palmer wrote a letter of protest to golf commissioner

Deane Beman, who fined Strange. Strange paid the money, then went to Palmer to apologize in person.

Strange's father, a professional golfer and owner of a golf club in Virginia Beach, Virginia, had died when Curtis was fourteen years old. Another professional golfer who was a friend of the family looked after Curtis, who was already dreaming of a professional golf career, after his dad passed away. But Palmer became something of a father-figure-from-the-distance for him. Strange had played with Arnold Palmer model clubs as a kid, and he went to Wake Forest University on a Palmer golf scholarship. Today, Palmer's signed photograph hangs in Strange's workshop.

When Strange went to see Palmer in 1982, the golf legend gave Strange a stern dressing-down about his behavior on the course, and Strange promised to reform. Strange worked diligently at controlling his outbursts and, on the advice of his agent, began smiling more on the course. Strange won eleven tournaments and three million dollars between 1980 and 1988, becoming successful enough that his agent could now secure him several million dollars a year in endorsements and appearances.

Strange's press began to change at the 1985 Masters tournament. When Strange put those balls in the water on the 13th and 15th holes, and squandered what would have been his first major tournament win, the reporters in the pressroom, knowing Strange's volatility, were expecting the worst during his interview. Strange was aware of what the reporters were expecting of him and, as he walked to the pressroom seething, he told himself, Let's not mess this up. Strange was pleasant in the pressroom, putting his rage on hold, and the reporters wrote stories about the new Curtis Strange.

Now a reporter was asking about the old Curtis Strange, the one who his twin brother, Allan, said, turned into a son of a bitch Allan fought violently with after their father died. The Curtis Strange who left Wake Forest in his junior year, married a pretty blond interior-design student from Salem College named Sarah, then washed out of the national qualifying tournament that would have allowed him to play on the tour. Curtis and Sarah went back to their hotel room that day and cried because they didn't know how they were going to earn a living. Curtis thought he was a failure, and Sarah felt helpless because she didn't know what she could do—this was the man's dream. All of a sudden they were nowhere. Strange had a wife to take care of and no job. Curtis and Sarah were twenty-one-year-old kids who were scared to death.

Strange, like many golfers who don't make the American tour, went to play the Asian and Japanese tours. His game didn't hold up any better in the Orient, and after screwing up badly in Japan one day, Strange started pummeling a hotel wall with his fists and cursing. Sarah sat there frightened, seeing in full form for the first time the intensity that had attracted her to him when they met. When Curtis saw that she was afraid, he swore he'd never let his anger consume him again.

Strange had been through all of this and back again because he wanted it, that preverbal *it,* so profoundly. It was desire and need and more. He studied the back of his hand at the front of the pressroom for a long minute before he answered the Houston reporter's question about his anger on the course. "No," he said, looking up. "I wasn't angry. I was just disappointed at myself that I didn't hit a better shot."

While Strange was talking to the press, Greg Norman was birdieing the 17th to tie Strange at thirteen under. Norman parred the 18th and headed for the pressroom while his playing partner, Ray Floyd, who had had a share of the lead a few hours before, went to the practice range in near darkness. Floyd had self-destructed, shooting a third-round 76 that dropped him into a tie for twenty-first place.

Norman bounced cheerfully into the pressroom while the reporters, who were sitting there with their questions about Norman's near-crash all prepared, looked at him in disbelief. "The double-bogey kind of took the wind out of my sails," Norman said, "but, big deal. One bad shot almost ruined my morning, but I came back. No worries about it at all. You're allowed to make one bad shot every now and then. No problem, except that it's so late my steak is now well done instead of medium rare."

During the summer of 1987, Curtis Strange had started wearing the same red golf shirt from his sponsor, Nike, whenever he was in contention on Sunday. It had helped him win three tournaments then, but he had been playing so badly during the 1988 season that, before Houston, he hadn't been in contention to try it out. Strange brought the red shirt out in Texas, and that made his wife Sarah happy. She had been riding her husband about wearing too many white golf shirts. Sarah was trying to get some color into him, to brighten him up on the course. Curtis had to admit the reds did show up nice on TV, but it was a lot of trouble matching the colors of his shirts and pants and socks when he was packing for a trip.

When Strange stepped to the 1st tee on Sunday, the intensity that radiated from his slim body indicated that he wouldn't have noticed if he had been naked to the waist. Strange was wired, and when that happened tension collected in his slim shoulders and propped them up like he had crutches jammed under his armpits. Strange was there to do a job, and that was to defeat Greg Norman and Tom Kite, the final member of his threesome, who was only one stroke off the lead that Strange and Norman shared.

The names at the top of the leaderboard on Sunday morning often don't include the golfer who will wind up with the trophy and the check when the grounds crew is collecting the flags from the holes Sunday night. That's not what happened in Houston. Strange and Norman and Kite battled it out, matching birdies with birdies, until they arrived at the 14th hole tied at sixteen under par. Nobody else was even close.

Strange birdied the 14th to go up one on Norman, while Kite bogeyed and effectively removed himself from the contest. Norman birdied the 15th to pull even with Strange, and he did the same on the 17th to claim the lead. Barring an error by Norman, Strange's only hope was to birdie the 18th and force a playoff.

Strange and Norman hit their drives on 18, walked to their second shots and stood in the fairway, weighing what they were to do. The surface of the fairway of the 445-yard 18th at The Woodlands becomes water three-fourths of the way down the hole. A yawning lake surrounds the green on every side but the left, and the pin was set well to the right and up near the front. The Shark hit first and took the safe way out, hitting well to the left of the water, leaving his ball ninety feet from the cup.

Strange stood there, eyes training over the water at the flag bumping softly in the breeze. Strange wanted this one and, even more, he didn't want to lose by backing off. If he hit a cautious shot and made par, to his mind he would be giving it away, and Curtis Strange did not give away golf tournaments.

Strange studied his yardage book with his caddie. It was 192 yards to the hole. He was thinking it was a four-iron shot, because there was a little breeze in his face. Strange grabbed a three-iron instead of a four-iron to create a margin for error. Then he jerked his right arm out, like a man trying to force the sleeve of a long-sleeve shirt up his arm without touching it, as he always did before he shot, even though he was wearing a short-sleeve shirt. Strange aimed a little to left of the pin, then cracked it.

Norman stood there watching the flight of the ball. The contact between the ball and the club had sounded a bit thin to Norman, and he thought the shot was going to terminate in the water. It didn't. The ball caught a tiny patch of fringe at the front of the green, just clear of the lake, and rolled, stopping four feet past the pin.

The tens of thousands of spectators who had collected around the perimeter of the hole roared their approval. They loved their Shark conditionally, and he suddenly wasn't looking like a winner. Strange dropped his birdie, Norman two-putted for par, and it was time for sudden death. The electronic scoreboard flashed the message that the action would resume on the 16th hole, and the mob trampled across the course as Norman and Strange hopped onto golf carts to ride to their showdown.

Strange had the honor of the first shot on the par-three 16th, and his ball landed on the green, thirty feet from the pin. Norman hit a perfect shot, and was only twelve feet from the flag. Strange put his first putt close to the hole, then marked the ball's location and stood back to observe Norman attempt a very makable birdie putt.

Norman studied the slope of the green, aligned himself over the ball and putted. The ball rolled slowly across the green, but ran out of force several feet before the hole. Norman, with victory in his grasp, had left his ball short with a weak putt. It was the kind of putt that male amateur golfers were hitting all over America on Sunday afternoon and, as soon as they had swung, they called out, For Christ's sake, Mary, hit the ball. Norman repeated his actions on the 17th hole, leaving another easy birdie putt short of the hole—as though he were afraid to put the ball in the hole—and Strange was still hanging on.

The golfers found themselves in the 18th fairway, staring at the water for the second time in less than an hour. Strange hit first, and as soon as he completed his swing he called out, "No . . . no," because he thought he had hit it over the green. He was trying a four-iron on the same shot he had hit a three-iron on earlier, and came over the top of it a little bit. But the wind caught the ball, and it landed in the middle of the green, twenty-five feet from the hole.

The pressure was on Norman. He was going to have to put his ball close to the flag to have any chance of staying in the match.

But in a replay of his earlier second shot on the 18th, Norman curiously and timidly put his ball way to the left, safely away from the danger of the water, but also well away from the hole. The end came quickly. Norman missed his long putt, Strange made his shorter one, and Strange had his first victory of the year.

Norman entered the interview room as reporters were finding seats. "Kind of exciting, huh?" someone said to him tentatively. The Shark had just lost the fifth of the six playoffs he had been in on the PGA Tour—while seeming to almost give the match away—and there was uneasiness in the air. No one was quite sure what to say.

"That was unbelievable," Norman said enthusiastically. "That's what golf is all about."

Norman loosened the laces on his new black and white saddle-style golf shoes, and wiped the top of a can of soda someone had handed him on a table cloth before opening it. The TV people turned on their lights, and Norman's wedding ring sparkled with multiple diamonds while a sound man knelt at his feet and extended a microphone at Norman like a supplicant.

"Greg," Dave Lancer, the assistant PGA Tour public relations director who was running press conferences this week, began. "You want to tell us about, ah . . . the . . ."

"That's why we play golf," Norman interrupted. "What happened here today was just fabulous. Three pretty good players from the first tee right down to the eighteenth, or for us the nineteenth or twenty-first hole. I think that's why we love to play the game. What you guys saw out there was an exhibition of what the players can actually play like under pressure.

"I just really enjoyed it. I'm disappointed I lost, but I really felt as if I didn't lose. I had one heck of a golf tournament, and Curtis obviously made the right putt at the right time. And hit one heck of a shot on the eighteenth hole the first time around."

"What were your thoughts when Curtis made that putt on the final hole?" someone asked, sneaking up on the tough questions.

"As I said before, it was one heck of a day, and I was sorry there was a loser. Three guys playing fabulous golf for eighteen holes, and as it turned out for twenty-one holes."

"Can you run through the birdies in your round real quick?" Lancer asked.

Norman recounted his round through the 17th hole of regulation play, his last birdie of the day.

"Greg, could you please go through eighteen also, and the three playoff holes?" a reporter asked.

"Go through the eighteenth?"

"Yeah, and the playoff holes."

"On the first playoff hole I hit a five-iron to fourteen feet from the pin," Norman said, skipping over the 18th hole, even though he had been asked specifically about it. "Next hole I hit a one-iron, then a seven-iron again to fifteen feet. On eighteen I hit a driver and then a six-iron, and two-putted from forty-five feet." In addition to failing to mention his play on the 18th hole, where Strange had forced the playoff, Norman did not volunteer any information about either of the putts on the first two playoff holes, which would have cinched the win had Norman not left them short.

Norman jumped from his chair and hurried from the room calling out, "Thank you, see you all later."

Strange accepted his bounty at a ceremony on the 18th green, and came to the pressroom to occupy the winner's chair. "Well, that makes you three for three in playoffs in Houston," Dave Lancer said.

Strange looked at the reporters. "You all look so solemn," he said in his Virginia drawl. "We had a great round of golf today, I'll start off saying that, all three of us, including before the playoff. It is really a shame somebody had to lose—I mean I'm tickled pink I'm the winner, it has certainly done a lot for my confidence.

"I think everybody enjoyed it and saw some good golf. I know I enjoyed it," Strange said earnestly, without a trace of a smile on his face. "Win, lose, or draw today, I know that I enjoyed it."

"Can you talk about your second shot on eighteen in regulation, the shot you hit . . ."

Strange interrupted the question like he couldn't wait to answer, and his face broke into a big, shit-eating grin. "Pretty damn good, wasn't it," he said, and the room broke into laughter.

"Actually, Greg said he thought you hit it short."

"There isn't much room there, and yeah, it hit on the fringe, so it only cleared the water by four or five feet, but that's why we are out here winning golf tournaments. It pretty much came out the way I pictured it."

"On the first playoff tee it looked like you guys had a really nice banter going before you teed off. It seemed like that put you guys in a really good mindset."

Strange worked his jaw from side to side as a doubtful look came to his face and he cast his eyes downward. "I wouldn't . . . ah . . . give it that much credit. All the players get along, and Greg and I are friends, but we still have our mind on golf."

"Was having won here twice before in playoffs an advantage?"

"No. I feel like I beat the best player in the world today. That in itself . . . is tough to do," Strange said, as he struggled for the words that reflected his image of himself. "Not that I'm chopped liver, but . . . anyway . . . I did, as far as I am concerned, beat the best player in the world today."

"Would you say the second shot on eighteen in regulation took a certain amount of *cojones*?"

"Well, that's why I'm sitting here now, or a big part of it. Some people have their strong points, and I believe that's one thing people know me as, if you went around and asked. What it takes is not only a lot of intestinal fortitude or guts or . . . what you're talking about. It also takes a confidence in your game and a confidence in your ability to hit a shot like that."

Tournament Director Duke Butler had come into the pressroom, and he said to Strange, "Curtis, you seem to win all your tournaments in warm weather."

"The beginning of this season when I wasn't playing well, everybody was saying, Oh, you'll get going, don't worry about it. But it's tough when you're not playing well. I went down to Australia and won a tournament, then came back to the West Coast and played like shit."

There was a huge outburst of laughter in the room.

"I'll tell you how I really feel in a minute," Strange said and everybody laughed some more. People were looking around the room at each other and smiling quizzical smiles like, is Curtis Strange really a regular guy, or is this an act?

Strange gave Duke Butler a nice commercial for the tournament, telling the reporters how wonderful everything had been, and saying they shouldn't worry about the date change next year, and then it was over and everybody was happy.

Butler left the room smiling and went off to relax until tomorrow morning. That was when Deane Beman, commissioner of the PGA Tour, was coming to pay a call. The Woodlands had promised to improve the course as a condition of their contract, and Beman was stopping by to see how they were doing.

Fame

LAS VEGAS, NEVADA.
Golf prides itself on being a gentleman's sport, one played ideally
with an unwavering respect for, and observance of, the exacting
rules of the game—which are constantly reviewed and annotated.
Professionals have sometimes lost matches because of penalties
they called on themselves for infractions of the regulations that no
one, save themselves, witnessed. It's part of the British aura of the
game: stiff upper lip, fair is fair, and all of that. But the game's
creators hadn't reckoned on what could happen when amateur
golfers were allowed to participate in a professional tournament in
Las Vegas, where a little duplicity about one's handicap might
yield a ticket to televisionland.

The Las Vegas Panasonic Invitational was one of four matches
on the PGA Tour in which amateur golfers actually competed in
teams with the pros throughout most of the tournament, rather
than playing in a one-day ceremonial match the day before the real
event began. But while all the amateurs participated in Las Vegas
from Wednesday to Friday, only those with the twenty-five lowest
net scores got to play on Saturday, when NBC rolled the cameras
out. And the possibility of appearing on national television with
Greg Norman, and of having a famous commentator admire your
swing, proved to be a powerful measure of a man's integrity concerning his handicap.

The amateur golfers came hobbling into Bob Kostelecky's office on Tuesday of tournament week like supplicants to a mon-
arch. Kostelecky was a vice chairman of the pro-am at the
Panasonic Las Vegas Invitational, and his purview included com-

paring the handicaps—the number of strokes between one and twenty-one that got whacked off an amateur's actual score to yield a net score—amateurs had reported to the tournament with those on record at their home course. When the numbers didn't coincide, and it happened in Vegas more than once, the lower figure prevailed.

"Look at this," one man demanded, yanking up his shirt to reveal a surgical scar à la Lyndon Johnson. "How can I play to my old handicap when I'm still recovering from surgery?" The next petitioner insisted his handicap was two strokes above that reported, but the only person who could verify it was the teaching pro from his home club, and that man had died last fall.

This was the routine stuff. The nothing-ventured-nothing-gained guys who gave it a shot and, when they got nabbed, backed off. There were also some intransigents like the guy with a history of a floating handicap, ranging from two to fourteen strokes, who had been banned from pro-ams in other cities after winning tournaments with bogus scores. Kostelecky had words with the man in his office at the course on Tuesday, which ended with the golfer marching out, shouting that he was going to sue.

Kostelecky had tried to get the guy on the phone to tell him the machinations were over, but he couldn't locate him at any hotel in town. Apparently the man had registered, with his wife and children, under an assumed name. On Wednesday, Kostelecky had to confront him on the 1st tee. It was distressing stuff, and then, just as Kostelecky was getting calmed down, a rocket-fuel-component chemical plant ten miles outside of town blew itself off the earth and a lurid cloud of God-knows-what filled the sky as hundreds of golfers played their rounds.

Pro-am fees often contribute substantial amounts to the cost of operating a tournament, but in Las Vegas, more than anywhere, the amateurs paid the freight. There were 624 amateurs in the field, whose $3,000–$3,500 entry tariff comprised a $2 million take. That money combined with Panasonic's sponsorship allowed Las Vegas to offer a $1.38 million purse, with $250,000 to the winner—the second-largest pot on the tour in 1988, and the key to getting pros to tolerate four days of amateur partners.

Traditional Wednesday pro-ams are genteel affairs in which the amateurs are customers or employees of mainstream corporations. They are being rewarded by the company that is paying their way, so everyone behaves well. Half of the Vegas field, however, was comprised of high-rolling gamblers who were being comped by their favorite casino, and many of the remaining slots were filled by individual golfers who were paying their own fee, and this created a special atmosphere. There had been fistfights on the golf course during the tournament at Las Vegas, and the clientele tended not to include many Harvard MBAs.

When the weather got chilly at the Las Vegas Country Club on Wednesday morning, one of the golfing gamblers slipped into the pro shop to buy himself a jacket. He was a street-smart-looking guy in his forties: darkly good-looking with wavy hair and a heavy beard it was difficult to keep clean shaven. He chewed on a broken toothpick as he scanned the clothing racks for a coat, selected one that pleased his eye, pulled it on and walked to the cash register without looking at the price.

The clerk said, "That will be fifty-five dollars, please," and snipped the plastic cord that attached a tag to the garment. The tag fell to the counter, and the man picked it up and tossed it into a nearby trash receptacle with a casual flick of his wrist to show that he was considerate, while being careful not to appear weak. He nonchalantly placed separate rubber-banded wads of hundred- and fifty-dollar bills on the counter to get to his stash of twenties, pulled off three, and returned the cash to his pocket vault, where he could feel its heft and sense its bulge, and be reaffirmed in his wealth.

Out on the course, men with rings of substantial mass, as many as four per man, and watches that prominently displayed their cost, were teeing off. It was one of the few places in America where, during a PGA Tour event, you could see a hair-on-the-fringes-only middle-aged man in baggy green Sansabelts with an eight-inch cigar clamped between his teeth attempting to drive an orange golf ball in the company of a professional golfer—and missing the ball entirely during his swing.

The amateurs loved the Las-Vegasness of playing with the tour stars, and the tournament organizers worked hard to keep them enchanted. There had been a welcoming party on Tuesday evening, a simple English Renaissance affair for 1,300, with trumpeters, red carpets, the Southern Utah State College Scarlet and Black Ceremonial Band, Scottish bagpipers, a Shakespearean troupe, mimes, jugglers, games of chance, and guest celebrities. The amateurs had been presented with golf bags and Panasonic electric bread makers, which no one seemed to know quite what to do with, at the course on Wednesday. Caesars Palace was hosting a fifty-thousand-dollar bingo party Thursday evening, where the golfers' wives and girlfriends would compete for mink coats, crystal, and Gucci products, while the former host of *The Dating Game* made double entendres and soap opera stars dropped by. Friday there would be an awards dinner with Waterford decanters being dispensed. And if ennui struck anyone along the way, the Hilton casino hotel had an ongoing rooftop party, with a little five-thousand-dollar side tournament to keep things interesting. To amuse the pros, Baron Hilton threw in a Rolls-Royce for the first hole in one on the par-three 17th at Las Vegas Country Club, which his hotel overlooked.

One of the amateurs had been scheduled to attend the wedding of friends in Japan during tournament week, but he persuaded them to alter their nuptial plans and be married in Vegas so he wouldn't miss the tournament. If he had dropped out, there were fifty men on the waiting list who were dying to get his tee times on the three days when the little guys joined the big guys inside the ropes.

It was a clear May morning in the desert when the amateurs climbed out of their beds in the cocoonlike casino hotels to ready themselves for their second day of participation in the Panasonic Las Vegas Invitational. The temperature was nearing 70, and it promised to climb only a bit higher as the afternoon arrived. The men dressed, ate, climbed into their rental cars or limousines, and reported to their assigned courses.

Robust desert winds were starting to whip through the barren land that surrounds Las Vegas as the golfers arrived at the courses. The gusts pushed over the mountains that ring the town, and rushed through the foothills toward the settlement. By ten o'clock the wind was rocking the distressed cars that sat, crammed with well-used belongings the owners didn't feel certain enough about the future to discard, outside transient apartments where people who hadn't found what they came looking for in Vegas lived.

Over at the Desert Inn Country Club, the second of the three courses being used in the tournament, what passed for restraint in Vegas—muted bells in the slot machines—was being disturbed. They had lost twenty elms to the wind earlier in the week, and had restored the course to its manicured best. Now the carefully coiffed sunbathers who decorated the perimeter of the pool but never swam were hurrying to their bungalows to escape the gale, and the three-dollar hot dogs at a food stand near the course were going begging.

Jim Van Vleck was on the Desert Inn practice range, trying to decide whether he should pack up his Swing Check machine and call it a day. His backer in California was saying it was time to come home unless something happened this week. It was getting too breezey to play golf, let alone practice. But Van Vleck had company on the driving range and, well, maybe he should stay. An inventor of his acquaintance from Utah had brought his Instant Replay machine to Vegas, and a sports trade magazine was out with a back-cover ad for a golf-course video unit Sony was introducing to the game. Van Vleck was not the only one to whom this idea had occurred.

Meanwhile, out west of town, beyond the casino strip and the service station offering free aspirin and sympathy, where you pick up Interstate 15 into Devils Playground and the Mojave, the wind was becoming surreal at the Spanish Trail course, site of "incomparable luxury living." Spanish Trail was a master-planned, gate-guarded community with Bel Air-like mansions, cluster condos and townhouses edging against the foothills of the mountains, and fronting the impossibly green desert fairways of a championship course. Everything was terra cotta and pale stucco, save the five-foot cinderblock wall that kept the desert at bay along the back nine.

The course was elevated and exposed, the mountains feeding wind to the fairways like a funnel to its neck, and the few immature trees that dotted the young community were bending to the earth. The wind speed indicators were bouncing past 60 mph and golfers, depending on their bearing to the wind, were gaining or losing a hundred yards on every shot. Balls were being blown right off the greens. Spectators were few—amateur golf is something to be played, not observed—except for the three hundred people who watched Greg Norman drive a ball 429 yards with the wind at his back just before play was called at 4:44 P.M.

Norman was three over for the day, and one under for the tournament, when play was canceled after he had completed ten holes. Norman was livid about the conditions he had competed under and, uncharacteristically, he had some harsh things to say. He told reporters that those playing at Spanish Trail had been blown out of the tournament, and then, despite a selectively enforced PGA Tour ban against public criticism of tournament sites by players, he suggested that the Spanish Trail course be dropped from the venue, and the tournament be reduced to four days in future years, so everyone played under comparable conditions at the other two courses.

Norman wasn't the only one who was unhappy. Tournament officials, learning that high winds were also forecast for Friday, decided to simply complete Thursday's round on Friday, move Friday's round to Saturday, and limit the 1988 tournament to four days. The change meant that Larry Cirillo, NBC's coordinating producer of golf, was going to have to make a Saturday afternoon television show out of a tournament round that would feature 624 amateurs playing golf on three different courses. It was not the stuff of which high ratings are made.

Cirillo was a solidly built, graying from the front, mercurial man who had the perpetually preoccupied air of someone who had had the complex task of producing television golf for fourteen of his twenty-seven years at NBC. He had rolled into Vegas at the beginning of the week with fifty engineers, twenty production people, and five announcers, with another fifty people lined up to be scorers and spotters over the weekend. A work crew had unloaded eight stationary cameras, four Minicams, and four hand-helds, and strung miles of cable at Las Vegas Country Club, where the pros had been scheduled to play on Saturday and Sunday. Now, in addition to all the amateurs in the field, the pros they were going to be paired with would be scattered all over Vegas, with random starting times that were unrelated to their positions on the leaderboard.

Once he learned of the new schedule, Cirillo thought about the broadcast he had done at the Bay Hill tournament in Florida three years ago. When rain came and washed out a round of that tournament, Cirillo put together a panel of golfers and had a talk show. People wrote more letters to NBC about that talk show. Even golf commissioner Deane Beaman asked Cirillo if they could do that for a half hour each week.

Cirillo decided to try it again. Not that he had much choice. He could send cameras over to the other courses, but that was expensive and he wasn't sure how much it was worth. He had spread cameras around at the Bob Hope, another multiple-course pro-am, and bounced the picture back and forth. But he'd watched the ratings there over the past five years, and they didn't change whether he went to the other golf courses or not.

Cirillo made arrangements to use a large tent near the NBC trailers as his studio, and asked the people who ran the tournament to assemble an audience for his show. He wanted people who were golf-knowledgeable, so they could ask good questions, and, he kidded, sober. This was, after all, live television, and all he needed was for some beered-up guy from the gallery to start screaming and yelling on camera.

He'd put announcer Jay Randolph in the audience with a portable microphone and tell him to make like Phil Donahue, and then Cirillo would hope some golfers with marquee value would create drama out on the course to build an audience for Sunday's broadcast. Cirillo knew that nobody loved second place in America, and if the right golfers didn't create story line of competition on the course for the broadcast, remote control units would be clicking throughout the land. If one guy was running away with it by ten strokes, Cirillo could do anything he wanted with his technology, and people were still going to switch to bowling or baseball or whatever.

It was the same with who the players were. Cirillo thought journeymen golfers like Mike Reid, Morris Hatalsky, and Scott Simpson were fine fellows, but they didn't create an audience. Viewers saw those guys on the leaderboard, and they might all be within one stroke of one another, and they'd say, "Okay, it's just another golf tournament." The serious golf fans of America tuned in for the beginning every week. If Cirillo had a horse race building on the course, he'd keep them for the duration. If he had a runaway, he'd lose half of them. Only the total hardcores would stay with him until the bitter end just to watch golf shots.

Even then he couldn't make all the viewers happy. They'd write that he had shown too many putts and not enough other shots. Cirillo had statistics to prove he aired 60 percent tee shots, second shots, and chips, and only 40 percent putts, but viewers would still insist that wasn't so.

A lot of people wrote about commentators too, and there was no gray area. They either liked a commentator or they didn't. Some people called Jay Randolph a buffoon, and others thought he had improved this year. "Vin Scully talks too much," they'd say, or, "Scully's great." Cirillo didn't know who was great and who wasn't according to the mail.

One lady from Seattle wrote to Cirillo after the Bob Hope and went on a tirade. She said she was an avid golfer at her club, and that she tuned in NBC to see the Bob Hope at one o'clock, and what was on but basketball. She was forced to watch fifteen minutes of basketball, with coaches jumping up and down like children, when what she wanted to see was the Bob Hope. That was why NBC golf got the lowest ratings, she said, and added that she hated NBC golf.

The woman hurt Cirillo's feelings when she said those things about his golf programs, and he telephoned her from his home in Florida. Cirillo got her at 8:30 in the morning, her time, and the woman proceeded to tell Cirillo everything that was wrong with his show. When Cirillo didn't hang up on her, the woman began to calm down. Now she and Cirillo have a running commentary. She sends him a critique of each show. How many shots he showed, how many commercials, what everybody said—the works.

All of this left Cirillo only one option: to do golf the way he thought it should be done—for the average guy. There were a multitude of ingredients in Cirillo's recipe for golf, and one element that was banned. NBC commentators are forbidden from ever, under pain of dismissal, whispering into their microphones during a telecast. They were to stay far enough away from the golfers so they could talk the way they do in normal conversation. Golf is a serious game, but nothing is that serious. And another exclusion. Announcers with grave British accents were not allowed on Cirillo's golf broadcasts either.

Greg Norman was tied for fortieth place when he stepped to the 1st tee at the Las Vegas Country Club at 8:30 A.M. on Saturday. He was off to a less than propitious start in the tournament after his disastrous, windblown second round, and he knew he needed to play catch-up golf. He had a confident, lets-get-down-to-business jut to his jaw as legions applauded his arrival at the tee, and that translated into a long sweeping whack with his driver that sent a ball flying down the fairway and into a bunker on the right side of the par-five hole. His second shot was also poorly executed, and the ball caromed off a tree on its flight out of the sand.

Norman's progress was carefully monitored by the NBC production staff in their trailer adjacent to the course. The heavily air-conditioned, windowless trailer was crammed with electronic equipment, but still had enough comfortable chairs and good lighting in the area of the control boards to make it seem as though it were located in midtown Manhattan rather than in the desert.

Norman was one of the scheduled guests on Larry Cirillo's talk show, and people were trying to estimate how soon after the program's 1:30 P.M. air time Norman would complete his round and be free to come to the tent that was serving as a studio. There was also some discussion about whether a tape with dramatic pictures of Wednesday's chemical-plant explosion should be replayed during the telecast. Some of the production people argued that using the footage would make them look foolish because the explosion hadn't affected the tournament, and as a news event it was four days old. Cirillo, knowing that television is pictures, wanted to use the scene, which resembled the detonation of an atomic warhead in its intensity, but he was beginning to waver under pressure from the staff.

Out on the Las Vegas Country Club course, Akiya "Andy" Imura, president and CEO of Matsushita Electronic Corporation of America, the parent company of Panasonic, was learning what it was like to be a celebrity golfer during a televised match. Imura, along with country singer Charley Pride and Denver Broncos quarterback John Elway, had been seeded into the Saturday round, and Panasonic, which had purchased three fourths of the commercial time on the broadcast, let NBC know they wanted their man to appear on the screen.

Imura is a slight, thin man, dressed that day in plum slacks, a green sleeveless sweater, and a blue baseball cap with a plastic adjustable tab in the back. He was as inconsistent a ball striker as any amateur, and he was just one of the boys on the course, raking the sand traps—which he visited frequently—after his shots, until the television camera and sound people found him. Suddenly he was the target of people who charged in from the gallery ropes, dragging cables and pointing equipment, as he approached a shot. The cameras would follow the flight of the ball—down the fairway, or into water, or off the course—before the operators would retreat to the sidelines, tear down the course in carts, and position themselves to record his next swing.

In the tent home of Cirillo's talk show, the audience, guests, and commentators were anxiously watching television, rooting for either the San Francisco Giants or the Chicago Cubs to win their baseball game, so they could go on the air at their scheduled time. Fuzzy Zoeller, who was to be a panelist, had already finished his round, and he studied the studio monitor and asked how long the golf show would be on the air. "An hour and a half," was the reply, "but it might end up being only an hour by the time this baseball game is over."

"Don't say that," golfer-turned-announcer Lee Trevino said, directing his attention to the screen. "We lost about ten minutes last time."

Jay Randolph walked around the tables where the audience was seated, asking people what their questions to the golfers were going to be. "We'll make one up later," one table told him.

"We have to screen these questions," Randolph said with concern. "This is a family show."

"Two outs, man on first," Trevino said. "Come on, strike out."

"I hope he hits it out of the park," Charlie Jones, Trevino's co-announcer said. "That will put us right on the air."

"There it is," Trevino said. "He's out. It's over," and everyone applauded.

"Don't forget," Randolph said to loosen up the audience as the network went to commercials, "when Charlie introduces Fuzzy Zoeller, boo profusely."

The show began with footage of Las Vegas and the surrounding countryside, as the announcers struggled for a positive way to explain to the viewers, who had tuned in expecting to see a golf tournament, that they weren't going to be seeing a golf tournament.

After the announcers were introduced, the picture went to the course where it caught John Elway hooking his tee shot into the trees on 15, as an announcer noted that Elway had also been a baseball player, and baseball players usually hook because of strong wrists. Then they showed Charley Pride, like Elway a ten-handicap golfer, teeing off on 17. The announcer said that Pride plays a big slice, just before Pride hooked the ball off the fairway, over a cart path, and almost into someone's courseside front yard. Then it was Andy Imura's turn to hit a ball and holler "fore" as it bounced into a front yard.

The cameras cut to Greg Norman on 18, before Jones said, "We said this was a tournament for both professionals and amateurs, and coming up is a true all-time amateur swing."

The picture cut to a man with vibrant plaid slacks resting under an overgrown stomach, standing much too far back from his golf ball, with his arms almost parallel to the ground rather than diagonal, and with a swing more native to a baseball field than a golf course, as he hit a ball into the water on the 17th hole.

"Oh, my God," an announcer called out.

"That's how you get distance," Trevino cracked. "You see how far he is standing from the ball."

Golfers Mark McCumber, then Roger Maltbie, joined Fuzzy Zoeller on the panel, and the men talked about the wind and the tournament. Maltbie was the only golfer wearing a sponsor's visor, and the cameras cropped his face tightly when he spoke to avoid having Michelob's name splashed all over the telecast without charge.

After returning from commercial, the leaderboard was shown and an announcer said, "Let's go back to Charlie with a special guest."

Greg Norman had arrived for the program, and the audience clapped for the first time when he was introduced. "You were not all that pleased with conditions at Spanish Trail," Jones said, referring to Norman's remarks to the press on Thursday.

Norman smiled, looked away, and mulled his answer for a moment before saying "No" in an "okay, let's be frank" voice. "We got caught in the bad weather, and I have played in wind before, but not like that wind. The wind was gusting to sixty-four or sixty-five miles per hour, and that is pretty stout stuff."

"In addition to the problems with the wind," Jones continued, "on Wednesday we had the explosion of a rocket fuel plant about fifteen miles away in Henderson, and it did have an effect as far as the players were concerned," Jones said, as the sight and sound of the blast filled the screen to the delight of Larry Cirillo.

There was a question about playing in the wind for Zoeller, then Jay Randolph asked from the audience, "Why aren't there any drugs on the tour?"

"It is an individual sport, and you can't lean on anyone else," Lee Trevino said.

"There was a very nice commentary here in the newspaper in Las Vegas on that very fact, and on the rapport that the athletes have with the media," Charlie Jones said. "The writer said, maybe it is dull and clean and white and nice, but it really is . . ." Jones began to stumble as he realized what he had said, and he hurried to correct himself.

"But maybe it is plain vanilla, that type of thing, but it is nice, and the writer said that is, a very ah . . ." Suddenly commercial lead-in music began playing loudly, as Jones continued. "Attitude . . . that he, ah . . . and has great respect for the professional golfers, such as the ones who have joined us today . . . it was very, very nice. We'll be back with Fuzzy's last win at the Anheuser-Busch."

Later the cameras returned to Panasonic's Imura on the course, as Imura hit an iron shot with such a violent swing the follow-through pulled him off his feet, as the ball sailed toward a sand trap.

"Bob Goalby, tell us about that swing," courseside announcer Mark Rolfing said.

"Actually he was setting up the ball nicely, and when he took the club away it looked like he was going to hit a nice shot. Let's take a look at it," Goalby said as a slow-motion replay of Imura came on the screen.

"He's set up to the ball very nicely, and he takes it away from the ball very nice, two-piece, right back there to the top of the swing it is perfect. Whoa," Goalby said as the picture showed Imura almost hitting himself in the back with his club on the backswing. "A little too far on the backswing, a nice move with the hip, down and through and good contact. Perfect position there."

Imura's follow-through was so forceful his club flew straight up over his left shoulder and pulled him off the ground like it was a hot-air balloon. "He should have locked his legs and elbows," Goalby said. "He just didn't follow through with relaxation."

"That's part of the fun here at the Panasonic Las Vegas Invitational," Mark Rolfing said. "The amateurs playing with the professionals."

Back in the studio, a woman from Las Vegas asked, "With all the video cameras being used, do you go out and check out your swings with video cameras?"

McCumber said he bought a video camera and used it to tape his kids, but he didn't want to see his swing. Maltbie said he used one infrequently, but found it helpful in working with his instructor. Zoeller said he didn't take golf that seriously and didn't want to see his swing either.

"Greg, do you use a video?" Jones asked Norman.

"Yeah, I do actually . . ."

"We're talking about golf now," Zoeller interjected to riotous laughter.

Norman looked over at Zoeller challengingly for a second, then relaxed. "That's all right, I use it in both," he said and slapped

Zoeller on the knee. "I don't have a teacher over here, so I keep records of my swing."

"Jay, you have a follow-up question?" Jones said to Randolph.

"Yes, we have Jim Van Vleck here who works with video with a lot of young players on tour, and I think he wants to respond to what these great players have said."

The camera switched to a close-up of Van Vleck. "I see a lot of the young guys out there working with the Swing Check video unit, out there on the driving range, and a lot of the old . . . I say this with respect . . . the older guys they kind of shy away from it, and they're kind of set in their ways. And yet I see the young guys with these great swings, and they're the up-and-comers, and I see them on the leaderboard there, and they use it a lot. And I just wonder between feel and video, in other words, you can get too technical and lose the feel by studying the video too much, but there is a happy medium there, and it is very interesting to work with them. And I just wanted to get your comments in relationship to feeling your swing as you see the swing, and I wondered how you feel about that?"

"I've always played by feel," McCumber said. "I can't tell from video what I am doing in my swing."

"When I started they didn't have video machines," Trevino said. "I always revert to old film of winning golf tournaments under the gun. You can video your swing all you want, but when old Joe Choke grabs you around the throat, that guy's video is not going to be there to help you.

"This guy's not going to run over and say, 'Look at this, man, this is what you were doing this morning on the practice tee,' " Trevino continued, mimicking a man with a camera to howls of audience laughter. "There is no substitute in golf for time. Practice gives you a tremendous amount of confidence. Ben Hogan once said, this is a game of misses, the guy who misses the best is going to win."

"And we're not going to miss a commercial," Jones said. "We'll be right back in just a moment."

Jim Van Vleck returned to his seat when the camera cut away. His season in the glare of the national television lights had lasted two and a half minutes. Later that afternoon, he would insist to a pretty woman with large green eyes who was working at a concession stand that his answering service at home had been jammed with calls after his command performance, but the next morning he would pack up and make the long drive home without having sold a Swing Check license, his days on the tour over.

Greg Norman came to the pressroom after the broadcast with a vastly different demeanor from the one he had when he last talked to reporters on Thursday. "Conditions were ideal," he said. "There was hardly any breeze to think about. You can put such a tight spin on the ball on these fairways that you should be able to stop it on the road. I knew that the greens would be putting great. They are probably the quickest Bermuda greens I've ever played on."

Norman then went over his round. He had shot a 66 on Saturday to put him seven under for the tournament and five shots off the lead. Norman was playing erratically, as he often did, but he said he wasn't troubled by it at all, as he had said he wasn't concerned about—or even aware of—his standings in the myriad of statistics the tour keeps on players' performance, when he was asked about that on Wednesday.

"Let me tell you this," Norman had said, "the only stats I care about are paychecks and victories. To me those are the only things that count. I play aggressively. I don't believe in stats. If you win a tournament, then obviously you have done everything right. The number one stat to me is victory. I don't really care about any others."

"What do you think your chances are of pulling this out on Sunday?" a reporter asked.

"The thing I have on my side is my confidence in my game. I'm not going to be backing off at all. I don't get intimidated just because it is Sunday. Golfers who don't play well on Sunday don't have the same push, and play the same aggressive golf that I do. I'd much rather play in front of fifty thousand people than five thousand. If you don't perform well they won't be out there. I give them the best show I can. The more people around me the better I play."

"At five shots off the lead, and with a lot of players shooting well, wouldn't you have to record quite a low score to win the tournament?" a reporter asked.

"I feel you can shoot a fifty-nine here if there is no wind and you're really on your game. A fifty-nine is a distinct possibility," Norman said of a score that had been shot only once in tournament play in the fifty-year history of the PGA Tour. "That's a positive thought, but I feel every time I walk on the course I can do something special. The beautiful thing about golf is that we are the ones who control our own destinies."

Peter Jacobsen came into Sunday eleven under and one shot off the lead. It was not a position he was used to occupying. Jacobsen had won only three tournaments in his eleven years on the tour, and the last two of those triumphs had occurred just after he turned thirty, in 1984. Jacobsen ruptured a disk in 1985—back injuries are rampant in the professional game—and his golf hadn't been the same since. Yet he had rehabilitated the impairment without surgery, instituting an exercise and stretching regimen and altering his swing, so he knew he couldn't hang everything on that.

Sometimes Jacobsen thought that, like Fred Couples, he wasn't tough enough on himself about winning. He thought he let too many things get in his way. He was the class clown of the tour, with a gift for imitating the swings and mannerisms of other golfers, and there was a seductiveness to the attention that brought. Every time somebody yelled out to him on the driving range, "Do Arnold Palmer," there was a temptation to forget about practice and do his little routine. The gallery, and even the other golfers, would laugh and Jacobsen would take his bow and smile, but all the time he would be wondering what had happened to his game, and when he was going to win.

Jacobsen wouldn't tell anyone he was worried about his game. He had always believed that when someone asked how he was playing, he should say he was doing real well, thanks. It was part of the front—jolly Peter Jacobsen, the entertainer of the tour, who could go into character with a moment's notice and still have his real self there when he came back. It started to become addictive and self-deceptive, until he got to where he couldn't even admit to himself that his game had gone to the dogs. Hey, he could still make people laugh at will.

Jacobsen knew that when he was strongly motivated, like when he began working with sports psychologist Chuck Hogan in 1984, he played well. The week after he spent some time with Hogan he went out and won a tournament. Now he talked with Hogan two or three times a week on the phone, and told him about his game. Sometimes they played a round and Hogan pointed out that Jacobsen was moving too fast, or that there was a nervousness in him.

Hogan taught him that hitting golf shots was like driving a car.

You learn how to work everything, then you don't think about it. If you get hung up on the mechanics, you'll end up standing on the 9th hole in the middle of a round trying to figure out your swing. When you're playing golf, Hogan told him, play golf.

Hogan also taught Jacobsen to improve his concentration on the course by visualizing that he was playing his shots in nonpressure situations. Sometimes Jacobsen would walk up to a putt and see an old shoe, like the one he putted into on the rug at home, rather than a cup. Sometimes he saw the ball as being attached to a stretched-out rubber band that was anchored to the hole, and when he let the ball go with his stroke, it went straight into the hole.

During the last tournament that Jacobsen had won, he had a four-stroke lead over Mark O'Meara after ten holes of the final round. O'Meara birdied 11 and 12, and Jacobsen parred and bogeyed. Walking from 12 to 13, Jacobsen started panicking because his lead had diminished to one stroke in two holes. He thought he was done. Then he told himself, No, I'm not, and he turned the whole thing around in his head. He told himself that he had been one stroke behind going into 11, and that he had then made two birdies, like he had fought back to go one ahead. He made himself believe that. Jacobsen parred all of the remaining holes and won because he didn't let the negative affect him, and he thought that showed character.

Jacobsen worked with Hogan for three days before he came to Vegas this year, and he was feeling highly motivated again. He wanted to win this one and get some respect. Players judged other players on the respect their peers had for them, and one of the things Jacobsen had been really working for was getting back to playing well, so the guys he looked up to would say, "Hey, great playing, good to see you back." The peer acceptance was very important to him.

The lead changed hands frequently coming down the stretch on Sunday, with six different players holding or sharing the lead at various times, none of whom was Greg Norman. While Norman was shooting a one-under 71 that would leave him tied for twenty-third place, Jacobsen was struggling to keep his name on the leaderboard on the front nine, and Gary Koch was scoring five under on the first ten holes to close in on the pack.

Koch, after twelve years of life on the tour, had suddenly found himself wondering why he was doing such a thing for a living last year. Twelve years of twenty-five to thirty weeks on the road started to seem like a long time when you had a wife and two young children who, unlike most pros' families with children younger than school age, didn't travel with you much. One Wednesday before a 1987 tournament he had called his wife in Florida and told her he didn't enjoy playing anymore and didn't want to be there.

Koch had earned $733,268 during the previous four years, and he knew of no other job that paid as well, so he stayed on the road and kept going through the motions. With the level of competition on the tour, that approach put Koch 175th on the 1987 money list, with $33,727 for the year—less than travel expenses.

Koch went home to Tampa then to do some serious soul searching. Like most tour players who aren't content with their lot, he went looking for help. He talked to sports psychologist Bob Rotella, who told Koch he had to want to continue or he should move on to a new part of his life. Koch went to visit golf instructor Peter Kostis to see if he could help, and Kostis decided Koch's problems were partly mental. Kostis told Koch to get away from it for a while to improve his attitude, and then come back to see him. Kostis later switched Koch from a wood to a metal driver, and got him to fade the ball to the right off the tee rather than draw it left, and that seemed to help.

The real catalyst for Koch was when January came and all the other pros went off to play, while he was at home shooting blanks on the practice range. By failing to finish among the top 125 on the money list, Koch had lost his exempt status to play in whichever tournaments he chose. Now Koch would have to write to each tournament he wished to play in and beg for one of the scarce spots the tournaments can allocate to nonexempt players. Although PGA Tour fields normally comprise 154 players before the cut, local tournament organizers have a free hand in selecting only eight of those golfers, using what are called sponsor exemptions. The remaining slots go to players on a meticulously defined priority list established by Deane Beman.

The fear of being left behind motivated Koch to find enough sponsor exemptions, and play enough good golf, to come into Vegas with $66,000 in his pocket, four months into the year. Yet he had not won a tournament since 1984, and doubts about his abilities as a golfer were always in his mind.

While Jack Nicklaus and other journeymen players frequently

chastised golfers on the American tour for their lack of desire, no one denied that the level of talent ran deep and wins were tough to come by. Peter Jacobsen had found himself distracted from his game by lucrative appearance and endorsement opportunities that came his way after he won a few tournaments. Almost without noticing, Jacobsen, like Koch, lost his competitive edge, and it was taking him many months to recover it. Yet Koch had a more serious obstacle to conquer. He had lost his exempt status and, in a game that is predominantly mental, he didn't even know if he could play at the pro level anymore.

Koch had arrived at the course on Sunday morning, three shots off the lead and, using the pressure-alleviating approach recommended by many sports psychologists, told himself it was just another day. The sun was shining, and it felt good to be there. He knew he was playing well, and he wanted to just let it happen. Let's just see how well I can do, he told himself. If that's good enough, great. If it isn't, that's fine too, I'll go on down the road and try again somewhere else.

Koch hadn't been able to establish the rhythm and the pace he wanted while he was warming up, and he walked out on the course feeling uncomfortable with his swing. But it didn't seem to matter, he knocked down birdies at the rate of one every two holes. His nonchalance continued until he looked at the leaderboard and saw that he was tied for the lead, and the $250,000 first prize—more than he had won in eleven of his twelve years on the tour—on the 10th hole. That's when the distancing techniques failed as panic struck.

All Koch wanted to do was hang on to the lead and win the tournament—he didn't give a damn about setting records. On each tee he tried to get the ball to where he could hit it again, and then get it on the green, where he could putt for par and go on to the next hole. He accomplished that, and by the time he finished the 18th hole, he had a one-stroke lead in the tournament.

Peter Jacobsen, who was playing in the group behind Koch, came to the 18th tee knowing he needed a birdie to tie Koch and force a playoff. He could feel the excitement bursting out through his fingertips, and he could feel a pounding in his chest. He felt like former Portland basketball star Bill Walton, who said the first three quarters of the game were fun, and he liked that because he loved to play basketball. But give him fifteen seconds on the clock, and his team has the ball, and he wants the last shot. That's why he plays basketball, because he wants to hit the last jump shot and win the game. He wants the glory.

On the occasions when Jacobsen had been in this position before, he had found himself thinking, If I hole this to get the birdie I win, and I get the winner's jacket, and I get all the adulation of the people in the pressroom, and the check, and I'm on television, and boy, won't I be something. He knew that he had to concentrate on what he was doing—Chuck Hogan had told him that repeatedly—but he was excited and having trouble remembering.

Jacobsen hit his drive on 18, a par-five with water in front of the green and sand behind it, 284 yards into the middle of the fairway. He knew he had hit a good shot when he left the tee, and all the way to the ball he was arguing with himself about what to do with his second shot. He could lay up short of the water, or go for the green. If he laid up, people would say he had no guts, and he didn't want that, so he decided to rip it.

At that moment, while he was standing out there peering at the flag, Jacobsen started having visions of grandeur. All he could think was, Well, I'll hit this three-wood 240 perfect yards, over the water, onto the green and into the cup. Just knock it into the hole, and saunter off the course, soaking up the noisy worship of the multitude of fans packed in around the 18th hole.

Gary Koch was standing near the 18th green waiting to see whether Jacobsen would take the tournament, and the automatic two-year exemption to play tournaments of his choosing that came with it, away from him.

Jacobsen slugged the ball like it was guided by God's hand. It hit the green, bounced and rolled into the back bunker. He blasted out of the sand, missed his birdie putt and parred the hole for second place and $122,222. Jacobsen waved to the gallery and came off the course patting backs and shaking hands as though he had just won the tournament by ten strokes.

Koch talked with the reporters, after failing in his attempts to reach his wife by telephone to share the news of his victory, before going off to celebrate with the tournament's organizers. Then there would be a flight to Dallas for next week's tournament. The people in Dallas had given him an exemption to play in their tournament when he needed it, and Koch didn't want to stiff them, even though he had just won a quarter of a million dollars, but it was going to be hard to be motivated.

Koch was feeling more relieved than exhilarated. Now that he was an exempt player again, he wouldn't have to go begging for a game. His money worries were gone as well. But after that wore off, he would start looking at himself as a tournament winner and expect, rather than hope, that he would win again soon. Sometimes he would try harder and put more pressure on himself than he should, attempting to live up to his Vegas performance, using that one week as his criterion. He would expect to shoot fourteen under par every week, and be disappointed when he didn't, even though he knew that wasn't going to happen.

In some aspects Peter Jacobsen was better off. He came into Vegas with about fifty thousand dollars on the year, doing his exercises and stretching, and he played great. He came to the last hole with a chance to tie with a birdie and failed to get it up and down. But that seemed to be kind of okay to him. He thought he was over the hump now.

When Jacobsen had started on the tour in 1977 and only the top sixty money winners were exempt from weekly qualifying, he had to learn how to survive Mondays, then how to make the cut on Fridays, then how to make money and then how to win. When Jacobsen's game became a joke, he had to relearn how to make the cuts and how to make money. He had mastered those skills a second time. And now, he thought, he was learning how to win again.

Jurisdictions

IRVING, TEXAS.

Only the absence of business-suited salesmen wearing snakeskin cowboy boots prevented the parking lot of Las Colinas Sports Club from looking like a suburban Dallas Cadillac dealership. The lot was gorged with lines of factory-fresh thirty-thousand-dollar Sedan de Villes, Broughams, Sevilles, and Fleetwoods, in either white or dark blue, which officials of the GTE Byron Nelson Golf Classic had obtained from the auto manufacturer as courtesy cars for the contestants in their golf tournament. Other tournaments provided new cars for golfers which bore decals proclaiming the occupants to be tournament participants, and sometimes the cars had special, consecutively numbered vanity license plates, but only in Dallas did each of the over one hundred cars bear identical, offical Texas license plates that read simply: NELSON.

The cars looked incongruous when they were moored down the road at the thirty-dollar-a-night Red Roof Inn, where some of the less prosperous golfers were staying, but here at Las Colinas, with its Four Seasons Resort, they formed an appropriate backdrop for the men from the Salesmanship Club, the nonprofit sponsor of the tournament, who walked past in their red pants and white baseball caps with scrambled-egg embroidered peaks, checking that everything was going smoothly for the pro-am.

Workers at a courseside building were using a crane to raise an "Allstate Welcomes the Byron Nelson Classic" sign to a prominent, rent-free position on the facade. Las Colinas, like most modern courses on the PGA Tour, was real estate driven. The course was created to inflate the value of the land surrounding it. Las

Colinas was exceptional in that, rather than being encircled with homes, it was lined by a Dallas-style office development, one featuring commercial buildings that proclaimed "architect-designed" the way designer jeans call attention to themselves with prominent stitching on the seat. But the oil business wasn't doing much to lubricate the Texas economy these days, and, despite the self-proclaimed designation "America's premier master planned development," many of the modish structures on the perimeter of the course were vacant.

On the golf course, players' agents enduring silk suits and cinched neckties despite the torrid sun and 90-degree temperatures pushed in among the picture-taking galleries at the driving range and putting green. The agents, clutching briefcases, were forced to wait patiently behind the gallery ropes for a moment of their young clients' time, as the golfers tarried disdainfully at their practicing. Black and Hispanic men from a temporary-employment agency threaded through the crowd that was heavy with paging beepers and jewelry, picking up trash, while wearing T-shirts with the ironic name of their employer: Moore Options, Inc.

As noon approached, a group of squarely built men with careful haircuts marched to a line of golf carts outside the clubhouse, while repeatedly scanning the crowd from behind their sunglasses. They wore casual clothing topped by overblouses that did an inadequate job of covering devices the men had attached to themselves, and their steps produced glimpses of coiled wires running to their ears, handcuffs dangling from their waists, and pointed bulges near their armpits. They were Secret Service agents, here to protect pro-am contestant and former President Gerald Ford—a man with a history of bruising spectators with misdirected golf balls—from any harm the spectators might try to do to him.

Ford emerged onto the course, waving and signing autographs, in the company of one of his playing partners, Tom Landry, the soon-to-be-former Dallas Cowboy football coach who somehow managed to look as starched and pressed in golf clothing as he did in the coat and tie he always wore on the sidelines. Ford, Landry, and their partners chatted amongst themselves as the Secret Service men loaded an ominous-looking two-foot blue nylon sack into one of the golf carts the agents would be occupying, and the entourage headed for the 1st tee.

Ford's play had improved since he left the White House and, if he wasn't getting tremendous distance on his shots, he kept his ball

in play, while receiving an endless stream of acquaintances between swings. The Secret Service agents, who were deployed in a
triangular formation of three carts around Ford, tensed in their
seats each time someone approached the former president, but it
was the unknown people outside the gallery ropes—those lacking
the proper credentials to pass under the lines—who held most of
their attention. The early afternoon passed uneventfully until, as
Ford's cart drove to his second shot on the 423-yard 4th hole, the
eyes of the agents holding down the left flank locked upon imminent danger.

She was a short, thirtyish blonde with immoderate makeup and
expansive, unsupported breasts that pushed mightily against her
thin white T-shirt, suspending the bottom hem of the shirt an inch
above the waistband of her tiny denim skirt, exposing a flash of
tanned stomach when she stood upright. When the woman felt the
eyes of the Secret Service on her, she stretched her right arm out
and rested it on a gallery-rope stake, lifted her left hand up to her
waist, and jutted her chest forward until the hem of her shirt rose
to disclose her navel. Her movements were precise and carefully
executed. It was an outfit, and a pose, she had spent a good deal
of time rehearsing.

The left-flank Secret Service men turned toward each other,
shaded eye met shaded eye, and they exchanged silent, knowing
looks. These men, who legend had it would throw themselves in
front of a bullet to save a president's life, knew how to react when
an aging ex-president out for a harmless afternoon of golf was
threatened this way. The agent who was driving mashed the ac-
celerator and propelled the cart forward with a start, then braked
to an abrupt halt three feet away from the suspect. The agents,
hardened to long hours of tedious surveillance, sat and stared
pointedly but speechlessly at the woman's breasts, while their president selected a club, took a practice swing, then swatted his ball
toward the green. Only when Ford had returned to his cart and
was safely headed up the course did the men break their gaze. They
advanced their cart slowly, and looked back frequently, as the
woman stood locked in her stance, a dangerous situation having
been defused without a word having been exchanged.

When Ford's party reached the back nine, where workers had
assembled television-camera towers near the greens in preparation
for the weekend broadcast of the tournament, the Secret Service
men in the lead cart would rush ahead when Ford hit his tee shots,

and scramble up the stairs of the towers to scrutinize the galleries. All the men could observe were thousands of prosperous-looking people drinking beer from cans encased in foam-insulating sleeves, who followed Ford for a couple of holes to see what a former president looked like, and wandered off to watch more accomplished golfers. It all seemed innocuous enough.

What the Secret Service agents didn't know was that William King, a forty-two-year-old man from Peoria, Illinois, who lived out of a well-used van and carried a copy of *Born for Battle* in his hip pocket, and who had designs on being the president of the United States himself, was walking around the course disguised as a pro-am caddie, studying those very same television towers, and calculating how he might use them to get his message across to the millions of people who would be watching their television sets on Saturday.

"Cripes, with the blue drapes and all the flowers, this place looks like a funeral parlor," Arnold Palmer said as he was led into the photo-opportunity-ready interview area of the media room by a flock of GTE officials. In exchange for putting up about half of the tournament's $750,000 purse, and buying an equal portion of the commercial time on the telecast, GTE had received the right to affix its initials to the front end of the tournament title, along with twenty spots in the pro-am and two thousand tickets for the event. By paying Palmer many hundreds of thousands of additional dollars to become their spokesman, GTE secured the right to compel him to play in their pro-am, and to escort him into the pressroom afterward, where they could sit smiling like proud parents—they had, after all, bought themselves a little piece of Arnie's tail—while Palmer held court and gave the news boys a few quotes for their stories.

Palmer was an infrequent visitor to the regular PGA Tour, and the interview room filled to capacity the moment he appeared. The fifty-eight-year-old grandfather was a member of the senior tour, where over-fifty golfers competed among themselves, rather than against youngsters who still had the fine motor control that delicate shots around the green required.

Palmer hadn't won on the regular tour in fifteen years, but no one who had anything to do with golf, save Palmer himself, really cared about that. Sam Snead, Jack Nicklaus, and Ben Hogan all had more than Palmer's sixty-one victories on the regular U.S. tour and, given the size of recent purses, twenty-five golfers stood in front of him on the career money list. But only Palmer could compel a young female reporter to blurt out in spite of herself, "I want to come sit on your lap," in a pressroom full of her largely male colleagues. And only Palmer could instantly and sincerely reply, "Well, come on," and not have anyone in the room think ill of the interchange.

Palmer dropped into a chair at the front of the room, hunched forward with his elbows on his knees and began flexing and rubbing his burly hands and wrists. Palmer has virtually no definition or taper between his hands and forearms, they seem to simply meld into an undifferentiated masses of flesh and muscle. They are not the sculpted appendages of a bodybuilder; rather they resemble nothing more than the shovel on the front of a bulldozer.

"What's it like for you to play on the regular tour now?" someone asked.

"It's getting so I know more of the people in the galleries than I do the golfers in the locker room," Palmer said with his easy smile.

"You should have seen him out there with those galleries today," a GTE man bragged. "He was terrific. Couldn't sign enough autographs."

"Signing autographs is part of the business," Palmer said, "especially on pro-am day."

"How do you spend your time, Arnie?"

"My time is divided up between golf course design, commercials, and senior tournaments. I probably spend the most time on course design, then tournaments, then commercials. I find myself busy a lot. Most of my days are scheduled far in advance."

Palmer had not become one of the wealthiest men in sports solely because of his golfing skills. The charisma and fan identification he brought to the game when golf and television were discovering each other had begun to make him affluent in the 1960s but, now that his game had diminished, his personal qualities were making him very rich. Palmer's companies include Arnold Palmer Enterprises for licensing and endorsements; ProGroup, Inc., for sporting goods; Palmer Golf Course Design Company; Arnold Palmer Aviation; as well as a string of auto dealerships.

"Will the time come when you don't play on the regular tour anymore?" someone asked.

"Yes, that time will come soon. I don't have a lot to accomplish on the regular tour anymore, so I will only play one or two a year." Palmer stopped for a moment then, noticing the corporate row in his audience, added hastily, "Being here for GTE and being their spokesman is something I enjoy, of course."

"Do you still practice?"

"I practice occasionally, but I miss being able to go out there and just hit balls and forget about everything."

"Do you miss being able to just play golf, without the business deals?"

"I can't remember when I was able to just play golf," Palmer said wistfully, and stared at his hands as though he could feel the grip of a favored club in them. "I'll tell you what I miss. I miss the way we used to play the tour. We drove cars around the country. We'd leave Dallas or wherever on Sunday night after the tournament, and drive to the next town. On the winter tour we played events from Arizona to Florida, and it was seven days a week. First you were driving, then the pro-am, then the pros would play together for two days. Those two days out there playing with your friends, I liked those two days a lot."

"How much course design work do you do, Arnie?"

"We've designed over a hundred courses, and we have contracts for forty more," Palmer said of the construction projects that brought in one million dollars per course at the minimum.

"Is there any competition between you and Jack Nicklaus in course design?" a writer asked.

Palmer looked at the man and grinned broadly. "Jack and I have never done anything that hasn't been competitive," he said.

"Here's your chance," the barker called out, "win valuable prizes in the long-drive competition. Have your swing analyzed by a computer. Ten swings for only five dollars."

There was a steady line of customers at the Special-Tee Enterprises, Inc., tent on Thursday afternoon, as men from the galleries fell prey to the siren call of the barker to test their manhood. Special-Tee had leased a tent on the tournament grounds, and installed an electronic tee that was wired to a computer with a television screen. When a golfer drove a ball off the tee and into a net ten yards away, the TV screen would display the clubhead speed at impact, the time ratio of backswing to follow-through, the distance the ball would have traveled in the air, and a graphic depiction of the clubhead's squareness to the target at impact. A chart listing the names of the men hitting the biggest drives of the video tournament was prominently displayed at the front of the tent.

Men would be walking by the tent with their wives or buddies, stop to half-snicker at the awkward swing of the man currently at the machine, eye the chart listing 274 yards as the longest drive, and reach for their wallets, knowing they could hit the damn ball further than that. They'd wait their turn, grab a driver, do their waggle over the ball, then whip the club at the ball like they meant to shatter it, only to have it roll impotently out of the stranglehold of the net while the TV screen blinked in calculation. Two hundred and four yards, it would read. All right, first swing is a mulligan anyway. Each successive swing would produce a more counter-productively violent flail, and an incremental change in simulated ball travel. By the fifth swing they'd be calling out to the man who took their money, "Hey, buddy, what the hell's wrong with this goddamn machine? I know I can hit a ball further than two hundred yards. This thing isn't accurate."

The barker would sympathize, while explaining the machine was calibrated regularly, and suggest that for a few dollars more he could provide them with a videotape of their swing, which they could examine for swing flaws. The customers would take the bait or not, but always they would walk away mystified about why they couldn't routinely hit a little dimpled ball with a specially designed club and make it go where they wanted it to. If the amateur golfers had had access to the pressrooms on the professional tour, they might have found solace in discovering that the boys who played for a living were often equally as confounded on the same issue.

Jeff Sluman thought he was a pretty good golfer, that he could play a little bit, when he finished his junior year at Florida State University in 1979 as the number one man on the team. But when his senior year came he wasn't swinging well or practicing hard, and he didn't even make the team. That wasn't good for his golfing ego, and he still hadn't fully recovered from it.

But Sluman persisted and practiced on his own, and when the guys who did make the golf team graduated and started their business careers, Sluman qualified for the U.S. Open as an amateur, and won a spot on the pro tour at the 1982 national qualifying tournament. Sluman knew that he could play some then, but he earned only $13,643 during 1983, and he lost his playing privileges.

There are two means of obtaining playing privileges on the PGA Tour, by winning enough money in tournaments played under sponsor exemptions to place on the top 125 on the money list—something few golfers ever do because sponsor exemptions are scarce—or by paying two thousand dollars to enter a three-stage national qualifying tournament. About eight hundred hopeful golfers add more than $1.5 million to the tour's coffers each year with their qualifying tournament fees. Half of them are dismissed after the first round of regional tournaments. The remaining four hundred are cut by half at the next round, before the surviving two hundred compete for about fifty available tournament players' cards in the finals. These top fifty are then eligible to compete in those tournaments during the next year that have room for them—usually about half of the year's events—after players with higher priority exemptions have decided which tournaments they wish to enter. Once a player earns his playing privileges with a top-fifty finish in the qualifying tournament, he must place in the top 125 his first year out, or he is back on the street again.

Sluman took a year off after he lost his card, went back to another qualifying tournament, and now he was standing outside the interview room at the Nelson tournament, waiting to be interviewed as one of the first-round leaders.

Sluman, at five feet seven and 135 pounds, was one of the smallest men on the tour, and he looked even more diminutive as he paced nervously back and forth in the entryway to the interview area, his arms tightly crossed on his chest, waiting for the media to finish with another golfer. Although Sluman had yet to win a tournament, he had been moving up the money list steadily. He had made it into the playoff at the 1987 Tournament Players Championship, only to lose on the third playoff hole, after having missed a winning putt on the previous hole when a spectator dove into a greenside pond as Sluman was about to stroke his ball. Sluman had tried to regain his composure, but he couldn't and he had to settle for second place.

Sluman was currently facing a situation that must have seemed as testing as the playoff at the Tournament Players Championship. His improved performance of recent years meant that he had been invited into the media room often enough to know the difficulties—and possibilities—it held for a young golfer, but not frequently enough to know how to handle them.

An uncomfortable silence always crept over the interview room the moment a lesser-known golfer finished going over his round. The easy questions about course conditions and such would be consumed quickly, and then everyone would sit there as flustered as freshmen at their first mixer.

The golfer, knowing the tremendous value of media exposure to an unknown on the tour, would be painfully sincere and eager in his attempts to please the reporters, but the reporters wouldn't know enough, or sometimes care enough, about the golfer to have a basis for questioning. The media people had plenty of golfers with known audience-appeal to write or broadcast about, and more often than not the neophyte golfer's spot on the leaderboard would evaporate by the end of the next day's round anyway. The result was usually a brief interview that resulted in little coverage, and a missed opportunity for the golfer.

Sluman came to the front of the interview room in Dallas and sat uncomfortably on the front edge of his chair, as he went over his round while playing with his watch. "How's your year going?" someone asked when Sluman had recited his last birdie.

Sluman said he had been playing consistently, and had only missed one cut, then talked of his elusive search—which was epidemic on the tour—for the perfect game. "I haven't been putting well the last few weeks, but I was putting well today. This is a goofy game, you're always satisfied with one part of your game and dissatisfied with another. You're always fiddling with something."

Sid Wilson, the public relations director of the tour who was conducting the press conference this week, looked around the quiet room for a moment. He was about to ask if there were any more questions, the signal for all that the interview was over, when Sluman unexpectedly said, "The strangest things happen to me every time I come here."

"Oh, like what?" someone asked, more out of politeness than curiosity.

"Well, last year a friend of mine named Doug, and my brother, and some other people came down to see me play. Doug met this girl at the tournament who tried to kill him. She gave him animal tranquilizer and left him for dead in his room at the Four Seasons hotel on the grounds of the golf club here. He was in a coma when they found him, and they rushed him to the hospital to pump out his stomach."

Notebooks flew open and pens hurried across paper as the

reporters were jolted out of their boredom. "Who was the girl? What was this about?" someone asked.

"The girl was part of a ring called the Rolex Girls," Sluman said. "There was a story about them on *60 Minutes*. They hang out at expensive resorts and pick up men who look like they have money. The women act like they're going to sleep with the men to get to their rooms, then they drug their drinks and rob them."

"Was the woman caught?"

"They caught her leaving the hotel, but they let her go before my friend came out of the coma the next day, so she was never prosecuted. They got his credit cards and stuff back, but she stole a ring from him that my friend had been trying to get off his finger for a couple of years and couldn't.

"The worst part of it was I got stuck with his five-hundred-dollar hotel bill," Sluman added.

"How did that happen?"

"The hotel said they would take care of the bill. They took care of it all right, they sent it to me because I had made the reservation for him through the tour office."

"What other things have happened to you here?"

"Two years ago my clubs were stolen from outside the club-house on the morning after the tournament," Sluman said. His words were flowing quickly, as if he were afraid he might not have another audience this receptive again anytime soon.

"Everybody said something like that couldn't happen at Byron Nelson's golf tournament," Sluman said sarcastically, "so I guess the clubs must still be around here and I just can't find them."

Reporters asked Sluman the full name of the man who was drugged, what city he lived in, and where exactly he met the woman, and all the while Sid Wilson sat there motionless and powerless. Wilson's flaccid cheeks normally pushed the ends of his lips downward, giving him a vaguely dyspeptic look, but as Sluman gave his testimony to the existence of real life on the tour—all the while committing the gravest transgression imaginable of the tour rule against a player saying anything potentially embarrassing about a tournament site or sponsor—Wilson appeared to go into a state of suspended animation. His gaze was fixed on infinity, his hands were pinned to his lap, and his skin tone held to its normal coloration.

The tour wields enormous power over powerless young men like Sluman—it can fine and suspend players at will—and golf commissioner Beman and his minions unleash their might freely when they feel the PGA Tour way of life is threatened or questioned. But Wilson knew any censorial display in full view of the press would be perilous. So he sat there like a man in meditational bliss, while the inquisitors from the media took Jeff Sluman's virginity. Wilson would handle Sluman later.

Sluman's stories would hardly have raised an eyebrow in most metropolitan police precincts or newsrooms, but the PGA Tour is the Disneyland of sports: a carefully controlled arena in which corporations rather than families can plunk down their money and have a life-affirming experience. Golf television broadcasts perennially attract the smallest audiences of any televised major sport, but tournaments have little trouble selling sponsorships and commercial time. The demographics of the viewers are above average, but more important is the perceived wholesomeness of the professional game. Corporations can invest their money without fear of drug or sex scandals tainting their name by association, present their best clients with a round on the links with a pro and, for an extra $7,500 or so, arrange to have one of the stars walk through the corporate hospitality tent, hard by the 18th green, after he completes his round. Attempted murders and stolen property had no place in the vigilantly protected world of the PGA Tour.

Jeff Sluman was still enjoying the attention of the press, but at the first lag in the interrogation Sid Wilson stood up and said, "Any more questions?"

"I have one more question," a reporter said to Sluman. "Why do you keep coming back here?"

"When I tell people these things they always ask me that," Sluman said. "I don't know. It's a nice course and there are some good people here too, I guess. My friend says he isn't coming back to Dallas anytime soon, but I'm just hoping to get through the week without anything strange happening."

Wilson walked from the interview room to the photocopy machine in the adjacent area. The PGA Tour public relations official who conducts the group interviews during a tournament takes notes during the questioning, then reproduces and distributes a summary of what was said for the use of journalists who missed the interview. The handout Wilson distributed from Sluman's session made no mention of the near-murder or theft. Instead, the closing line quoted Sluman as saying, "I love this tournament and this golf course."

Sid Wilson then embarked on a saunter around the media room in an attempt at damage control. Dallas was turning into a minefield for Wilson. Stories had been running in the local papers all week about the tour's maneuvers to influence Home Box Office's filming of a movie based on Dan Jenkins's 1974 novel *Dead Solid Perfect,* which was set on the golf tour. The cable television network had announced in April that local tournament officials had consented to have some of the filming take place at the Nelson tournament, and at the Colonial Invitational the following week in Jenkins's home town of Fort Worth. The telemovie was to feature Ben Crenshaw and Peter Jacobsen playing themselves as golfers, and ABC's Jack Whitaker, Dave Marr, and Ed Sneed playing sportscasters.

Jenkins, in addition to being a novelist, was a contributing editor of *Golf Digest* magazine, a podium he used to relentlessly criticize golf commissioner Beman, his policies, and the corporate tour sponsors. Such words of disparagement were issued infrequently by the golfing press, and Beman was a man with a long memory, but Jenkins nonetheless talked blithely about filming not only at tournaments, but also at PGA Tour headquarters in Florida. Between the announcements and the proposed filming dates, however, Beman decided that the film, which would contain nudity, adultery, and prodigious amounts of profanity, was not in the best interest of the tour.

Before the first camera was in position, seventy-six-year-old Byron Nelson was informed that scenes from an R-rated movie were to be filmed at a tournament bearing his name. Nelson, who belongs to the Church of Christ, had in his youth received a junior membership in the Garden Glen Country Club near Fort Worth because he was the only caddie there who didn't drink, smoke, or curse. Banning the sale of alcohol was still a local option in Texas, and a bottle of liquor was hard to come by in some neighborhoods close to Las Colinas—although considerable quantities of inebriants were available at the tournament itself.

Nelson told tournament officials he didn't approve of nudity in movies, and that he hadn't cursed in his life, and that was the end of filming in Dallas. Beman called officials from the Fort Worth tournament and reminded them that their contract with the tour forbade any type of photographic, television, or motion picture work during the week of a tournament event without permission from the tour. ABC, which purchases the right to broadcast tournaments from Beman's office, hastily cautioned its sportscasters about the clause in their contracts which prohibited them from appearing on a rival network, and golfer Ben Crenshaw was preparing to phone Jenkins to tell him he had to bow out because he was afraid his fans might wonder why he was in a movie with dirty words in it.

Deane Beman couldn't do anything to prevent the ultimately little-noticed film from being made in other places, just as Sid Wilson couldn't do anything about the two short items that would run in the Dallas newspapers the next day about Sluman's adventures. But Wilson could make sure Sluman was reminded about the PGA Tour code of silence.

When Sluman was brought into the media room later in the week, reporters were quick to ask if anything unusual had happened to him yet. "No," Sluman said brusquely, the delight with which he had told his stories a few days earlier long gone from his voice.

When the reporters pressed Sluman, as Wilson sat at his side, Sluman interrupted them. "Look," he said, "I just want to play golf. Let's leave the other stuff out of it."

When Arnold Palmer came to the 1st tee on Friday at even par for the tournament, with a decent chance of making the cut—something he seldom did on the regular tour anymore—his gallery was massive but respectful. No one hooted or hollered at the elder Arnold Palmer on the golf course. People might call out quietly, "Atta boy, Arnie," or, "Go get um, Arnie," while they wildly applauded his every move, but that was it. Palmer gave the spectators a bewildered grin after teeing off, shook his head to indicate the ball hadn't gone precisely where he wanted it to, then hitched up his pants and went lumbering down the fairway.

Many theories have been postulated about Palmer's popularity which, although it had peaked over two decades earlier when his tremendous galleries were dubbed Arnie's Army, still assured him of one of the largest followings on the golf course whenever he appeared. People talk about Palmer's dogged, never-say-die intensity on the links, or his common-man lack of pretension in dealing with the public. But the place where Palmer provoked the most visceral response from people was on the tee when he had a driver in his hands.

There are a number of cults on the pro tour. Some golfers—

cool guys—always flip the collars of their golf shirts up at a rakish angle. A very small group always wear pants with enough cotton content to actually hold a wrinkle. One contingent of golfers seldom practices and believes the golf swing is intuitive. But the largest collection is the mechanics—men who profess that golf is physics, and once they have mastered the application of the principles of leverage to the swing, they will never have another bad day on the course. The mechanics spend a lot of time on the practice range, freezing their motion in the middle of their backswing to study the position of their arms relative to their torsos. They eventually develop swings that are as aesthetically pleasing as a well-executed arabesque in ballet, even if they take home the big check on Sunday only infrequently.

When Arnold Palmer reaches the top of his backswing, he lurches at the ball with a force and ungainliness that is more appropriate to the descent of an axe on a felled tree than a golf club on a perched ball. He swings the club hard, the way every untutored golfer in the world does reflexively, and somehow he manages to keep the club under control in his viselike hands so the clubface ends up square at the moment of contact. He applies a little twirl to the club at the top of his follow-through, then lifts his head up with a look of naive fascination to discover where the ball has gone, like a kid who has just chucked up a stone and cracked it with a stick. It is one of the most visibly forceful swings in the professional game, and golf fans love that, inexplicably, it works so well.

Palmer was pressing hard to make the cut on Friday, and as he crouched on the 3rd green to study a birdie putt his shirt was already stained with sweat. He looked at the putt carefully and uncertainly. Putting, once a Palmer strength, had become his frailty, and when Palmer dropped this putt to go one under he sighed in relief as the crowd cheered.

The people in Palmer's gallery began to murmur among themselves when he went over to talk to paramedics on the medical cart after coming off the 6th green, and when he walked down the 7th fairway wincing and rubbing the right side of his midsection. Palmer reared back with his driver on the 8th tee and the painful tic in his side that had been troubling him since the previous night grabbed him, and his ball sliced off the right side of the fairway and into a patch of trees.

Palmer walked down the fairway determined not to let the pain bother him, and he hit a tremendously curved recovery shot from the midst of the trees to the edge of the green. Rolling applause greeted Palmer when he walked to the green. Palmer pulled off his visor to give the crowd a courtly salute, then turned back to look at the trees he had maneuvered his ball out of, not seeming to believe the shot himself.

The medical cart reappeared as Palmer approached the 9th tee, and he waded through the gallery to get to it. Palmer talked to the paramedics for a minute, then the man whose ferocious swings used to yank his shirttail out of his trousers modestly pulled up the right side of his shirt so the medics could apply an analgesic cream. Hundreds of fans swarmed around the cart, stretching up onto their toes to get a glimpse of the proceedings, as a wintergreen smell drifted through the air and Palmer looked around self-consciously at the hordes gawking at him.

Palmer came to the 9th tee with his shirt out—he would wait until he was heading down the fairway, away from prying eyes, before tucking it back in demurely—and a woman in the gallery said to her friend, "It doesn't look right anymore, does it? Arnie on a golf course with his shirttail hanging out."

Palmer was hoping the cream and two pain pills he had taken would let him continue in the match but, after double-bogeying the 10th, he came to the 11th tee and put his first shot into a lake that ran down the left side of the fairway. He told tournament officials that no good would come of his continuing in the tournament, and they found a cart to drive him back to the locker room.

Palmer sat in the cart, smiling ruefully at his fans, as it picked its way through the mob of people around the tee. He had just withdrawn from a golf tournament for the third time in his thirty-four-year career.

William King arrived at Las Colinas on Saturday afternoon just as the ABC telecast was going on the air. He rotated the beak of his baseball cap to the back of his head to lower wind resistance and ran the two miles from the front gate to the 10th tee, where he knew the tournament leaders, and thus the cameras, would be. King had been a 4:40 miler in high school, but that was more than twenty years ago and, although his spirit was desirous of moving that rapidly, his flesh was weak.

King reached the 10th tee, perfumed with sweat and winded,

but with his eyes shining fervently, only to discover the area surrounding the tee was hopelessly clogged with people. The last
twosome of the day was about to tee off, and it included tournament leaders Jeff Sluman and Ben Crenshaw, who was a native of
Austin, Texas.

Texas newspaper editors appreciated the sensibilities of their
readers and, in their coverage of the tournament, the editors in-
sured that each reference to a golfer employed any possible relationship the man might have with Texas as an adjective before his
name was stated, halting just short of such terminology as "frequent Dallas visitor," "grandson of Irving native," "former Southern Methodist University applicant," or "look-alike to Waco
resident."

The Nelson tournament had turned into a chauvinistic Texas
love feast after two rounds when local boy—Austin was, after all,
only two hundred Texas miles away—Ben Crenshaw had turned
up on top of the heap. On Saturday morning over fifty thousand
people had poured into the parking lot of Texas Stadium, where
marshals without horses herded them into roped-off holding pens
to await chartered buses that would transport them to the golf
course. Now William King was trying to get into camera range at
the 10th tee, and every last one of those people seemed to be in
front of him.

King knew from experience that if the tee was this jammed, the
10th green was only going to be worse. And he remembered from
caddying in the pro-am that the entire left side of the 11th hole was
lined by water, so all of the spectators would coagulate on the
right. He had no choice, he had to write off the 10th and 11th
holes, and run to the 12th tee to establish a good position opposite
the camera operator.

King waited serenely at the 12th tee and made small talk with
the spectators, who seemed not to notice the intense, blissed-out
laughter that punctuated his conversation, or that he had unbut-
toned his shirt, but was holding it closed over his chest. Finally,
when Sluman arrived at the tee and was about to strike his ball,
King dropped to his knees to be in direct line of the camera, pulled
open his top shirt, and displayed his T-shirt to an audience of
several million people. It read: *John 3:16.*

King was a TV hit man for God. For the last four years he had
endured a subsistence existence on the road and devoted the better
part of his energy to getting clothing adorned with scriptural ci-

tations on television at sporting events. It was not a vocation he took lightly.

King had studied under master TV hit man for God Rollen Stewart. Stewart had been getting his face on television since 1977, but he didn't become a Christian until 1980, and until then his appearances were sheer vanity, and devoid of higher purpose. King met Stewart in a hallway at the 1984 Republican National Convention. King was looking for a new gig, having just bowed out of the race for the Democratic presidential nomination after receiving thirty-four votes in the New Hampshire primary, and Stewart had found a niche appearing at televised sporting events wearing a rainbow-colored Afro-style wig and shirts with biblical citations. When the two were photographed talking together and the picture appeared in a newspaper the next day, King knew he had found his calling. King apprenticed with Stewart, and now considered himself to be Stewart's partner in their couch-potato ministry.

King found the PGA tour to be an especially fertile ground for TV proselytizing, thanks to the cooperation he received from the golfers who were members of a tour Bible study group, a collection of several dozen pros who held services each Wednesday in the city where the week's tournament was being staged. The group had once been only a minor embarrassment to the unreborn majority on the tour when, on the rare occasion a member was a tournament leader, he would walk into the pressroom and call out something like, "Praise Jesus."

At a 1987 tournament in Ohio, marshals and spectators had organized to stand in front of King everywhere he went. People shadowed him around the course, blocking him so he couldn't dart from hole to hole. But when the final putt was in the cup, Don Pooley had won, and when they handed him the trophy he said, "I'd like to thank the Lord Jesus Christ for this trophy," and King was vindicated.

Then 1987 turned into a bountiful year for the Christians, when three of the year's four major tournaments were won by members of the Bible study, and Scott Simpson told the press that he had won the prestigious U.S. Open by reflecting on a biblical passage he had carried in his wallet. Now study member Steve Jones took it upon himself to make sure that any time he was in a tournament King would have a free pass waiting for him. And when Jones wasn't at a tournament, as was the case this week,

King merely had to go to the Wednesday meeting and ask the first guy he met for a pass, and he would be rewarded with one.

King rose to a half-crouch position, shooting his left leg out and rolling his chest toward it, while stretching the bottom of his T-shirt to keep the lettering taut, and staying in camera range as a man with a portable camera followed Crenshaw through his tee shots on 12, then King fled down the course. King performed with the zeal of a first-tour-of-duty missionary when the cameras were rolling, but he was having trouble keeping focused on golf these days.

King was distracted by his efforts to start a mail-order business to peddle a radiant barrier that people could install in their attics, which he called the eagle shield. The shield was purported to bounce heat right out of people's houses in the summer, without the heat rays even touching their insulation, let alone entering their living space. And he was equally preoccupied by the upcoming 1988 Summer Olympics.

The whole world would be watching TV from Korea, and King had been crafting the message he would send to them for three years. It was going to be the heaviest message that had ever been sent on television. It wouldn't be John 3:16. John 3:16 was the shallow end of the pool, where people came in. It was a nice opening message for a guy who had never read a Bible, and was sitting there with a can of beer. King wanted him to see the message, find a Bible, and open it up to read the passage. In Korea, King wanted to really confront the whole global system that Satan was putting together in a very powerful way, and that was going to require an entirely different, more omnipotent message.

King's presence in Crenshaw's gallery did not bestow any blessings on the golfer's game. Crenshaw had picked up three strokes on the course on the front nine, only to lose each of them on the back nine. He came to the pressroom at nine under for the tournament, tied for the lead with Bruce Lietzke.

"I had such good fortune through the front nine, everything was going great, then the couple of bogeys at thirteen and fourteen really stopped my progress," Crensaw said. "It seemed to go the other way just like that. I suppose it was my turn, but I was very disappointed that I dropped three shots."

Someone handed Crenshaw, who was known as Gentle Ben for his soft-spoken manner, but who could bend a club with the best of them on occasion, a cup of iced tea and a packet of sweetener.

Crenshaw emptied the sweetener into his drink, looked unfruitfully for a place to put the empty packet, then slipped it between his fingers and the cup.

Crenshaw had been distressed a lot lately, particularly during the closing round of tournaments. He had never been a strong finisher, having lost six of the seven playoffs he had been in during his fifteen-year career, but now he was crashing and burning somewhat regularly and, like every golfer on the PGA Tour who wasn't winning, he hadn't the faintest notion of what was wrong. After falling out of contention at Las Vegas, the frustration got to Crenshaw so bad he said he had wanted to jump into a pond on the course.

The guru Crenshaw sought out was his former college roommate, who was now a country club pro. The man came to Dallas, observed Crenshaw during a practice round, and determined all Crenshaw needed to do was reposition his clubface at address a fraction of an inch. Crenshaw made the change and charged to the top of the leaderboard on Thursday and Friday. Now it seemed the bromide didn't work on weekends, and Crenshaw was searching for another explanation.

"I was playing along nicely coming into the thirteenth, and I started thinking that with a few more birdies I was going to finish with a three- or four-shot lead. But," Crenshaw said, "it wasn't meant to be."

The wind would come up Sunday afternoon at Las Colinas and make the golf tricky, but the first storm of the day developed in the pressroom. The *Dallas Times Herald* had asked Payne Stewart, who had played his college golf in Dallas, to write a column for the paper during the four days he participated in the tournament. And in Saturday's edition of the paper, Stewart had voiced that familiar golfer's refrain that tournament officials were deliberately drying out the greens to drive up scores.

"I think they're letting the course get out of control," Stewart wrote. "If it's hot like it was today and one of those big Texas winds blows through, the course could get unplayable. It's ridiculous. As hard as the greens are getting, they better watch it. It's obvious they're close to dying. And then they sprinkled the greens with water during play today, and that's just bad preparation. I blame our field staff and the greenskeeper. It was like playing golf on Central Expressway."

Byron Nelson, a quiet gentleman, was so irked by Stewart's remarks that he made a rare and unannounced visit to the press-room to hint, but never actually say, that the year's drought rather than maliciousness might be responsible for the dry conditions. Nelson was asked if he had spoken to Stewart about his remarks. "No," said Nelson, who understood that tour discipline was ad-ministered in the back shed rather than the pressroom, "but I think someone will enlighten him a little bit."

Payne Stewart was also on Bruce Lietzke's mind later that afternoon. After the wind blew Jeff Sluman into a six-over-par round that landed him tied for thirteenth, and Ben Crenshaw into a one-over round that was good for a tie for third place, Lietzke found himself standing in a bunker near the 18th green, needing to get his ball in the cup in two strokes to win the tournament, or three strokes to force a playoff with Clarence Rose, who was waiting in the scorer's tent. Chances were good that Lietzke would be able to accomplish one of the two, but all Lietzke—staring victory in the eye—could think about was Payne Stewart. Stewart had been in the same bunker at the same tournament needing only a bogey to win in 1985, and as soon as Lietzke stepped into the bunker he remembered that Stewart had double-bogeyed, and then he lost the tournament in a playoff.

Lietzke wanted to go for the pin and get it over with, but Stewart's ghost persuaded him to play a safe shot out. Lietzke figured his ten victories during his thirteen years on the tour would give him a decided edge in a playoff with Rose, who had never won. Lietzke holed the ball in three, went to the scorer's tent, and then walked out to find his transportation to the 16th hole for the beginning of the playoff.

The only time professional golfers routinely use golf carts dur-ing a round at a PGA Tour event is at the commencement of a playoff. The television broadcast is usually in overtime, and the first playoff tee is often some distance from the 18th green. When it appears a playoff is possible, tournament officials will ferry a few carts over to the scorer's tent so the golfers can hop into them. Or at least that's what they do everywhere else but Dallas.

What Bruce Lietzke found when he emerged from the scorer's tent was not a golf cart, but three huge, brand-new, thirty-thousand-dollar Cadillacs with NELSON license plates—*and* a mo-torcycle policeman. Lietzke slid his sweaty clothes across the supple leather upholstery, dragged his dirty spiked shoes through the plush cut-pile carpet, and settled back in air-conditioned comfort as tournament officials stormed into the other cars. Somebody gave a signal to the motorcycle cop, who kicked his bike into gear with his shiny leather boots, and the motorcade of behemoths went tearing down a cart path on the side of the golf course, the cars bouncing and wallowing and throwing up clouds of dust on the spectators, while the folks from the GTE Byron Nelson Classic demonstrated that they knew how to do things with style in Dallas.

Lietzke's conjecture that his past victories would give him a decided edge over Rose proved correct, and the playoff ended in a Lietzke victory at the 16th hole. That meant that everyone got to pile into the Cadillacs for a motorcade back to the award ceremony on the 18th green. Doors slammed shut, a motorcycle engine revved, dust flew, spectators ran for cover, and an unidentified voice seemed to be calling out from the distance, "Hi yo, Silver."

Lietzke emerged from a Cadillac and walked onto the 18th green, where a long line of members of the Salesmanship Club stood waiting to greet him.

Dee Brown, president of the club, stepped to a microphone and addressed the crowd. "Thanks to you golf fans," he said, "we've had record crowds, and we not only appreciate your attendance, but we appreciate your courtesy and the way you've conducted yourself during this exciting tournament. Thanks to your support, we've had record sales, and as you may or may not know, this tournament gives more money to charity than any other tournament on the PGA Tour. The proceeds from your support will continue to support our work with kids at our camps in East Texas, and at our educational center in Dallas."

The Nelson tournament was indeed a significant, if not the premier, producer of funds for charity, having passed more than $6 million in funds to the club's wilderness survival camps for socially and emotionally disturbed adolescents—kids the club said were one step from prisons or mental institutions before they intervened. The camps claimed that 85 percent of the kids who attended their programs went on to become good citizens. The Salesmanship Club was proud of the kids they helped, and they had pictures of some of them on posters around the tournament to demonstrate that.

Dee Brown continued with his speech, and noted that some of the disturbed children who became Salesmanship Club campers had been invited to the tournament. "And I'd like to welcome, and I'd like for you to join me in welcoming, some of our kids that are with us today," he said. And then Brown pointed across the lush 18th green of Las Colinas Sports Club, over to where the Salesmanship Club members were standing in their blue blazers and red pants, and there, kneeling on the green in front of the men in the blazers, was a long line of disturbed children, whom the Salesmanship Club had brought out to the tournament and now were proudly putting on display.

Rocky Johnson, chairman of the board of GTE, also addressed the crowd. "We certainly enjoyed sitting up there in the skybox and watching everything, and the playoff was just frosting on the cake. Besides that, it gave us an extra chance to give a couple of more commercials, and we enjoyed that very much also," he said. "This was a great tournament, but we look forward to making it the greatest tournament on the PGA Tour before we're done."

Fires in the Bellies

When Jack Nicklaus's Muirfield Village Golf Club in Dublin was dedicated on May 27, 1974, Nicklaus told the one thousand people who attended the ceremony that the completion of the club, which took almost nine years to accomplish, meant more to him than his brilliant golfing career. When Nicklaus won the second Memorial Tournament held on the course in 1977, he said the win was his biggest thrill, and his greatest accomplishment in golf, despite having won sixteen major tournaments to that point. When he won the match again in 1984, he said again that it meant more to him than any other tournament.

Some of the sportswriters who were present to hear Nicklaus's remarks scoffed at what he said, and insisted that Nicklaus was engaging in hyperbole. What the reporters didn't realize was that Muirfield Village, named after the famous Scottish course of the same name, was Nicklaus's monument to himself and the exalted position in golf he had single-mindedly pursued since childhood. There was only one thing that Jack Nicklaus ever wanted out of life, and that was to be recognized and remembered as the greatest golfer who had ever inhabited the earth.

Nicklaus had begun playing golf at ten, when he first accompanied his father, the owner of several pharmacies and a one-time scratch-handicap golfer, to Scioto Country Club outside of Columbus, Ohio. Bobby Jones, whose record of thirteen major-championship victories Nicklaus would one day eclipse, had won the 1926 U.S. Open at the course, and Nicklaus entered the world of golf hearing the club's members recount every shot Jones had hit on the course. The young boy took careful notice that a man's golf game could make people recall him that vividly twenty-four years after the fact.

The young Nicklaus proved to be a golf prodigy under the tutelage and unflagging encouragement of Scioto's teaching pro, Jack Grout, who took great pains to impress upon Nicklaus that he had been blessed with a special talent. Nicklaus broke 70 for the first time, from the championship tees, when he was thirteen. Later that summer, he shot 63 on five different occasions. Nicklaus decided then that he wanted to break Jones's record in the majors and, like Jones, do so while remaining an amateur. Nicklaus's father was strongly supportive and, in 1950s money, he laid out the first of what would be thirty-five thousand dollars over the next eight years for his son's golf and travel expenses.

Nicklaus thrived on athletic competition, and when he was in junior high he told his father that he wanted to go out for the football team. The senior Nicklaus advised his son to forget about football, saying he wasn't fast enough to play the game. His father's disparagement became yet another challenge for Jackie to vanquish. So his father thought he was too slow for football? Rather than trying to succeed immediately on the gridiron, Nicklaus went out for the track team instead. After he had won a host of medals in track, Jackie brought them home, taunted his father with them, then asked if he still thought his son was too slow for football.

At fourteen, Nicklaus's golfing exploits were making headlines in the local papers, where he was being called the next Sam Snead. But Nicklaus would scoff at that. He was going to be better than Snead, and he didn't need newspapers, or anyone, to tell him that. Nicklaus's father was driving his son to a golf match when the boy was fifteen and, wanting to give his offspring some reassurance, the father informed the son that he was good enough to win the tournament he was about to enter. Jackie told his father that he already knew that, and to please be quiet.

While the other sixteen-year-olds around Columbus were delighting in the prospect of their first driver's license, Nicklaus was defeating a field of professional golfers to win the Ohio Open tournament. By the time he queued up for freshman registration at Ohio State, Nicklaus was an international amateur golf phenomenon, and his name and reputation preceded him at every event he entered.

Mark McCormack, the founder of International Management Group, was in the early stages of building his player management colossus at this time, which he had started by representing Arnold Palmer exclusively. Television, Arnold Palmer, and President Eisenhower had sparked a golf boom, and there was suddenly far more money to be made in the game than ever before—especially through corporate tie-ins. McCormack approached Nicklaus in 1961, while the golfer was still in college, and told him his agency could promise Nicklaus a first-year income of $100,000, exclusive of tournament purses, if he would turn pro.

Nicklaus resisted the idea mightily. Going pro meant that he wouldn't be able to surpass Jones's accomplishments with the special standing that golf confers on amateur champions. But Nicklaus had married the year before, and his first child had been born in July. Nicklaus was shuffling from playing golf to selling insurance—the golfer's occupation of choice in those days—to attending classes at Ohio State when he found time.

The university eventually tired of Nicklaus's neglect of his studies, and the president of Ohio State informed Nicklaus that he would no longer allow him to remain a student if he wished to follow these other pursuits, and suggested that he withdraw. Nicklaus—a man of some intelligence—bitterly left the college and joined the tour in early 1962. Within weeks, Mark McCormack obtained a clothing endorsement contract, a book contract for an autobiography, and a deal with General Motors that would have a new Buick waiting for Nicklaus at every stop on the tour. Endorsement deals in Great Britain and Australia soon followed.

Nicklaus arrived on the pro circuit, chubby and far more confident than established people in a field like a twenty-two-year-old newcomer to be. He immediately became an unwelcomed rival for Arnold Palmer, whose brash game and attending popularity were at their zenith. Nicklaus played poorly his first few months out. But he told reporters, when they asked, that he expected to earn thirty thousand dollars in purse money as a rookie nonetheless. Few veteran golfers on the tour were making that kind of money, but Nicklaus hadn't meant to boast. To his mind it was a reasonable assessment of his abilities relative to the field. But the other players, the ones who called Nicklaus "Ohio Fats," screamed about the kid's presumptuousness when they read his words.

Nicklaus ignored them, just as he overlooked the fans who rooted for his defeat when the upstart rookie wound up in an eighteen-hole playoff with Palmer to decide the 1962 U.S. Open championship. Spectators urged Palmer to walk around on the green while Nicklaus was putting, and Palmer himself chastised Nicklaus for playing too slowly. Nicklaus disregarded them all, kept the stoic expression on his face, and remembered the hours he had spent a decade before hitting ten buckets of balls on the driving range when the other twelve-year-olds in his golf class were hitting one.

All of that toil had been in preparation for what was to officially begin that day, in a most auspicious manner. Jack Nicklaus defeated the king, Arnold Palmer, by three strokes—in a major tournament—to record his first professional win. Columbus, Ohio, threw a Jack Nicklaus Day. There was a parade to the state house with confetti, ticker tape, and all the rest. The next week, twenty-two-year-old Jack Nicklaus was on the cover of *Time* magazine.

Nicklaus won three other tournaments during his rookie year, finishing third on the money list with $61,869 in earnings. He would not finish lower than fourth in annual revenues during the next sixteen years of his career, nor win fewer than two tournaments a year—despite an ever expanding off-course business empire—and he would attain the money title for five of the six years between 1971 and 1976. By 1988, he would have won seventy-one PGA Tour events, eighteen more outside the U.S., and finished second fifty-eight times. He would add eighteen majors as a professional to his two U.S. Amateurs. Three of the wins in the majors would come after he had turned forty.

Yet amidst a life of statistical monuments erected around the globe, Nicklaus reserved his fondest words for a golf course/housing development and tournament in the flatlands of central Ohio where, during his boyhood, Nicklaus decided the world was never going to forget Jack Nicklaus.

Nicklaus sired three of his five children by 1965. He transplated his young family then to the balmy climes of North Palm Beach, Florida, and, at the age of twenty-five, immediately formulated plans for the golf course and tournament that would be his shrine in the town he had just vacated. He enlisted a friend to fly over Columbus to identify a site for the course, brought in a course architect to examine potential locations, then purchased 180 acres in suburban Dublin when the designer pronounced the setting to be the best inland location for a course he had ever seen.

Unfortunately, financiers did not agree, and the project floundered for years, even after Nicklaus resigned himself to surrounding the course with a housing development. But such was the span of the shadow that an absent Nicklaus cast at home that a group of local businessmen, feeling honored to be able to participate in Nicklaus's dream, worked long hours at what became their second job: enlisting other people in Nicklaus's drive to create a masterpiece in their midst, and to develop a tournament on it that would rival the majors.

When the last deal was cut and the course was completed, it bore more than a passing resemblance to Augusta National, home of the Masters tournament and brainchild of Nicklaus's hero Bobby Jones. The fairways followed the long up-and-down sweeps of Augusta, they were built with ample width off the tees, but with quite difficult greens.

The tournament, too, took its cues from the South. Nicklaus called his event the Memorial Tournament, and honored a figure from golf's past with a ceremony each year, but that was the veneer. The essence was Nicklaus outdoes Augusta. Horticulturists splashed tens of thousands of brightly colored, winter-nurtured flowers over the grounds, caddies were issued uniform coveralls, and when there wasn't the budget to bury the television lines as they were at the Masters, a workman was dispatched with green paint and brush to camouflage the 1,600 yards of yellow cable that ABC strung out over the course. The field of golfers receiving invitations was reduced from the weekly norm and the greens were made very fast, so the participants would learn a new respect for the meaning of the word par. During the first decade of the tournament, only ten percent of the contestants shot better than par over the four days.

Nicklaus had put his money where his mouth was when it came to Muirfield Village. He had complained bitterly about the decline of the American tour for years, and in Muirfield Village he had built a golf course that the spoiled American pros, with their high-tech clubs and golf balls, couldn't decimate even if they were at the top of their game. The Memorial Tournament had one of the $900,000 purses the boys were accustomed to, but they were going to earn their money here—and maybe learn a little bit of gumption as well.

Of all the aspects of the modern game that troubled Nicklaus, and there were many, nothing galled him more than the failure of the American tour to produce an heir apparent to approximate—rather than replace—him atop the world of international golf. Nicklaus had risen from the backwaters of Ohio to make the PGA Tour the ne plus ultra of golf, and now the Sony World Rankings—

even the rating sponsor was foreign—listed Australian Greg Norman, Scotsman Sandy Lyle, German Bernhard Langer—who was having an unproductive 1988—and Spaniard Seve Ballesteros as the four premier golfers in the world respectively.

The most galling blow of all came in September of 1987 when the Ryder Cup, a biennial competition between American and European golfers that is played alternately in the States and in England, unfolded on Nicklaus's own sanctuary in Dublin, Ohio, with Nicklaus serving as the nonplaying captain of the U.S. team. The Europeans took the match for their first victory here since the competition began in 1927, then linked their arms and danced joyfully and defiantly on Nicklaus's 18th green like a chorus line. Nicklaus had earned his first ignominious entry in golf trivia books: Name the U.S. course on which an American Ryder Cup team first lost to their European opponents.

Nicklaus's American team had hopes of a miraculous comeback until the closing minutes of the final round. The Yanks needed to win nine of twelve possible points that day, and they managed six of them with three twosomes—each worth a point—still on the course. Nicklaus still had hopes of avoiding disgrace until Curtis Strange, the Masters choker, lost to Seve Ballesteros and, with two groups left, it became statistically impossible for the Americans to pull it out.

Nicklaus said his boys weren't as tough as the Europeans, and that the team didn't have any dominant players because, with 125 golfers exempt from weekly qualifying—thanks to Deane Beman's all-exempt tour policy—the Yanks could make six-figure livings without having to learn how to draw blood. Nicklaus sang: Where are our dragon slayers of tomorrow?, and the refrain was, No one in America wants to be Jack Nicklaus, and it's driving Jack Nicklaus nuts.

But none of that mattered this week, for Nicklaus had his clubs back in his hands and there was another milestone on the horizon. Nicklaus was within $2,450 of becoming the first man in the history of golf to earn five million dollars in his career, just as he had been the first to earn two, three, and four million dollars, and he would be able to achieve this in front of his mother on his own course at his own tournament. Last place paid $2,500. All Nicklaus had to do was make the cut, which he had done in all previous twelve Memorials, and he would be one step closer to immortality.

* * *

During his first year as golf commissioner in 1974, Deane Beman saw Jack Nicklaus's caddie, Angelo Argea, enter the clubhouse at a tournament in Pinehurst, North Carolina, in violation of PGA Tour rules. Caddies, thought to be of questionable repute and virtue, were—and still are—forbidden from entering clubhouses or locker rooms at tournament locations. Beman immediately issued an order suspending Argea's caddying privileges for thirty days. Argea had entered the forbidden zone only because he had an urgent message to deliver to Nicklaus, and only after the guard at the door—who had refused to deliver the message for the caddie—authorized Argea to talk to Nicklaus in the clubhouse briefly. Nicklaus later explained these circumstances to his friend Deane Beman, certain that Beman would rescind the suspension. Beman didn't. He told Nicklaus rules were rules, and that the commissioner's decisions were final.

Deane Beman didn't need Jack Nicklaus or anyone else to tell him how to run the commissioner's office when he arrived on the job. Beman asserted his new authority instantly and, after one near-rebellion among the players early in his regime, unwaveringly. When a magazine published an article in 1975 alleging that a California resort that was a tournament site had mob connections, Beman unilaterally canceled the twenty-three-year-old tournament that was held there. The tournament was a favorite of the players, and they were distressed that Beman had acted summarily—without even a token consultation with the players' advisory board. Resentment and anger, stoked by locker-room bitch sessions, grew among the players until Beman was forced to rescind his decision.

Since the tour is essentially an association of independent contractors who play golf for a living, the golfers own the business Beman runs, and he served at their pleasure. The PGA tour was a small and loosely organized entity then, with minimal assets and an annual income of several million dollars that was derived almost exclusively from television revenues. With seemingly little to lose, the golfers were ready to face Beman down when he attempted to deny them one of the chief pleasures of their lives—playing golf and having a good time.

Beman yielded to the players then, and went back to work on expanding the business. Beman knew that the organization was living at the caprice of the TV networks, and he didn't like that at all. Hat-in-hand was not Beman's style, so he set out to redefine the balance of power by transforming the tour from a collection of matches into a self-sufficient conglomerate over the next fourteen years.

Beman discovered sports marketing just as the economy and interest in golf were expanding. Corporations were hungry for new, safe outlets for their advertising messages, and Beman was there waiting to tell the marketing folks his boys didn't even put their fingers in their noses, much less drugs. The sponsors loved that the golfers were independent businessmen who didn't get paid unless they produced, and the audiences for the matches were as upscale as they came. It was a perfect fit, and Beman lured corporate sponsorship to golf to such an extent that 70 percent of 1988's tour-sanctioned events bore company names in their titles.

Beman was simultaneously pressuring tournament organizers to continually increase their purses if they wanted to retain their events and, when TV networks complained that golf ratings were too low, Beman went back to the tournament organizers and told them they would have to sell much of the television advertising for their tournaments themselves if they wanted the tour office to negotiate with the networks for rights fees on their behalf.

When courses that were the sites of successful tournaments raised the $100,000 to $300,000 rents they charged the tour, Beman responded by moving the tour into golf course development by building or licensing his own courses, called Tournament Players Clubs, and relocating the tournaments to them. These courses pioneered a concept called stadium golf, in which fairways and greens were bounded by large earthen gallery mounds to give spectators an unimpeded view of the action on the courses. But, given Beman's bent for standardization, the courses also had an assembly-line quality to them, and Jack Nicklaus thought the sameness of the challenges they presented was another contributing factor in the declining prominence of American golfers.

In an attempt to spread the wealth he was accumulating in the PGA Tour's nonprofit coffers, Beman contracted with tour players to serve as consultants to the architects who designed the TPC courses, regardless of the players' past course-design experience. The design teams never lacked for direction, however, for Beman had stacks of blueprints and guidelines that specified exactly what he had in mind. What Beman decided he wanted, after one false start at the first TPC, was a good, serviceable golf course that would accommodate spectators and television well. If meeting those concerns resulted in courses that presented golfers with the same challenges and shots every week, that wasn't so horrible. It simply meant that golf became the equivalent of a well-insured life: a series of experiences in which there are no surprises.

Golf course and real estate developments are fraught with financial risks, however, so Beman had local real estate developers do the financing and construction on the Tournament Players Clubs, while the tour oversaw the courses and retained a piece of the future appreciation of some courseside properties that were sold. The tour then used the courses one tournament-week a year and hawked memberships for up to thirty thousand dollars for amateurs to use them the rest of the time. Beman took a commission on the memberships for the tour, then passed the remainder of the funds on to the developers, with the proviso that each dollar the developers received reduced the price of the tour's purchase option on the properties by an equal amount. The deals Beman structured varied from course to course, but they had one shared feature: the PGA Tour never had money at risk in any project.

Beman utilized local volunteers to work his tournaments, persuaded sponsors and tournament operators to make contributions to charity in the name of golf, sold resorts the right to call themselves official golf destinations, started an in-house television and film unit to produce commercial programs—with an eye toward possibly producing their own nonunion tournament telecasts in the future—and created 1988 assets of $70 million and annual revenues of $125 million in the process.

With new waves of cash flowing into the tour's headquarters complex on the Florida coast at every change of the tide, golfers who kept their top-125 exemption had an annuity, and the best— or most popular—became rich. It was hard for any golfer to argue with money like that, and Beman's authority became virtually unquestioned. When Beman learned that Tom Watson, Jack Nicklaus, Greg Norman, and Ben Crenshaw had been criticial of TPC courses in an interview they taped during a 1987 tournament, Beman simply ordered the TV segment quashed, and the disparaging words disappeared as though they were never spoken.

None of this bold empire building or stern domineering, however, seemed to prevent Beman from acting like a man who had nightmares featuring lawyers shouting, "Restraint of trade," when he talked about attempting to control the equipment PGA Tour players could use.

Beman, now a plump man with silver-frame glasses and thinning gray hair, was addressing the golf press corps from the stage of the interview room at the 1988 Memorial Tournament. Beman told the reporters, in precise and cautious language, that the tour's policy board had voted to consider banning the use of certain golf clubs during official tournaments beginning in 1989. Up until this time, the United States Golf Association (USGA), an amateur body, had been the sole organization to approve or disapprove equipment.

"Have you consulted with the USGA?" a reporter asked when Beman finished his presentation.

"No, we haven't. This action and our research, even though we have invited outside associations to make comments on our testing and provided them with data, is being taken completely independent of other associations. This is not a joint action."

The USGA and the Royal & Ancient Golf Club of St. Andrews, Scotland, are the official writers and interpreters of the rules of golf in the United States—the R&A handles the rest of the world without the USGA—and, although their pronouncements have no legal status in the States outside of USGA events, most amateur golfers and all pros on the tour abide by their decisions. The USGA had innocuously decided to sanction clubs with U-shaped grooves inscribed on their faces, in addition to clubs with the traditional V-shaped ones, in 1984 when a new club-manufacturing process called investment casting caused grooves on new clubs to vary from the V-shaped specifications. Shortly thereafter, manufacturers began exploiting the ruling by designing U-shaped or square grooves into their clubs, and golf had a controversy to rival surrogate motherhood.

U-shaped grooves provide additional space for water and grass to collect in when golfers attempt to make clean contact with balls they have driven into the tall grass adjacent to the fairways, thus allowing the golfers to impart some additional spin on the balls and increasing the odds that balls which land on the greens will stay there. These new clubs were quickly adopted by the younger players on the tour, and when they started winning tournaments with them veteran golfers squawked that the equipment was unfair. Soon the clubs became emblematic of everything older generations inescapably find wanting with younger ones.

The USGA remained mute on square grooves until 1986, when the organization's tests found that one brand of clubs, the Ping Eye 2, had nonconforming grooves. Ping Eye 2's were being used by numerous pros on the tour, but they found the sharp edges of the club's square grooves were cutting the soft, balata-covered balls they favored. The manufacturer of the clubs, Karsten Solheim, rounded the edges of the grooves to correct the problem, but the USGA determined that in doing so Solheim had made his grooves too wide. The USGA asked Solheim to reduce the size of his grooves and, when he refused—saying the USGA was measuring incorrectly—the USGA banned them from USGA championships beginning in 1990, and from all play under USGA rules in 1996.

In early 1988, amid continuing howls from the journeyman golfers on the tour that all square-grooved clubs should be banished, the USGA announced that it had retested the clubs and had again found only inconsequential differences between clubs with V- and U-shaped grooves, and reiterated its ruling that, except for Ping Eye 2's, they were acceptable.

The USGA's caution on the issue was related to a lengthy and expensive legal wrangle the body had to endure in a similar case involving a banned golf ball. When a manufacturer produced a golf ball in the late 1970s with a dimple pattern that was resistant to hooking and slicing—at the price of decreased distance—the USGA disallowed the ball. The manufacturer took the USGA to court for violation of the Sherman Anti-Trust Act and won its case. The USGA had the ruling overturned on appeal, but when the manufacturer began preparing a challenge to that ruling, the USGA offered a $1.375 million settlement to end the dispute and to avoid even larger legal bills, while still having the final legal opinion on the case in their favor.

Although the USGA had backed off on the issue of clubs with square grooves, millions of which were already in use, the old hands on the tour refused to allow the matter to die and, just prior to Beman's announcement, the tour's policy board had voted to take a vote on breaking from the USGA on the issue at their upcoming August meeting.

"Do you think the players are going to agree with this?" a reporter asked Beman.

"I don't think we could make any ruling that the players are going to agree with one hundred percent. I think that a number of players will support the principle of the decision, but will be uneasy with us departing from the USGA rules of golf, and they will think that we made the wrong decision because of that, and we are uneasy about departing from them."

"Are you going to work with the USGA on this at all?"

"It is possible that could be constructive if our respective lawyers would allow us, but that is why it is important to understand that this decision, even though we informed them what we were doing, was not done in conjunction with or as a result of any discussion with any other organization," Beman repeated, before leaving the meeting with his objective accomplished.

As long as the tour could be seen as acting unilaterally, it was unlikely the club manufacturers' lawyers would come after them for restraint of trade, since only a few hundred PGA Tour golfers were affected. And, by making an announcement that the tour was only considering taking action, Beman was putting pressure on the USGA to act before the tour issued its ban, if the USGA wanted to maintain exclusive control of equipment approval in the game. It was Beman at his feisty, strong-armed best. As an amateur golfer he learned never to take a shot without knowing the yardage to the flag, and as commissioner he never took an action without knowing who he could leverage against whom.

Greg Norman's mother gave him two of Jack Nicklaus's instructional books when Norman took up golf as a teenager in Queensland, Australia. Norman gleaned the fundamentals of the sport from those publications but, oddly enough, he also found some surprising biological information within the pages that set his mind at ease.

Norman was a strong and lanky lad on the cusp of manhood who loved athletics and physical challenges. But he was also a shy boy who was quietly concerned about the size of his appendages. Norman had small hands and feet, and short, stubby little fingers. It wasn't something a boy wanted to talk about much, but when he opened Nicklaus's book and found reproductions of Nicklaus's hands on the pages, Norman couldn't resist pressing his own hands to the paper to see how he measured up to the master. In the moment that Norman saw his hands were the size of Nicklaus's, his worries evaporated. Nicklaus had stubby little fingers too.

Norman passed his high school years waiting for his education to be over and wondering futilely what he was going to do with his life. His golf game was improving rapidly, but Norman's parents firmly opposed any notions he had of turning pro. Norman's father was a strong-willed mining engineer, a man who, when he wanted to do something, did it *now*, his son would say, and the man wanted Greg to follow in his footsteps. But when the boy's indifferent academic record made further education unlikely, and when Norman's bent for spending endless day surfing off the Australian shore threatened to become a vocation, Norman's parents gave their resigned blessing to golf.

Norman left home in 1975, shortly after his twentieth birthday. He was off to face the most terrifying challenge of his young life: Did he have what it took to become a professional golfer? Norman kissed his mother goodbye and set off down the long road to Sydney, where a job as a trainee club professional, the required first step to becoming a pro golfer in Australia, awaited him. Norman made it only three hours down the highway when he had to turn around and return home. Somehow, on the day he was to embark on what he thought he wanted most, a professional golf career, Norman had managed to leave home without his life savings.

One year later, Norman had advanced in golf quickly enough to find himself paired with Jack Nicklaus in the opening round of the Australian Open. Norman had had his picture taken with Nicklaus the previous day, but their real first meeting, where the man would take his measure of the boy some were calling Australia's new Nicklaus, was on the 1st tee. Norman addressed his ball, as the huge gallery that Nicklaus had attracted watched judgmentally. Norman flailed at the ball and proceeded to catch only the top part of it with his swing. The ball rolled to a stop a mere thirty yards from the tee. Norman stood there feeling inadequate and inferior before his countrymen and his hero.

Norman rebounded the next day and outshot Nicklaus by two strokes. Nicklaus, liking what he saw, encouraged Norman to come play in the United States, a piece of advice he reinforced by inviting Norman to his 1977 Memorial, one of Norman's first American appearances. But Norman avoided playing the U.S. tour full-time for six years. He first played the Australian, European and Asian tours, where he became a frequent winner and a wealthy man. Finally, in 1983, Norman came to the States with his American wife, a former airline stewardess he had met while traveling, and signed on for his big test.

Jack Nicklaus was delighted with Norman's arrival. Nicklaus hadn't been able to secure, after several false starts, an inheritor of the throne at home, but he believed he had discovered one from the other side of the world in Norman. Nicklaus was impressed with Norman's raft of overseas triumphs, but it was Norman's self-proclaimed hunger and guts that reassured Nicklaus that he had found the real thing this time. Nicklaus thought Norman was a young man after his own preoccupation.

Norman had won only five times in the States when he arrived at the 1988 Memorial, but that didn't appear to trouble Nicklaus, who had embraced Norman as his protégé and Florida neighbor. The boy had the right attitude, Nicklaus believed, and with all that talent it was just a matter of time until he started winning here more frequently.

Norman had come to the 1988 Memorial after winning the Italian Open, where he had received a $100,000 appearance fee— more than he had won for his victory—just for showing up. Appearance fees were forbidden in the States, so Norman played a limited schedule here, supplementing it with frequent paid overseas visits each year. "How are the golf courses in Italy?" a reporter asked when Norman was brought into the media room after his first round.

"The course we played, Monticello, is a nice course, unfortunately we had a lot of rain on Wednesday and Thursday and they couldn't get out there and clear it off. I'd like to get on it when it was dry, because I think you could shoot quite a good score. It's one of those golf courses that you get on and drool."

"What kind of galleries do they have in Italy?"

"They had quite a few on Sunday. How many I don't know, but the first fairway was lined three or four deep in the afternoon."

"Do you get the same kind of reaction over there?"

"Yeah. Golf is not that big in Italy, they only have eighty-some golf courses in the whole country. They're still feeling their way, and I think that's why they wanted to promote the game by bringing in somebody from the outside. They said they sold twenty thousand more tickets this year than last. I don't know if that means they sold twenty-one thousand instead of twenty thousand."

"Did they say your presence was responsible for that?"

"Oh, yeah. They told me that one night at a dinner I had with . . ." Norman said and stopped. "It makes you feel good that you can sell that many tickets."

Norman didn't seem to be in a hurry to identify the tournament officials he had dinner with, perhaps because the tournament was operated by his business agent, the International Management Group (IMG), which hires its own players to play in the fifteen tournaments it operates in Europe, Japan, and Australia. It was business deals like this that caused the head of IMG's golf division to joke that IMG was where the term "conflict of interest" was coined.

"Were Seve Ballesteros, Sandy Lyle, and Bernhard Langer there?" a reporter asked, wanting to gauge the difficulty of the field Norman had beaten.

"Seve didn't play, no. But we had all the other top players from Europe. Sandy didn't play. But Woosnam and all the others from the European tour were there." Of the thirty-six highest finishers at the Italian Open, only one fourth were in the top twenty-five on the European money list.

"Why did you go over there, because of the appearance fee?"

"The Italian Federation wanted me to play," Norman said, referring to the entity that sanctioned rather than owned the tournament, "and I hadn't been there for a few years and my wife has never been to Italy. Milan is one of the fashion capitals of the world, so she liked that. Another factor was that the Monte Carlo Grand Prix was the weekend before, so we decided to take a four-day break and go watch Nigel Mansell drive. I've never been to Monte Carlo. It was all part and parcel. The Ferrari factory was just down the road, so I had five or six good reasons to go."

"If she went shopping, it's a good thing you won," a reporter said with the easy familiarity the golfing media had with Norman.

"What do you mean," a second reporter said, "he went shopping at Ferrari."

"I spent more than she did," Norman said. "I'm the one who has to make those putts, you see."

"Did you buy a car?"

"I bought two," Norman said and everyone laughed. "You want to know the truth, don't you? I bought an F40, which is a very limited model to celebrate Ferrari's forty years of making road cars. They're only making nine hundred or nine hundred fifty of them I think. It's a very expensive car that is just a purebred fast car. A two-seater with an engine right alongside you."

"What's the other car?"

"A Testarossa."

"What was first place at the Italian Open worth?"

"Seventy thousand dollars, U.S.," Norman said, although reports in the European press put that sum, at the prevailing exchange rate, at closer to $65,000.

"What did the F40 cost you?"

"We really don't know. You pay the price when it lands in the country. I would say it will be between three hundred thousand and three hundred fifty thousand dollars," Norman said.

"What's the top speed?"

"About two-twenty. That's miles per hour, not kilometers," Norman said, although reports in automotive enthusiast magazines were placing the car's price at $260,000 and its top speed at 201 mph.

"If the car cost that much, you lost money on the trip."

"I think I can afford it," Norman said flatly.

"How much did the other car cost?"

"Oh, about a hundred and thirty thousand I think."

"That's not bad," a reporter said, and everyone laughed.

"Oh, that's not bad, huh?" Norman said with amusement.

"Will you drive either of these cars?"

"Hell, yes. I'll drive the Testarossa all the time. That will be my fun car. The other one I'll only drive about thirty miles a year."

"They will be thirty fast miles."

"No, if I ever drive it fast it will be on a racetrack. There is no point in driving it fast on the highway. I know it goes fast. I don't have to prove it to myself or anybody. Honestly, it's a coffin on wheels. It's lethal. The guy asked me if I had ever driven a Formula One racing car. I said no. He said this is the nearest thing to it. It's not a car that . . . I'm not capable of driving the car. I mean, I don't know my capabilities and I don't know the car's capabilities, so I'm just going to buy it for an investment. If somebody like Nigel Mansell wants to, and knows how to handle a car like that, sure he can take it for a drive when he comes to the States. But it's not worth risking my life or somebody else's life to get out there and run the car at its potential."

Norman's diatribe about motoring safety was uncharacteristic for a man who seemed to take every magazine journalist who interviewed him at his home on a breakneck run in one of his cars or speedboats. His prudent stance did, however, coincide with the publication of an article in *Golf Digest,* which quoted Norman's wife as saying that her husband had once taken her on a 140 mph ride over country roads while she was pregnant, and had ignored her entreaties to slow down. People had told her, she said, that Norman would change once they were married, but she knew now that he wouldn't, and she had learned to live with it.

"How's that boy you gave your trophy to at Hilton Head?" a reporter asked.

"Jamie is doing well. He's in the hospital right now, I think he is going for his bone marrow. I spoke to him from Italy. I haven't spoken to him since I got home."

"Did you get a lot of mail about giving the trophy to Jamie?"

"Oh, yes, plenty of mail. And even here people mention to me that they are happy about it. That's a natural reaction on their part."

"With all the international travel you do, how do you deal with jet lag?"

"You don't really think about it," Norman said dismissively. "If you think about it, then you're going to get into trouble. I just drink a lot of fluids before I take off—water, that is, not beer or anything else. You hydrate your body. Get as much fluid in there as you can, because you lose about eight ounces of fluid per hour on the plane. That's where you get your jet lag from.

"Drink lots of fluids and don't think about it," Norman said with great assurance, "and you'll have no problems with jet lag."

When Jack Nicklaus walked off the 18th green on Thursday after shooting two over par, a group of reporters asked Nicklaus how he felt about his round. "I played like a guy who hasn't shot a full eighteen holes in seven weeks," Nicklaus said, "which is exactly the case with me. I started off shaky, but things got better as I went on. Besides, that isn't a bad score, since no one shot lower than sixty-nine today because the course is playing so difficult."

When Nicklaus shot four over on Friday, including a double bogey on 18, and missed the cut—by one stroke—in his own tournament for the first time, reporters asked him how he felt about losing his chance to break the five-million-dollar barrier. "What does it mean?" Nicklaus asked, and pointed out that with today's purses his record would soon be obsolete in any case.

"What will you do with your weekend now?" a reporter asked.

"I'll be here. I'm not going anywhere," Nicklaus said, and walked stoically off to the locker room.

When Jack Nicklaus's friend Greg Norman finished the tournament on Sunday well out of the running, he came to ABC's broadcast booth to be interviewed by Nicklaus, who was serving as a commentator. "I don't want to make excuses for you," Nicklaus said to Norman when he arrived, "but was your uncompetitive finish due to your being tired from running to Italy and back?"

"In hindsight, I shouldn't have gone," Norman said to the man he had just, in a small way, failed. "I like Italy, but I wish I hadn't gone."

As Norman and Nicklaus talked, Curtis Strange was playing Nicklaus's course like he owned the place. After shooting 73 and 70 the first two days of the match, Strange had tied the course record with an eight-under-par 64 on Saturday and, wearing his lucky red shirt, he was on his way to winning the tournament with a final-round 67.

Strange edged out tour veteran Hale Irwin for the victory, and when Irwin, who was sick to death of all this talk of foreign golfers, walked off the course, he stunned reporters by telling them that he had just been beaten by the best golfer in the world. Strange had an impressive record in regular tour events over the past eight years, winning thirteen times and finishing first on the money list twice, but he had never won a major tournament and he was listed fifth on the Sony Rankings, behind Norman, Lyle, Langer, and Ballesteros. Strange was a respected competitor, but no one had ever called him the best golfer in the world before.

"You were talking to some of the fellows out there and said that, right now, Curtis Strange is the best player in the world," the tour's director of information, Tom Place, said to Hale Irwin when he entered the media room.

"I think that absolutely, Curtis Strange is the best player in the world right now. You can talk all you want about Mr. Ballesteros. He doesn't play over here regularly. Greg Norman does and we just saw Curtis beat him in a playoff not long ago. Curtis is a very intense individual who is tough to beat because he never lets up. He always hits the ball well, he doesn't hit wild shots, he doesn't get himself in situations where he is going to come out with a bad score, and he is an excellent putter. He makes them when he needs to."

"Elaborate on what you said about Curtis. Does he have to prove that to the other side of the ocean?" someone said.

"I think we have heard a lot about how the Ryder Cup team lost, and how hard the foreign players work on their game and all of that. No one is disagreeing with that. All I am saying is, bring them on. You back your man and I'll back my man and we'll go play. I think that Curtis is currently playing as well as anyone. That may change next week, but he is playing very well and getting wins out of it. He isn't finishing second and he isn't finishing third."

"Does this make him a favorite at the U.S. Open?"

"It's a toss-up. I'm not going to fall into that trap of picking favorites. Not out here. He would be one of the players I would pick, but he wouldn't be the only favorite."

The tour's Tom Place left the interview room and was replaced by Jack Nicklaus, who had come to conduct the interview with the new champion of his tournament, Curtis Strange. This was the same Curtis Strange who, if a man chose to look at it that way, could be seen as carrying a heavy burden for the U.S. loss in the Ryder Cup match that had been played on this very course. It was the Curtis Strange who had taken Nicklaus's archrival, Arnold Palmer, as his golfing hero. And now it was Curtis Strange people were trying to foist off as a better golfer than Greg Norman.

"Hale Irwin just said he thinks Curtis is now the best golfer in the world. Do you agree?" a reporter said to Nicklaus when he took a seat on the stage.

"Well, Curtis's record as of late has been awfully good, I don't know how you would . . . rate . . . you really start . . ." Nicklaus hesitated. He had brought trouble on himself more times in his career than he could remember by being as forthright as he was inclined to be. He wasn't going to make that mistake again, and be a poor host on top of it, but this was not going to be easy.

"I don't know how to answer that," Nicklaus continued. "Curtis's record has been awfully good, but I think . . . Curtis hasn't won a major. Greg's only won one major, and if you count Greg as being the best player in the world today . . . so I suppose they both have a while to go as it relates to record.

"If Curtis should happen to win some majors, I think that would solidify his position as being . . . what they're talking about," Nicklaus said, finding himself unable to say the words "best player in the world." "Obviously from the way he is playing, I think he is going to fall in that category the way he is playing right now. I think Norman falls in that category, and I think Ballesteros falls in that category."

After a long silence, Nicklaus looked at the man who had posed the query. "I don't know whether that answers your question or not."

"They said on ABC that if you look at Curtis's record here

prior to this year it wasn't anything special, but that he got to know and like this course at the Ryder Cup last year."

"That's what I just said at the presentation ceremony. Curtis said that he never liked this golf course, that it was a little too long for him. Last year at the Ryder Cup the course was real fast, and he said it played identical to that this week. He played very well in the Ryder Cup against Ballesteros," Nicklaus said, then corrected himself. "He played pretty well . . . he just didn't come out with . . . with the win."

"Is it set that this tournament will be two weeks earlier next year, or does it have to be approved by the tour policy board?"

"They're the ones who gave the date. I'd just as soon stay where we are, or move a week one side or the other. CBS had contractual rights to keep our event, and for them to give up the event—I wanted to move the event to ABC because I am working for them, and I felt like ABC would give us greater coverage. For CBS to give up our tournament, they said, Okay, for the next three years we want the four weeks prior to the U.S. Open so we can have golf and the NBA."

At that moment, a side door to the interview room slammed shut as Curtis Strange, the man who had just won Jack Nicklaus's tournament, entered. Nicklaus continued talking without looking up or acknowledging Strange's presence in any way, as Strange walked onto the stage and took a seat beside him.

"That was the only date we could play," Nicklaus said, "so we knew that we might get hit with some weather.

"We went back and looked at the history of the weather for that period versus this week, the average temperature difference is one degree and the average rainfall is identical over the last twelve years," Nicklaus said, as Strange cleared his throat. "Maybe we'll get lucky and it will be just fine.

"We have the chance of having a cold spring and not having full leaf on the trees at that time," Nicklaus said as Strange coughed. "There is a plus to that too, in that it allows us to have the European players. There was a comment made in the paper as to, what does he want, the U.S. players or the European players? It isn't a question of whether we want the U.S. players or the European players. It isn't an either-or. We'd love to have both players, and honestly we want to have everybody who is eligible to play to bring their golf clubs and play."

Strange finally broke in. "Jack, may I say something on that? I think Jack wants the best players in the world, and there are a couple of guys who didn't play this week who are among the best players in the world. It makes the tournament better, and if I win this year with the best players in the world that makes my victory even better."

"I don't think any of the good players ever object to having the best players here," Nicklaus said.

"Jack, what did you do the last two days, and did you enjoy yourself?" a reporter asked.

"I had a miserable time if you want me to be honest. Yesterday morning I got up and went down to see a guy in the hospital, and he left a half hour before I got there. I came back and exercised a little bit in the afternoon," Nicklaus said as Strange shifted uncomfortably in his chair.

"Today I got up and came over and had some conversations here on business things, and then I went out and practiced after everybody teed off, and my son Gary came over and he wanted to hit a few balls with me, so we hit a few balls. Then I went up and did the telecast. I'd much rather be playing."

There was a long silence, and when it was apparent that no more questions were forthcoming for Nicklaus, he said, "Enough of me, let's get on to Curtis. Curtis, do you have a mircophone there?"

"Go ahead, I'll just interrupt anytime I feel like it," Strange said archly, and everyone laughed.

"Jack didn't enjoy the Ryder Cup at all because he couldn't play, I'll tell you what," Strange said, reminding everyone that he had played and Nicklaus hadn't. "It is a hell of a lot tougher to sit there watching it on TV."

"Every time," Nicklaus said. "You can control it."

"But you were a wreck at the Ryder Cup," Strange said in his Virginia drawl.

"I was? I was a rat?" Nicklaus asked with a lowered voice that sounded hurt, but not all that surprised, that Strange would call him a rat.

"A wreck," Strange said.

"Okay, I wanted to make sure whether you spell it r-a-t, or w-r-e-c-k."

"Curtis," a reporter said. "Hale Irwin just said that right now you are the best player in the world. How do you react to that?"

"It's a great compliment coming from a great competitor and

a great player. But I don't look at it in terms like that. I go out and play golf and do the best I can. If that is written, then so be it. I want to win as often as I can, but I don't pay much attention to ranking systems."

"Curtis, is it true that if your back hadn't been bothering you at Las Vegas, and you hadn't taken a few weeks off, your original schedule didn't have you playing here this week?"

Strange hid his face behind his hand sheepishly, as Nicklaus looked over with a measured smile and watched carefully for Strange's answer, which was slow in coming. "My original schedule was to play Colonial and see what happened from there," Strange said. "I have a busy schedule. I'm going to be playing at least eight of the next ten weeks, and you have to skip somewhere. In all honesty, you look at your schedule and you have to see where you've played well and where you're comfortable, and that didn't include Memorial at one point."

"Curtis, you sort of gave your putter a javelin toss on the 14th hole . . ." a reporter began.

"It deserved it too," Strange interrupted to roars of laughter.

"Overall, though, are you more relaxed on the course? Has there been a change in the way you approach the game?"

"No, I don't think so. I still think you need that fire in your belly. I especially think I do. I'm at a level now that I feel that if I keep going and keep working, and keep that fire in my gut, and keep trying to improve, I think I can get to that next level, I really do.

"But it is extremely tough. When you think of great players in the game, they all have something special. They either have length, which translates into strength, or they are tremendous putters, or they have something that stands out. If you look at my game, and I have read it too many times to think about, I don't have anything that stands out. I don't hit the ball three hundred yards down the fairway, I don't hit two-irons up over the clouds and land on the green softly. So I have to do what I do best—reaching down in my gut and getting something extra down the stretch."

"Is the next level to win a major tournament?"

"Whatever the level is. Jack can answer that better than I can."

Nicklaus, who had been periodically yawning behind his hand and cleaning his fingernails as Strange spoke, looked up with a start at the mention of his name.

"Sometimes I'm blind to what you all think," Strange said to the reporters, "or what Jack . . . or whoever is from the outside looking in. Coming down the stretch what I wanted to do was make that putt at fourteen, and I hit a godawful putt. There was a flip of the putter, but it wasn't so much missing the putt as it was, Damn, I hit an awful putt, and I wasn't supposed to putt like that coming down the stretch."

"Let me say something about Curtis's game," Nicklaus volunteered, sensing that this was the place for him to speak from his senior statesman position.

"You asked if the next level is major championships, and it is surprising to me with as many tournaments as Curtis has won, and as well as he has played, that he hasn't won major championships. Curtis is a good straight driver, he's very good around the greens, a good iron player, a good putter, and he recovers well," Nicklaus said, stopping short of saying that Strange was a wonderful little golfer. "Maybe the level he has played at will propel him into a major championship very soon."

Nicklaus turned to Strange and said, "You're just approaching the prime of your career, really."

"I was just going to say, I'm not old yet," Strange said.

"No, you're not like I am," Nicklaus said. "You have gray hair, but you're not like I am."

"Be careful now," Strange countered, enough being enough. "I still have a microphone on too."

"Did you debate your club selection on the second shot on the par-five fifteenth?" a reporter asked.

"Yeah, for me to have hit the ball that far off the tee, I thought I had to be hitting downwind. I could have gotten onto the green in two today."

Strange looked over at Nicklaus and said, "That was a good drive."

"I saw you," Nicklaus said.

"You were watching?" Strange asked in surprise.

"Sure I was watching," Nicklaus said.

Strange laughed nervously, like, how about that, Jack Nicklaus was watching me play. "So anyway, for my ball to have gone that far I thought we were downwind, but on the second shot the wind was blowing into me, and I wasn't sure what club to hit."

"If you're not certain what the next level is, Curtis, what's the next thing you want to do?" a reporter asked.

"Win a major," Strange said immediately

Art

Most people at Westchester Country Club knew that Lawrence
Taylor, the hulking and notorious New York Giant linebacker,
was a man with an innate capacity for violence. His preferred
methods of tackling opposing players—driving his helmet into
them or attempting to cut them in half with a sweep of his
forearms—had been well publicized. Yet Taylor managed to look
deceivingly delicate this warm June day as he strolled the rich
fairways in white linen knickers, white knee socks, a white cap,
and a red, black and gray argyle sleeveless sweater. Taylor was a
celebrity entry in the pro-am at the Westchester Classic, and he
looked every bit the part.

Taylor had been playing corporate outings and pro-ams for
several years because his agent thought the contacts he made in
them might be beneficial financially. Then golf had taken on another role in Taylor's life when he developed a substance abuse
problem and, finding traditional detox centers too confining, Taylor went on a six-week cross-country golf outing to purge his
system of cocaine, while simultaneously avoiding the reporters
who were on his trail. The sportswriters had crucified Taylor when
they learned of his self-prescribed rehabilitation on the links, and
their criticism would sound anew two months hence when Taylor
again went for his clubs after being suspended by the National
Football League for continued drug use. But none of that mattered
today.

Taylor had already shot a morning round of golf before coming to Westchester for his 12:58 P.M. starting time, and he ap-

peared tired and drawn during his first holes. Taylor was an addictive golfer, often playing thirty-six holes a day during the off-season—occasionally nine holes each on four different courses. He carried an eight handicap, but he scattered balls wildly at the tight Westchester course, and he found himself behind trees more often than in the fairways when he was taking his shots at the greens. Nonetheless, he gave the spectators what they wanted from him, chugging down the numerous beers that were offered, signing autographs, humoring the heckling drunks and the leering husbands who pushed their soft blond wives over to have their photos taken with the stud's massive ebony arm draped over their shoulders.

Fortunately, most of the fans had dispersed by the time Taylor trudged, with his four playing partners, to the tee on his twelfth hole of the afternoon. Taylor was bushed, and he flopped heavily on his golf bag the moment his caddie placed it on the ground. Taylor yanked his cap off and wiped his forehead on his arm with the sigh of a man who wanted nothing more than a moment's peace.

"Oh, look at the poor baby," a female voice ringing with mockery called out loudly. "He's all tired out from playing a few holes of golf and now he needs a rest."

Taylor turned his head and narrowed his eyes to identify the woman who was inciting him. She was a tournament volunteer in her late forties who was standing on the tee with a camera around her neck.

Taylor stared at her in bemusement, like, Who is this old lady?, then turned away.

"Come on, baby, get off your duff and get over here," the woman persisted in a raised voice.

Taylor stared at the woman hard for a minute, then, seeming to recognize that he had encountered an opponent far more formidable than a charging offensive lineman, he complied with her wishes and rose slowly from his perch on the golf bag.

Taylor was correct in assuming this was an encounter he was not going to win, for his tormenter was not just another tournament volunteer. She was a Westchester wife. A middle-aged woman from a good family and the right schools who knew her role in life—to be the spouse of a financially comfortable husband, to run a large house in a well-shaded suburb where her children's friends would always feel welcome, to be active in the community and to get all this done without a lot of fuss—and, by God, she was good at it. She had stylishly short graying hair, which she wouldn't for a moment consider dyeing. When you got older your hair was supposed to turn gray. She wore her skirt above her knees, even if her legs weren't quite what they used to be, because that's what made sense when you were charging around a golf course. And she knew how to handle a man, whether he was a partner in a major law firm over for drinks or a belligerent professional football player she had been assigned to photograph.

"Let's go, get your tail over here," the woman said to Taylor again, this time with a chiding smile, as she arranged the other four golfers for the group picture that would be presented to them as a memento of their outing.

Taylor dragged over and bunched up with the others, but his put-upon expression was not going to make a happy picture for the amateurs who had laid out big bucks to play in this match. Not to worry, the photographer was prepared. She knew that many of the pro golfers she would have to contend with hated playing with their almost universally golf-inept partners in pro-ams, and they, too, would often need a little something to perk them up for the pictures.

The woman nodded to her husband and adolescent son who were standing off to the side of the tee, and they walked up and stood behind her in close formation as the woman focused the camera. When everything was right, save Taylor's expression, the woman said to her son, "Okay. Now."

The boy reached for something he had been concealing, then whipped up a placard on a board, like a picket sign, over his mother's head. The woman waited two beats, then clicked the shutter, just as the golfers dissolved into hysterics. The indomitable Westchester wife's prop was nothing less than a lurid, full color, split-beaver centerfold from a men's skin magazine, which, presumably, the woman had purchased—give me the filthiest magazine you've got, one could imagine her saying to the clerk—and then pasted up on the kitchen table, perhaps while *Masterpiece Theater* played on the TV in the family room. It was all great fun!

The stock market might have gone to hell last year, and the tournament's sponsor might be having second thoughts about continuing their support, but none of that was any reason why the boys couldn't have a hoot out there on the course today.

The ploy worked on Taylor, but when he stopped laughing he

tried to get in the final word. "Hey," he said about the poster, "why don't you have the real stuff out here?"

"Next year," the woman shot back, dismissing the most feared linebacker in professional football with a wave of her hand. "We didn't have the budget for it this year."

The Westchester Classic was known for the way tournament organizers knocked themselves out to make the visiting professional golfers feel at home, and that was because of the Westchester wives. Westchester was one of the few tournaments that was actually run by a charity—most tournaments have a golf-related group that runs the event and they decide how much, if any, of the proceeds should go to a designated nonprofit organization. But in Westchester, United Hospital owned the tournament. They got Manufacturers Hanover to be the main sponsor and NYNEX to be the secondary sponsor, cut a deal with the PGA Tour office to be an official tournament, and rented Westchester Country Club for the event. And it was the hospital's women's auxiliary, called the twigs—"like branches on a tree," Mrs. J. Richard (Ann) Fabrizio, twig chairlady, liked to say, while splaying out her fingers to illustrate the concept—that ran the show. They accomplished their tasks efficiently enough to have added $12.7 million to the coffers of local hospitals over the past twenty-one years.

It was Fabrizio's job to get her chairladies to recruit their girl-friends and neighbors to complete the needed volunteer work force of 1,500, and to make sure the affiliated hospital twig groups sold more than 100,000 tickets—many of them from card tables set up in shopping centers—for the new-car raffle that would be held at the tournament. The lady volunteers would then participate in every aspect of pulling off a professional golf tournament with only one paid employee.

But Fabrizio's task was a relatively easy one. Mrs. Donald S. (Karen) Whamond, Jr., had been in charge of contestant services for the last twenty-two years, and she was the one who had to coax professional golfers into coming to New York to play golf for a $700,000 purse, an increasingly difficult assignment.

A decade ago Westchester offered one of the largest purses on the tour, but now the sponsors were balking at continually upping the ante each year, and the pot was in the second tier. Additionally, the tournament was saddled with a date that fell the week before the U.S. Open. The question of whether or not to play in a

tournament the week before a major was as replete with myth as
the dilemma over whether a boxer should have intercourse the
night before a bout. There were widely varying opinions about
what helped and hurt a golfer's performance in a major, but the
only hard fact was that staging a golf tournament in this time slot
was difficult. And when that tournament was located near New
York City, the burden was cubed.

Most golfers on the PGA Tour grew up in nonmetropolitan
areas of the South and Midwest, and to them New York City was
a malevolent place they read about in newspaper stories with dire
headlines. They didn't know that Westchester was the New York
of riding academies and country day schools, rather than the New
York of subways and boom boxes. Karen Whamond encouraged
the tournament's volunteers to always have smiles on their faces
when they ferried the golfers to and from the airport, and to tell
the golfers that yes, they were in close proximity to New York
City, but Westchester County was a collection of small suburban
towns like the neighborhoods they came from.

While the area was a pastiche of small burgs, they were far
more prosperous villages than any the golfers had known as children, and hotel costs in the area were high. So Whamond also
helped arrange free lodgings in private homes near the course for
a third of the 150 golfers competing in the tournament. The folks
who provided the rooms might not be interested in golf, but they
were civic-minded people who wanted to do their part for the
tournament.

When golfers' wives and children started traveling on the tour
more frequently in recent years, Whamond arranged family activities, and always tried to do something special for the wives. At
first she organized Westchester-wife kind of ventures, trips to
Broadway shows and to the Statue of Liberty, but they didn't go
over well. Then, last year, she sent a questionnaire out to the wives
and asked them what they really wanted, and that resulted in
programs that hit the mark: a guided tour and shopping spree at
Bloomingdale's; complete make-overs and haircuts by Revlon. The
make-overs were so popular that all the wives wanting them
couldn't be accommodated, and they started calling in weeks before the tournament requesting appointments.

But even with all of this, the field at Westchester had been
distinctly lacking in star-quality in recent years. Karen Whamond
wrote letters to the players when the U.S. Open was to be played

in the northeastern part of the country and pointed out that the weather conditions and grasses were similar at Westchester, so why didn't they acclimate themselves here, and they ignored her. Then, for reasons Whamond didn't understand, many of the top players, and particularly the crowd-pulling foreign players, suddenly decided that Westchester was *the* place to tune up for the Open this year, and Karen Whamond had her best field in ages.

Record-breaking ticket sales were all but assured, and Whamond was as happy as could be—except for one thing that always nagged at her when the tournament was over and the players stormed on to the next town. Some of the golfers, and particularly the young ones, never formally acknowledged the manifold efforts of the Westchester wives with a personal thank-you note. Whamond wished that the PGA Tour would take one day at their annual qualifying tournament and put these young guys in a classroom and teach them some manners. Some of them just didn't understand etiquette at all, and it irritated Whamond to no end.

Seve Ballesteros was the only notable professional golfer in the world who could be described as dashing. In a sport in which the young players were sometimes perceived as being colorless and overcoached products of scientific college golf programs, everything about Ballesteros was dramatic. He was given to matching bright golf shirts with dark, formal trousers; his play was often distinguished by erratic drives followed by amazing recovery shots; and the fine features of his handsome face constantly projected the bountiful range of Latin emotion which the game of golf evoked in him. Many players were aggressive with their clubs, but Ballesteros used his like a matador working the cape. His objective was not just to defeat the course, but to do it aesthetically.

The interview area of the media room filled quickly when Ballesteros was brought in after playing in the Westchester pro-am. The room had been crowded when Greg Norman and Sandy Lyle, the Scotsman who was currently leading the U.S. money list with three 1988 victories, were brought in for pretournament interviews, but Ballesteros outdrew them both. Ballesteros's appearance at Westchester was his first in the United States since he had finished tied for eleventh at the Masters two months ago, and one of only seven he would make during all of 1988.

Ballesteros had first learned golf by hitting stones with a homemade golf club on the beach that fronted his family's farmhouse in

Pedrena, a fishing and farming village on the northern coast of Spain. He began caddying at the age of eight at the private club near his home, sneaking in a few holes under the cover of near-darkness each day on the course he was prohibited from playing because of his caste. Ballesteros learned bits and pieces of the game from his three older brothers, who played some professional golf, and his uncle, who was the teaching pro at the golf course and a noted European pro. But mostly he taught himself and followed the instincts of his exceptional talent, hitting ball after ball wherever he could in a quiet village in which there was little else to do. Ballesteros became lost in golf, quitting school at fourteen and turning pro at sixteen.

Ballesteros's career was launched in 1976 when, at age nineteen, he tied Jack Nicklaus for second place at the British Open. Three years later, he won that major tournament and, the next spring, he became the youngest man ever to win the Masters. By twenty-seven, Ballesteros had claimed a second victory in each of these matches and he had become an international sensation.

Over the next four years, however, Ballesteros's temperamental nature, which allowed him to sometimes play golf that could only be described as inspired, and other times caused him to weep after winning or losing an important tournament, more often than not became his nemesis. He, like many another golfer, found water with his ball on the closing hole of the Masters, and missed putts when they had to fall. Despite several close finishes, Ballesteros turned thirty-one without winning another major.

"In Spain two or three weeks ago you said that you were thinking of playing a lot more in America next season. Have you finalized any plans?" a British sportswriter, who was part of the sometimes large contingent of European, Japanese, and Australian reporters who covered golfers from their countries on the American tour, asked Ballesteros.

"I didn't say that I would be playing," Ballesteros corrected. "I said that I was starting to think about playing a little more—maybe—next year. It is a possibility, but other than that I haven't made any plans. I haven't made my schedule for next year. It is too early."

"The only way you can play that frequently is to get your American tour card back and play the full fifteen tournaments required," a reporter said, referring to a PGA Tour rule restricting the number of tournaments nonmembers of the American tour such as Ballesteros could play—a stipulation that was enacted because of Ballesteros.

"That's the way I understand it, unless they change the rule," Ballesteros said.

"Have you ever spoken to anyone about the possibility of the rule being changed?"

"No."

"Well if the rule isn't changed, you'll have to play the full fifteen."

"I guess so."

"This doesn't mean you've signed a peace treaty with Beman, does it?"

Ballesteros twisted his face and shrugged his shoulders in a gesture that was Gallic in the magnitude of its indifference. "I don't care about that," he said.

Ballesteros's pressroom coquettishness on the issue of his playing more frequently on the American tour was the latest chapter in a saga that had its roots in the simultaneous ascensions to power of Ballesteros and Deane Beman in the early 1980s. Ballesteros had emerged then as the first young European golfer in years who had the makings of a true world champion, and the people who ran sometimes poorly attended European golf tournaments, and who were forced to pay appearance fees to visiting Americans to bolster their gates, were thrilled to have the captivating young Spaniard in their midst.

Ballesteros, who was neither a fool nor insensitive to personal affronts, quickly demanded that he be paid appearance money as well. The European tour rejected Ballesteros's ultimatum until he absented himself from the European circuit for a year, and tournament operators changed their minds. Ballesteros has since come to earn a princely living regardless of how he fares in competition. His appearance fee grew to eighty thousand dollars an event, except for a tournament Ballesteros's own company organized in Spain, where he paid himself ninety thousand dollars for appearing. He benefited from the usual assortment of endorsements and contracts that elevated his annual income to seven figures. And Ballesteros, who was born of humble, but not poor, farming stock, had become engaged to the daughter of a billionaire Spanish banker, a twenty-two-year-old woman who had attended convent school with Princess Caroline.

Meanwhile, Deane Beman, who had clung to the security of his career as an insurance broker for years before finally abandoning the less competitive amateur circuit to turn pro, was transforming the American tour into an egalitarian and lucrative entity that virtually guaranteed a comfortable income to the unquestioning players who lived by Beman's rules. The tour banned appearance fees, thus assuring that Beman, rather than powerful player management agencies like IMG, would decide who played in what tournaments, and also preventing superstars from syphoning money off the top of purses. Golfers who were Team Beman players, and who finished in the top 125 of the money list, received a virtual annuity on the gravy train.

To ensure that overseas players such as Ballesteros didn't work both sides of the street by showing up in the States only when they couldn't get an appearance fee elsewhere, Beman, in consultation with Ballesteros, enacted a requirement in 1984 that foreign players had to play fifteen tournaments here, and thus become official members of the American tour, to enjoy unrestricted access to U.S. tournaments.

Ballesteros, who was given to homesickness and impetuousness, complied with the ruling in 1984, then unilaterally decided it was too burdensome and played only nine American tournaments during 1985. Beman responded like a cuckolded husband. He ordered Ballesteros's name retroactively banished from the 1985 money list, barred him from playing in all 1986 U.S. tour-sponsored events except one in which he was the defending champion, and created a new rule that limited nonmenbers of the American tour to playing in five regular tournaments, the three non-tour-sponsored U.S. majors, and the World Series of Golf.

Beman had previously exempted individual players from the fifteen-tournament rule, and he would grant similar dispensations in the future, but not to Ballesteros. Ballesteros was everything Beman wasn't—a handsome, charismatic, exciting, and extremely talented golfer. Ballesteros took every chance he got to demonstrate that he thought those characteristics intrinsically entitled him to preferential treatment. Beman was a bare-knuckled negotiator who owned the keys to the gates of golf heaven. He never renegotiated a done deal, and he never buckled under pressure.

Ballesteros lobbied, and won the support of, established American stars like Jack Nicklaus, Tom Watson, Ray Floyd, and Curtis Strange—although foreign players like Greg Norman and Sandy

Lyle who abided by the fifteen-tournament rule, and won here in Ballesteros's absence, were not sympathetic—in an attempt to get Beman to rescind the fifteen-tournament rule. Nicklaus argued that the American tour needed Ballesteros—that a golfer as accomplished as he was an asset to any event. But it was to no avail. Beman seized every opportunity to show Ballesteros that the insurance man who became commissioner, not the artiste, ran the show. Beman told Ballesteros he could return when he was ready to follow the rules, and not before.

Ballesteros played his allotted one tournament and three majors in the States during his suspension in 1986, and returned eight times in 1987, earning $305,058 that year without a victory—the highest income per event of any golfer. When his overseas golf earnings, products endorsements, and business activities were calculated in, Ballesteros was a wealthy and, one would assume, a happy man. Nonetheless, Ballesteros carefully monitored press reports about the American tour weekly.

"What made you even think about playing golf here more often?" a reporter asked Ballesteros.

"I always enjoy playing in America. I never said I didn't like it. And the European tour has grown up a lot and I think it is almost as good as the American tour. It doesn't need as much support from me as it used to," Ballesteros said, sounding abnormally altruistic. "So if I come here to play fifteen tournaments—maybe, maybe—that means that I would have to reduce the number of tournaments I would play there. But that's not decided yet. Nothing is decided yet."

"What are your goals now?"

"My dream right now is to win the U.S. Open," Ballesteros said of one of the two majors he hadn't won.

"If you spent more time here, don't you think that would help you towards that goal?"

Ballesteros paused for a long moment to consider how candid he wanted to be. "That's probably one of the reasons that maybe I would change my mind about playing here next year—maybe. It is hard to come over for just two or three weeks and get settled down and be comfortable and play well. You have to get used to the conditions of the golf courses and everything."

Ballesteros had wanted to win the 1988 Masters, one of his favorite tournaments, so much that he had spent the week before the match practicing at Augusta National, sometimes as much as seven and a half hours a day. Given Ballesteros's stature, a victory in anything less than a major now was insignificant.

"When do you think you will make the decision?" a reporter pressed Ballesteros.

"Sometime before the season is over," Ballesteros said evasively, knowing all the while that his feeler would reach Deane Beman's ears before the last Westchester wife had cheerfully shuttled a golfer to the airport on Sunday. "Maybe September or October. I don't know."

It rained most of the day in Westchester on Thursday, and the temperature was in the low fifties—a rare and brief respite from the broiling summer temperature that prevailed nationwide during 1988—but that didn't prevent seventeen thousand fans from coming to the course. The Westchester wives who were working the tournament, and many of the spectators, pulled on their bright, school-days yellow rain slickers—rain slickers were supposed to be yellow, although a few parvenu faddists had forsaken yellow for bright red—and motored out to the club. Some of the club's members drove over for lunch and ate at the outside tables, under a canopy, despite the foul weather, because one would no more dream of lunching inside during June than one would consider coming to dine at the club in anything less than a coat and tie or a decent dress.

The lunch crowd glanced from time to time at the television monitors that were placed around the dining areas and the corporate hospitality tents, and watched the players tramping around the course in their rain gear, trying to make the best of a dismal day. The sound was turned low on the sets, but those sitting close to the monitors could hear the commentators analyzing the golfers' shots and their records on the tour in bright voices. Out on the course, the spectators weren't being so restrained.

The economic barrier of membership in a country club like Westchester might serve to assure certain standards of conduct in the clubhouse, but anyone with fifteen bucks in his pocket could gain admission to the grounds during the tournament. So working men from the boroughs of New York City who played some golf drove up the Hutchinson River Parkway to have a look at how the pros played the game on a fancy course. And, having parted with their fifteen bucks, when they had an opinion about what they saw, and they usually did, they voiced it.

If fans at the British Open quietly applaud virtually every shot that is struck and reserve their remarks to denote the exceptional stroke by exclaiming, "Well played," the New York working stiff holds his applause for the exceptional shots and comments directly to the golfers on all others, thus sparing the player the need to evaluate his game. And so it was that a golfer who hit over the green would be informed immediately that he had taken too much club, a golfer who sliced his shot would learn that he had come off of the ball, and a golfer who got lucky, like Tom Kite, would be apprised that he wasn't fooling anyone.

Kite hit a pitch on the par-five 5th hole on Thursday that was headed toward trouble at the right side of the green until it took an irregular bounce and rolled close to the pin. A fiftyish man in a windbreaker standing close to Kite removed his cigar from his mouth and, being careful to use his idea of country-club profanity, gave Kite an evaluation. "Cripes," he said, "that didn't look that good when you hit it, did it Tom?"

One hole behind Kite, Greg Norman, who was on his way to a two-over-par opening round, was in a funk as gray as the weather, silently mouthing curses to himself after his shots and ignoring his gallery. Norman had been frustrated to near his flash point with his game since Curtis Strange had beaten him in the playoff in Houston last month. He was convinced he had been playing well, but he was getting nothing more out of it in the States than a tie for twenty-third in Vegas and a tie for sixth at the Memorial. Some unknown force seemed to be holding Norman back, but he didn't know what it was. He could only roam the course like a panther without prey and wonder what was wrong and when he would be able to resume his mission of kicking in the door on the American tour.

Norman's demons were haunting him so at the end of his round that he quickly brushed past the reporters who were awaiting him. "Not a good round; not a good day," he said as he hurried away. "Not very pleasant. Cold and damp. Two over is not a very good score."

As Norman walked into the clubhouse, Peter Senior, one of Norman's three Australian countrymen playing in the tournament, was in the pressroom thanking Norman for making it possible for him to play at Westchester.

"I think Norman had a lot to do with getting me into this tournament," he told the reporters. "I played with him in the last

round of a tournament in Australia, and I told him I was coming
to the States for a few weeks. Norman asked me if I'd like to play
at Westchester and, when I said that I would, he said, 'I'll see what
I can do.' I got a phone call from the tournament the next day
saying they'd love to have me."

Westchester tournament officials felt they hadn't been sup-
ported by American players in recent years, and this year they
decided to allocate their four unrestricted sponsor exemptions—
half of the allotted eight exemptions are reserved for PGA Tour
members—more heavily toward overseas players. And when Greg
Norman, whom tournament officials were more than delighted to
have in their field, asked if they couldn't invite an Australian,
Westchester was quick to comply.

Senior had come to the states in 1986 after earning a tour card
in the national qualifying tournament. He played in twelve tournaments that year and missed the cut in every one. He then went
off to the European tour to improve his game. Senior had since
won several times in Europe, and he was hoping to be ready for the
American tour full-time in the next few years.

Australian Wayne Grady, who was three over after his first
round at Westchester, had followed the same route Senior was
now taking, and Grady had eventually won his American playing
privileges after spending six years roaming the world, trying to get
his game together.

Grady had had some trouble in school with his teachers as an
adolescent down under, and at age fifteen he told them to stick it
and went off to play golf. He didn't enjoy school. It wasn't where
he wanted to spend his time, so he turned to golf and was shooting
par at seventeen. There wasn't much of a pro tour in Australia in
the 1970s, but it didn't matter anyway. All Grady ever wanted to
do was play in the States. Anyone who entertained those sorts of
thoughts in Australia was told that he was crazy, that he would get
his head bashed in on the American tour. But Grady didn't really
care what they thought, he knew he was going to do it some day.

Grady started playing the Asian and European tours in 1978 at
twenty-one, with occasional forays to the Japanese tour. He found
things on the Asian tour he wouldn't experience again. They had
ten tournaments with ten different organizing bodies, all of which
had different ideas about how they wanted to run their tournaments. And, if you wound up paired with a local golfer in some of
these matches, you were in trouble. Sometimes when Grady played

with locals they would just straight out cheat, and he'd refuse to sign their scorecards. Then Grady would end up getting disqualified for his refusal to attest to his partner's score. There were times where his ball would disappear off the fairway. He'd drive one down over a hill and, because he was beating one of the local favorites, he'd get down there and his ball would be gone. Spectators would bang cans together on his backswing. Anything. He'd have to fight and scratch and scrape to buy a dozen golf balls because he couldn't get them anywhere. He'd wear a pair of golf shoes until they bloody well fell to bits.

Then he'd go home to the foundling Australian tour, fly to the location of a tournament and go searching for a hotel on his own. He'd have to take a taxi to and from the course every day because there wasn't any transportation, and his taxi bill for the week would be $100 when, at the time, the total purse of the tournament was $50–$100,000 and only ten guys a week would be covering their expenses. When he got to the course, the organizers would act like they were doing him a big favor to let him play in a golf tournament.

Grady came to the States in 1984, after winning in Europe, and played seven events on sponsor exemptions, just to see what it was like. After having been told all his life he wasn't good enough to play in America, he wanted to see for himself. Grady didn't do very well in those tournaments, but when he went out onto the practice field and watched the guys who were making a couple of hundred thousand dollars a year, he said, This is bullshit, they're not that much better than me. Grady didn't let it concern him that tournaments were won on the playing field, not the practice tee.

And the way Grady was treated while he was here! Everywhere he went there were signs up, "Welcome PGA Golfers." He could ring up a tournament and they'd book his accommodations and pick him up at the airport. If they had cars available they'd let him use one, and if there wasn't one there was always transportation. They put lunch on for the golfers, and manufacturers' reps came around to the locker room and gave out—free—three dozen golf balls and eight gloves every week, and the shoe people would give you a half-dozen pair. Clothing manufacturers were ready with a dozen pairs of slacks, a month's worth of shirts, sweaters, clubs, bags, and visors. Not only were all of these goods free, but some of the manufacturers paid for players to use their products. It was enough of a bonanza to bring Grady back to compete in the qualifying tournament at the end of the year, where he won his card.

Grady made $167,497 in 1985, his first year on the tour, before going into a slump and earning less than that in 1986 and 1987 combined. He commuted to Europe to play the required nine tournaments to keep his card there for insurance, and kept working on his game. If there was anything Grady had it was stamina; he had finished in second place twenty-six times worldwide and never gave up hope. Grady almost won a tournament in Japan over the 1987 winter break on the American tour, and that got him pumped up for the 1988 season in the States. But while he was home in Australia over the holidays, he broke his hand playing cricket and he missed the first six tournaments of 1988.

Now he thought he was very close to playing well, even if, after two top-twenty finishes earlier in 1988, he had missed five out of the last six cuts. Things would get better, he always told himself, if he just kept grinding away. Grady would finish tied for twenty-fifth at Westchester, picking up $5,460 for the week. He and his wife and their eighteen-month-old daughter would pack up and move down the road to the next stop. They were making progress. They had spent forty weeks of 1985 in motels; now they had a house in Florida and Grady was doing what the boys at home always told him he'd never do.

"Would you rather be good or lucky tomorrow?" a reporter had asked Ken Green when he was brought into the pressroom late Saturday afternoon as the one-shot leader of the Westchester Classic.

"Lucky," said Green, a twenty-nine-year-old who had won twice in his six years on the tour, without hesitation. "I've got enough good in me that if I get some luck I'll be all right. I can't hit all perfect shots, and I'll need the breaks on the bad shots if I'm going to win."

Green had gotten those breaks on Saturday, twice having balls that were headed for troublesome areas of the golf course strike trees and ricochet into the fairway. It was only the second time that Green had been leading a tournament after the third round. The last time, in 1985, he had prayed for heavy rains on Sunday.

"Will it bother you that somebody like Seve Ballesteros is only three shots behind you?"

"He is only a threat if he plays well and I don't," Green said. "Having a name player coming after you is overrated. You control yourself. If you are going to let the marquee players scare you, you're not ready to win."

Whether he was ready to win or not, Green was desperate to win—even a lucky win. He was a native of nearby Danbury, Connecticut, and a loud throng of friends and relatives had been shadowing him around the course all week. When a woman from a local radio station asked Green if she could do a telephone interview with him very early Sunday morning, Green had gladly given her the telephone number at his mother-in-law's, where he was staying with his wife and three kids for the week. Green had never been close to winning at home before, and he didn't know how soon he would be again.

"I'm going to be shitting bricks tomorrow," Green had told the sportswriters in a cracking voice. "To win around here would be the best win I could ever have. They can talk about the majors, but here and Hartford, Connecticut, are the two tournaments I want to win most. That is probably putting too much pressure on myself, but that's the way I am. If I don't win this golf tournament, it doesn't matter where I finish, I am not going to be happy—even if I shoot a sixty-five while losing."

On Sunday, the television announcers made fun of Ken Green's having said the Westchester Classic was more important to him than a major but, even if Green had been able to hear them, he wouldn't have cared. He was too busy trying to will a win that was beginning to look improbable. In the group ahead of Green, David Frost had take a one-shot lead from Green by the third hole, and Seve Ballesteros was threatening. Then tremendous roars began echoing back from the galleries on the final holes of the front nine. Six groups ahead of Green, Greg Norman, who, at six shots off the lead after the third round, had been written off as a contender, was in the process of pulling to within one shot of the lead at the halfway point with consecutive birdies on the 6th, 7th, 8th, and 9th holes. Norman was mounting another one of his final-round dives for the finish line, and he birdied the 17th and 18th holes to take sole possession of the lead, with Green, Frost, and Ballesteros, all tied at one shot back, still out on the course.

Norman would have a good forty-five-minute wait until the other golfers near the top of the scoreboard finished their rounds and, with the scores so close, there was a strong likelihood of a playoff. Yet Norman chose not to go to the driving range or the putting green to keep his swing in the groove, but to accept an

invitation from CBS Sports to join their announcers in the broadcast booth over the 18th hole, where he would answer questions
and watch the other players close in on his lead while basking in
the attention of an audience of several million on live TV.

When Green and the other golfers in the last group of the day
came to the 18th tee, fifty thousand people were huddled in around
the gallery ropes. Unlike the courses at Tournament Players Clubs,
Westchester didn't have earth mounds around the course to allow
spectators to look down on the action, a situation enterprising
entrepreneurs addressed by giving a device from golf's past a modern twist—they sold cardboard periscopes with advertising printed
on them. The perimeter of the fairway was a veritable forest of
alien-looking people with periscopes extending up from their fore-
heads like antennae and, with all the printing, they appeared to
have descended from a planet named Buick.

Green stood on the 18th tee waiting for Ballesteros and Frost,
who were in the group in front of him, to hit their second shots on
the 535-yard, par-five hole. Ballesteros was upset because his drive
had landed in the rough, and he pulled his three-wood from his
bag to shoot for the green in two. He wanted to steal the tournament away by scoring an eagle three. It was a high-risk gamble,
but Ballesteros played golf more with his heart than with his clubs.

"No, Seve," Ballesteros's brother and caddie, Vicente, told
him. "You have a bad lie and it might land in the bunker near the
green and be difficult to get up and down."

Ballesteros stood there with his three-wood in his hand, glancing from his ball to the green. He had built an international reputation on his aggressive play, and it pained him to think about
having to hit a safe shot and leave the ball short of the green. Men
like Seve Ballesteros did not take the coward's way out and lay up.

As Ballesteros hesitated, his brother continued to implore him
to do the smart thing, repeating his reasoning twice more. Ballesteros thought for a moment and finally relented, returning the
three-wood to the bag and yanking out a tame eight-iron, thinking, okay, I'll go your way. Ballesteros and Frost each chipped
their third shots onto the green, then dropped their birdie putts to
tie Norman for the lead at eight under.

Ken Green's pregnant wife and his sister were pressed in among
the masses along the 18th fairway as the roars went off signaling
Ballesteros's and Frost's birdies and, being unable to see, they
exploited the rank of their "contestant's guest" badges and pushed

their way under the gallery ropes and onto the side of the fairway.

Ken Green was in the fairway needing an eagle to win and a birdie to tie, and he was scared. Having watched his lead wither in the intense heat, which had returned on Friday, had shaken his confidence. The marquee players the press had questioned Green about had stormed right by him like, well, maybe they were better golfers. Green's wife, Ellen, wanted him to go for the eagle. She didn't want Kenny in a playoff with those guys with the big names.

Green hit a three-wood, under the immense pressure of the seventy-second hole, so well that it gave him hope that all was not lost for him—that maybe he could be a big-time player yet. The shot rolled to the rear of the green, where Green would have a difficult twenty-five-foot putt to win a tournament in front of his neighbors. All Green could think about when he stood over that putt was not leaving it short. He didn't. He rolled it to within a few inches of the side of the cup, then watched it roll five feet past. Green needed to drop the next shot to become the fourth man in the playoff.

As Green crouched to study the line of the short putt, Greensboro popped into his mind. Two months earlier, Green had had a two-foot putt to win that North Carolina tournament and $180,000. He had blown that shot, dropped into a tie with Sandy Lyle, and gone down in defeat on the first playoff hole. Up until now, Green had managed to rearrange the image of that final hole in his mind so that he remembered it as him making the final putt to get into the playoff, while forgetting the one before it that had cost him the tournament. There was no time for revisionist history now, however, because if Green missed this putt the big guys would go on to the next hole without him. He conjured every bit of concentration he could find and dropped the ball in the center of the cup.

The four players followed the marshals who were clearing a path for them to the first playoff tee, while fifty thousand people stormed across the now playerless 18th fairway to the adjacent 10th hole. The 10th hole was a par-four with the green just three hundred yards from the tee and potentially reachable with a driver. That drive had to be undeviating, however, because the fairway was lined with bunkers and trees that would consume errant shots.

With four players in the playoff, each knew that the probability was high someone would birdie the first hole and seize the match. There was no room for caution or timidity, yet every aspect of the situation—a 1.68-inch white ball sitting dauntingly on a peg waiting for the golfer to muster composure so sterling as to drive it three football fields away on a perfect trajectory between the lines formed by legions of people staring in intense silence—threatened to atomize the resolve of all but the most determined.

Greg Norman knew that feeling. He had come to his second shot on the seventy-second hole of the 1984 U.S. Open needing a birdie to put him in position to win his first major. Norman had been on a roll, having saved par on the prior two holes with spectacular recovery shots from the rough. On the final hole he drove onto the fairway and had an easy six-iron shot to green, and then birdie possibilities. But as Norman stood there and thought about winning his first major tournament, his courage began to dissolve. The Great White Shark, who had won dozens of tournaments everywhere but the United States, was also the Aussie boy who, when it was time to begin his pro career, had managed to forget his money and had to go home to retrieve it.

Norman had looked up at the 18th flag at the 1984 U.S. Open, and the test it represented, and, in his mind's eye, everything was transformed. The 18th green was no longer a closely mowed circle of grass, and he a champion golfer. The green was suddenly a dark room, and Norman was a little boy who was afraid to push back the door and walk into it.

Norman reared back with his six-iron and decided at some microsecond during his swing that the darkness represented more danger than he could manage. He sent his ball flying into the grandstands beyond the green, well away from the immense terror of the hole. Norman recouped and dropped a forty-five-foot putt to finish in a deadlock with Fuzzy Zoeller. In an eighteen-hole playoff the next day, Norman allowed Zoeller to demolish him by eight strokes.

Norman could admit now that he had choked on that six-iron shot, but only by adding the stipulation that he hadn't choked on another shot since. But all of that had been four years ago, and as Norman walked to the 10th tee at Westchester, he knew what he had to do, and he was convinced he was ready to do it.

The players drew numbered slips of paper to determine their order of play, and Green won the honor of the first shot. He pulled his driver from his bag without hesitation, even though he had stopped using it during his round because he had begun hitting slices with it. Green felt he had no choice but to go for the flag. The rest Green had given his driver during the final holes had not cured it of its slice, and he sent his ball flying down the right side of the fairway, where it came to rest behind a bunker and under trees, quite short of the pin.

Ballesteros, the second man off, was full of confidence as he hit. He had birdied this hole all four times he had played it during the 1988 tournament—even though, a year earlier, he had lost this tournament in a playoff with a bad drive on the same hole. Ballesteros caught the ball cleanly and he thought he was going to be close to the flag, but the ball veered left at the last moment, and came to rest in a bunker just short of the green.

David Frost had a one-iron in his hand. He was going to play it safe unless Green or Ballesteros was close to the pin. When he saw Ballesteros's shot, Frost replaced the one-iron with a driver, only to send his ball slicing off to the right near Green's.

Greg Norman was certain he could outdistance Ballesteros with his driver, and when he saw the Spaniard's ball in the bunker, he thought his drive was a sure thing to find the putting surface. It didn't. Norman hit long, but the ball curved well right of its target and landed behind trees.

Green, Frost, and Norman made bold attempts at recovery shots, but Ballesteros popped his ball out of a difficult lie in the bunker and took the victory with his first putt.

Greg Norman was the first player into the pressroom, and the reporters showed no mercy. They wanted to know why he had now lost six of his seven playoffs. "Although I never make excuses for myself," Norman said, having several at the ready, "I think I may have been a little stiff from sitting in the TV booth waiting for everyone to finish. Nevertheless, Seve birdied the hole and won. It wasn't that I gave it away, he shot one lower. My problem has not been beating myself, it's been the other guy beating me. I haven't done anything really wrong."

David Frost had registered his eighth second-place finish on the American tour—a record he had been questioned closely about recently—and, before a question could be asked of him, he informed the tour official conducting the interviews that he had a plane to catch and could only stay for a second. The sportswriters let Frost talk about how well he had putted that week, then one said, "You've come close a number of times now, David, when do you think you are going to break through?"

"I wish I could answer you," he said with exasperation.

Ellen Green was crying a little when she came in with her husband, not because he had lost, but because she was proud that he had played well enough to be that close. Her husband, however, spoke with his uncommon candor. "I lost the tournament," he said. "There shouldn't have been a playoff. It was my position to win and I didn't do it. We can call my playoff performance an abortion and let it stay at that. It's disappointing. I don't know if anybody here knows how much I wanted to win this tournament, but tonight I might shed a tear or two, or beat the wall and put a hole in it or something. You take these little disappointments and go on. That's all you can do. Sooner or later I'll poke back through."

Seve Ballesteros walked in, leaving the bravado that served him so well on the course in the scorer's tent. "Winning today helped me pick up some more confidence," he said in a voice heavily accented with the tones of his homeland. "I don't know how I will play next week because it is another tournament, and it is a major, which is always difficult, but definitely my confidence will be much higher.

"When I missed that four-foot putt and lost in the playoff at the Masters in 1987, I lost a lot of confidence in my game and in my putting. Then I started missing a lot of crucial putts, and I was always making mistakes at bad times. When I came here my confidence wasn't very good. I won once in Europe this year, but I missed two cuts here, and I missed one there for the first time in six years."

Ballesteros talked about his round, and then someone asked, "Do you enjoy the pressure of a final round like today, when everyone is making birdies and the score keeps coming down?"

"We all look for the kind of pressure where you are one shot ahead or one shot behind, and you try hard to hang on with all the excitement and the galleries," Ballesteros said. "That's what competition is.

"It's not the same when you walk up the last hole with a big lead. I won the Majorca Open this year, and I was six shots ahead, and I didn't have any feelings at all. I was happy, but there were no other emotions. It was a completely different situation today. This is what we all are looking for. It is why we play golf."

Mortality

BROOKLINE, MASSACHUSETTS.
Curtis Strange had been within a few shots of the lead, and he was
thinking he might still have a chance at winning his first major
tournament as he walked toward the 10th tee during the final
round of the 1987 U.S. Open. It was Father's Day, but any aware-
ness Strange had of the date was stuffed away in the remote reaches
of his consciousness. At the entrance to the tee, however, an official at the tournament who was a friend caught Strange by the arm
and, wanting to offer him inspiration, said, "Win this one for your
dad."

Thoughts of course strategies and swing keys were displaced in
Strange's mind by remembrance of early morning rides to the golf
course on summer days when Curtis was nine and learning his
dad's game. He and his father would open the clubhouse of the
course his dad owned, then Curtis would throw his golf bag over
his shoulder and go heading off through the grass that was still
heavy with dew to hit balls all day long, his father checking his
swing from time to time, rubbing his head the way fathers do when
they want to show affection. They'd ride home late at night for
supper, Curtis saying, "Dad, you should've seen the way I was
dropping putts today. It was great." His dad would smile and say
that was fine.

Curtis spent five years going to the golf course with his dad like
that. He learned the basics of the swing from him, and all the other
things that a father who is struggling to play some pro golf between running a club and giving lessons to the members can say to
a son about the possibilities and disappointments of life. Curtis

started competing in junior golf matches, and when a pro tournament would come on the TV at the club he'd watch for a half hour,
before running off to the course to play some holes, while imag-
ining himself one day doing better at golf than his dad had had a
chance to do.

Then his father got cancer and died, just when Curtis was
starting to need him the most. It made Curtis so goddamn angry
that his father was taken away from him that sometimes he wanted
to hit people without knowing why. The edge was always there,
even when the pain started to fade, and Curtis didn't know what
to do with it. Finally he did the only thing he could do. He kept
playing golf, remembering always what his father had taught him,
but sometimes finding no one to rage at but himself when he
couldn't play well enough for his dad.

Strange stepped to the 10th tee during that final round of the
1987 U.S. Open with tears in his eyes, still trying to find a way to
resolve his loss, all these years later. He finished the tournament
tied for fourth. The 1988 U.S. Open was also scheduled to end on
Father's Day, but Strange wasn't going let anything he could control get the better of him this year.

Strange took the week before the Open off and went home to
practice and to get prepared mentally. After starting off the year
playing like shit, as he had told the reporters in Houston, he had
won two tournaments in a month's time, and some respected
players were going around calling him the best golfer in the
world.

Strange didn't really need the extra pressure of having a label
like that, and all the media attention it brought, hung on him two
weeks before a major tournament—one he wanted to win very
much. It didn't suit his personality either. Strange prided himself
on being a regular guy, somebody who wasn't going to start drinking imported beer just because he won a few golf tournaments.
Besides, Strange knew that since he hadn't won a major, the idea
of his being considered the best golfer in the world was absurd. It
didn't matter how many weekly tournaments he had won, majors
were what people judged you by in golf.

So Strange forced all those thoughts out of his mind at home in
Virginia, concentrating on polishing his game and working up his
competitive juices. He succeeded so well that when he came to
Brookline and reporters saw him playing practice rounds at The
Country Club, site of the 1988 Open, they came back to the media

room and said to other reporters, "Have you seen the look in Curtis Strange's eyes?"

Greg Norman and Jack Nicklaus played a practice round together on Tuesday at The Country Club—an imperious name that was intended, its members insisted, to differentiate the club from its city counterparts in nearby Boston at the time of the club's founding in 1882—and their gallery comprised more than 90 percent of the spectators on the grounds that day. The dozens of other notable golfers on the course practiced in relative solitude, while throngs observed Norman and Nicklaus playing the course in oppressive 95-degree weather. It seemed unlikely that, here in the hub of Kennedy country, a foursome of Teddy and three of the Kennedy boys would have drawn more notice.

And what an attractive pair they were to follow: the Golden Bear, as Nicklaus with his midwestern cornsilk-blond hair was known, and the Great White Shark, he of the surfer's peroxide blond locks. The most accomplished golfer in the game, now in his declining years, and the most popular young linkster in the world, trying to find victory.

When Nicklaus and Norman came to their second shot on the 18th hole, the fairway was lined ten deep with sweaty bodies and the nearby bleachers that bordered the green were overflowing. As thousands of eyes focused on the two, Norman, a well-known Boston Celtics fan and friend of Celtics star Larry Bird, reached into his golf bag and withdrew a green baseball cap with the Celtics' name stitched on the front, and the gallery roared its approval as he waved it and put it on his head. Then Norman pulled a second cap from his bag and walked across the fairway to place it on Nicklaus's head.

Nicklaus smiled uncomfortably as the crowd doubled its volume, and Nicklaus tried unsuccessfully to find an angle at which the hat would feel less like a dunce cap to him than it did. It wasn't a matter of size, but one of appropriateness. Jack Nicklaus did not clown on the golf course any more than the Queen Mother wore shorts to afternoon tea—it simply wasn't done. Nicklaus left the hat on as he walked onto the green to tumultuous applause, but before he attempted to putt he feigned that it was interfering with his ability to read the slope of the putting surface and he removed it as inconspicuously, but as quickly, as possible.

Galleries had found much to dislike about Nicklaus in his first years on the tour. He was grim and remote—except for his cockiness—on the course, seeming to care little about the folks on the other side of the gallery ropes who paid to watch him play. Nicklaus was indeed concerned with the fans, just not as much as he was with winning. Nicklaus once tried to smile more during tournaments—after he got adjusted to the tour during the early 1960s—but it didn't work. When reporters asked Nicklaus about these attempts at projected warmth, Nicklaus explained that he wanted to smile more frequently, but that it seemed to be harder for him to arrange his facial muscles in that manner than it was for other people. Nicklaus's galleries grew in time as the mass of his accomplishments made him impossible to ignore, but Nicklaus knew it wasn't like rooms lit up when he walked into them, and he was comfortable with that.

Norman, however, never missed a chance to perform for the crowd, and the crowds, in turn, rushed to him as though the earth were pitched toward Norman wherever he walked, regardless of his standing in any given tournament. His treatment of the press was equally considerate and, for the most part, they always gave him the benefit of the doubt. Norman didn't lose tournaments often according to the sports pages and golf broadcasts; more frequently he was the victim of extenuating circumstances. Norman earned his acclaim through force of personality.

Norman and Nicklaus signed autographs and made their way through their gallery to the indoor tennis courts that were serving as the interview area for the 1,379 members of the media from twenty-one countries who were covering the tournament that was America's national championship of golf.

Nicklaus and Norman were scheduled to do separate pretournament interviews, but when they arrived together the USGA official who was the moderator of the interview sessions that week decided to modify the plan. The official routinely repeated all questions that were called out to the golfer being interviewed, since many reporters in the large, high-ceiling building were unable to hear them, but he decided to relinquish that task this time. "We're going to change the format," the man announced as Norman and Nicklaus took their seats. "Jack's going to play my role, and re-ask the questions Greg gets."

Nicklaus looked at the official as though the man were a teenager on a crowded bus who had felt sorry for the old-timer and stood up to offer Nicklaus his seat. "Well, okay," Nicklaus said in a what's-this-guy-trying-to-pull voice, "if I can't play the other role."

"This is Jack's thirty-second consecutive Open, which breaks the record previously held by Arnold Palmer and Gene Sarazen," the USGA man said before leaving.

"God, I'm thirty-three years old," Norman said with amazement, as though fully comprehending the fifteen years that separated him from Nicklaus for the first time.

"You that old?" Nicklaus responded quickly.

"That tells how old you are," Norman said. "Never mind how old I am."

"Greg," a reporter asked, "you seem to have fallen into a pattern of charging into contention on Sunday recently. How do you manage to turn it on like that?"

"I don't know if on Sunday you bear down a little harder and concentrate or what. My worst rounds have been my first two rounds. I seem to get out there and get lackadaisical about it. I put myself in the middle of the field, then the third round I have a fairly good round, then Sunday, bang. Whether I'm seven shots behind or nine shots behind, I still feel that I have confidence in my ability to come back and win the tournament."

Nicklaus spoke up, never having repeated the question to Norman for the audience as he had been asked. "I'd like to comment on what Greg is talking about. Greg went through a period where he led all the major championships and didn't win," Nicklaus said, referring to Norman's losses in the 1986 major championships. "He may have mentally backed off a little bit so that he didn't get so far ahead that he felt like he couldn't finish."

"Are you feeling any pressure to improve your record in the States?" a reporter asked Norman.

"I really feel that I'm three or four years away from the peak of my golf, and once I get to my peak I expect to play for another eight years at that level, so I feel like I'm fine-tuning myself. I can't wait to play golf in another fifteen years at a competitive level. Every time I come out I feel like I'm getting better. If I have that attitude in my mind, I know that I'm going to be completely satisfied for years and years," Norman said, apparently having abandoned his design to vanquish the American tour during 1988, and having altered his answer from Hilton Head, where he had told reporters he didn't play here frequently enough to win often.

"Jack, what do you think about that?"

"At Greg's age, what are you thirty-three . . . ?" Although Norman and Nicklaus were friends, Nicklaus paid as little attention to Norman's answers as he had to Curtis Strange's at the Memorial Tournament. Norman responded the same way when Nicklaus was talking, and both spent a good deal of time contemplating the ceiling of the room as the other spoke. Now Nicklaus had forgotten Norman's age, which he had been told only a few minutes before.

"Thirty-three, yeah," Norman said.

"Thirty-three. I think if you go back and look through history and look at golfers who were thirty-three they still had some very good years. From thirty-one to forty the guys played some of their best golf," Nicklaus said, referring to himself without mentioning his name.

"I have always enjoyed Greg's attitude towards the game and his desire to win and be the best. People have asked me who I think the best player is, and I think it is Greg. I think Greg, Seve, and Sandy Lyle, coming off the Masters, are probably the three strongest players that I can think of," Nicklaus said, no longer having to worry about being a gracious host. This was a topic on which he wanted to set the record straight. As the former best golfer in the world, Nicklaus believed it was his province to name his successor, and he didn't take kindly to other people intruding on that domain. In addition, if Norman wasn't the best golfer in the world, Nicklaus had erred in anointing him, and that reflected badly on Nicklaus.

"Jack, you didn't put Curtis in the dominant category," a reporter said.

"I think he falls in that category. I'm not trying to downgrade anybody. I think Curtis is a terrific player."

"But you didn't mention him."

"He hasn't won a major. It is simple as that," Nicklaus said with exasperation. "If he would happen to win this week we are going to talk an awful lot about Curtis Strange. Larry Nelson has won three majors and Lanny Wadkins has won one. You have to win that first one before you start talking about being in the same breath as great players. How many golf tournaments have you won, Greg?" Nicklaus said, looking at Norman.

"Fifty."

"Fifty. Here's a man who knows how to win golf tournaments. He may have only won one major, but he's won a lot of golf tournaments and he's going to win a lot more majors. If Curtis wins this, then he's won as many majors as Greg has won, but he hasn't won fifty tournaments. He's won what, twenty tournaments?"

"Worldwide, sixteen," a reporter said.

"That's pretty good," Nicklaus said. "Obviously that's going to raise his stock, but he has to keep winning."

The formal press conference broke up shortly thereafter, but a group of reporters pressed forward to the stage and circled Nicklaus to ask follow-up questions.

"Why is there so much interest in who's the best golfer now, Jack?" someone asked.

"Three or four years ago there was no one golfer. I said back then that guys needed time to develop and that the cream would come to the top. I said that Ballesteros and Norman would come to the top, and they have."

"Don't you think the fact that ninety percent of Norman's victories have come overseas factors into that?" a reporter asked.

"I think that Greg goes over and he destroys the fields overseas. He wins most of the tournaments he enters in Europe and Australia."

"But he doesn't win in the States," a reporter responded.

"I think that's here," Nicklaus said, tapping his index finger on the side of his head. "That's what he is trying to overcome."

If the PGA Tour, with its corporate tournament sponsors and endorsement deals, could be seen as the marketing arm of American business, and Augusta National Golf Club, presenter of the Masters tournament, was a club with a membership heavy with CEOs, then the executive members of the USGA, administrators of the U.S. Open, were the stockholders of corporate America. They were men, often lawyers, with privileged backgrounds and names like C. Grant Spaeth and William J. Williams, Jr., who looked like they had issued from the womb wearing miniature blazers, neckties, and wingtips, who provided the capital for the CEOs and the marketing boys to do their stuff.

They worked at their lawyering but, freed from the drudgeries of endless hours of corporate life by their trust funds and investment accounts, the men of the USGA volunteered their time, and paid their own expenses, to preserve the integrity and traditions of golf. The executive board of the USGA was the Daughters of the

American Revolution of golf, and they oversaw a hired staff of one hundred, headed in 1988 by Frank Hannigan, a man who brought his black Labrador retriever to work with him each day at the USGA's headquarters, Golf House, in northern New Jersey.

The USGA, through a phalanx of thirty volunteer committees, directs virtually all aspects of amateur golf for the six thousand golf clubs that are its members, from rules and handicaps to equipment approval and agronomy research. It maintains a technical center where a robot drives ten thousand golf balls each year to ensure that balls on the market do not exceed the limits for acceleration and distance the group has established. The organization also runs thirteen championship matches each year, including the point of intersection between the USGA and the PGA Tour, the U.S. Open.

The USGA doesn't offer much deference to tour pros when it conducts the Open. Only fifty-three tour members in the 1988 Open field of 156 professionals and amateurs had exemptions that got them into the tournament without having to endure at least the second stage of a two-part series of qualifying tournaments, which 5,500 golfers had entered around the country. During the past thirty years only two golfers who had entered the competition at the first level of the qualifying matches have ever won the tournament, but the open-qualifying approach did allow forty-seven players who had never participated in an Open before to make the field.

Once the golfers arrived in Boston, no one was waiting at Logan Airport with a courtesy car for their use. The pros had to ride a shuttle or schlepp over to the rental car counter with everyone else for a change. When they reached the golf course, they found that the host club and the USGA, in accordance with tradition—the Open is held at a different location each year—had been working with architects and contractors for the past three and a half years to make the fairways narrow, the greens slick, and the scores high. The eighteen holes they would play were a composite course created by combining various holes from the three nine-hole layouts that the members used. The only relief the pros would find would come, ironically, from the intense June heat. The thick, club-grabbing rough that had, in former years on other courses, been an Open feature, had been wilted into near-harmlessness by the sun.

If the USGA was an association that devoted itself to amateurism in golf, however, there was nothing unbusinesslike about the $15 million the U.S. Open would gross from the sale of TV rights, tickets, programs, concessions, and a corporate tent village where thirty-three corporate sponsors had paid $100,000 a pop for thirty-by-forty tents, where corporate logos were prohibited except for discreet signs at their entryway.

Nor did the USGA show any affection for the nonprofessional merchants who heaped card tables outside The Country Club with T-shirts, hats, visors, and other souvenirs bearing insignia like "Open, Brookline, Massachusetts," which seemed to approximate, but not duplicate, the USGA's "U.S. Open" trademark, which was reproduced on millions of dollars worth of items stacked on tables inside the club.

The USGA lawyers hustled into a courtroom in Boston on Wednesday and told a judge the free-lance retailers were selling duplicatous merchandise that seemed official at first glance and that, because of its inferior quality, would forever sully the name of the event and the USGA. The judge wasn't convinced that people didn't know what they were buying at discount prices—lawyers from the Boston Marathon had lost a similar case recently—and the judge told the lawyers they were going to have to do better than that.

The lawyers went back to the course in Brookline, hung out near the card tables, and collared people after they had purchased merchandise from the vendors. The lawyers asked the stunned patrons if they thought the items they bought were official U.S. Open souvenirs. When anyone said "yes," the lawyers produced an affidavit to that effect and said, "Sign here."

Thursday morning the USGA lawyers were back in court brandishing the affidavits, and Thursday afternoon they were accompanying federal marshals armed with a court injunction while they seized every unsanctioned souvenir they could find on the streets bordering the course. No one was arrested, but the merchandise was taken to the basement of the clubhouse at The Country Club for safekeeping.

It wasn't often that Greg Norman remembered his dreams, but he had had one in June of 1987 that was so startling it had lodged in his memory. Norman, who had fantasized about becoming a fighter pilot as a child, dreamt that he was up in a helicopter with his friend Larry Bird of the Boston Celtics. They were flying along as nice as could be, the stars of the golf and basketball worlds, when inexplicably the helicopter began losing altitude. They were falling out of the sky and were about to crash into the earth in a fiery explosion when—brrrrring—Norman's alarm went off and saved him from an unknown fate. It was the third time in Norman's young life that he thought he could have died.

Norman's first brush with death came when he was an eighteen-year-old surfer with shoulder-length hair. Norman was camping out on a beach in northern Australia when a storm passed through the area. After the winds died down, Norman walked out along a finger of land that extended into the sea, and dove into a storm-swollen wave to bodysurf back to the beach. The whitecap pushed him to the floor of the ocean rather than toward the shore, however, and Norman was left terrified and gasping for breath as he struggled to get to land, where he promised himself he would never ride a wave again.

The second incident occurred two years later when Norman was making a five-hundred-mile drive from Sydney to his parents' house in Brisbane during the middle of the night. About a hundred miles from his destination, a kangaroo leapt into Norman's path and Norman swerved his car into a directional post on the highway to avoid hitting the animal. Badly shaken, Norman managed to drive home, where he went to bed. Norman examined the car later in the day and discovered it was heavily damaged and the fuel tank was dripping gasoline as a result of the crash. Norman stood there looking at the car and told himself that he was lucky to be alive.

Norman had not only survived those incidents, but he had also gone on to become a man who was called the best golfer in the world. He was counted among the favorites in the 1988 U.S. Open, where no less a personage than Larry Bird, the fellow inhabiter of his near-fatal dream, had come to The Country Club the day before to walk in his first-round gallery.

Now Norman was in the midst of his second round and he had come to the resting place of his second shot on the par-five 9th hole. Norman found that his ball had stopped near a bridge over a creek, and that the bridge would impede his swing. Since the bridge was an immovable obstruction, Norman was allowed to reposition his ball, and he dropped it onto the trampled grass of a pedestrian crosswalk on the fairway. As Norman hit his third shot, a loud "thwack" resounded as his club simultaneously struck the ball and a rock that was hidden under it by grass. Norman felt a sharp pain and sensed something pulling in his left wrist, and he knew that he had just been injured.

Larry Mize, one of Norman's two playing partners, heard the sound of the impact across the fairway and walked over to ask Norman if he was all right. "We'll see," Norman replied, determined to persevere.

Norman managed to par the hole, but by his second shot on the following hole his wrist was beginning to swell and ache too much to continue. He wrapped his wrist in a towel, walked over to his partners and said, "Fellows, I can't play."

Norman was taken to a medical tent on the course, where his wrist was iced, wrapped in an elastic bandage, and put into a sling while the call went out for an orthopedic surgeon who was at the tournament to meet Norman in the locker room. Meanwhile, news of Norman's withdrawal from the tournament was being reported by ESPN, which was broadcasting the first two days of the tournament on cable TV, setting off a stampede to the locker room by Norman's wife, Laura, his father, who was in the States on business, members of the news media, and Hughes Norton, the head of International Management Group's golf division and a man who, as the Shark's agent, derived a rather substantial portion of his ample income from Greg Norman.

Hughes Norton's identification with Norman was such that he kept a life-sized cardboard cutout of Norman from an advertising campaign in his Cleveland office. Norman's Spalding golf bag rested in front of him in the picture, and the bag was turned so that Norman's name was clearly visible on it. Next to the cutout, Norton kept an identical red and white golf bag that was positioned in precisely the same manner, with Norton's own name spelled out on it, but nobody was standing behind this bag.

The forty-one-year-old Norton had begun his career with IMG just a few miles from The Country Club. Norton met IMG founder Mark McCormack when McCormack came to speak to Norton's class at the Harvard Business School. Norton later drove McCormack to the airport, where he asked him for, and received, a job.

Norton now personally represented Norman, Curtis Strange, David Graham, and Mark McCumber, and oversaw other IMG agents who represented several dozen of the top players on the tour. IMG offered golfers a full range of service from preparation of taxes to investment advice, bookkeeping, insurance, and estate planning but, more important, they cut deals for some of them to make millions of dollars off their reputations. In return, IMG took 25 percent of everything the golfers made. And the agency was getting a double-dip at the Open. In addition to having its players participate, IMG also had negotiated the sale of worldwide television rights to the tournament, and would be taking a chunk of the more than three million dollars that brought in.

IMG fancied itself as wielding such tremendous clout in the golfing industry, primarily because of the prominence of its stable of golfers, that Norton had once called himself the most hated man in golf. The IMG corral was deep with talent, but there was no question who the principal horse was. When Norton came to The Country Club, he brought one press handout with him, entitled "Greg Norman: Facts and Figures." Now the lead stallion had come up lame.

When Norman got to the locker room he called his orthopedist in Florida. "Dr. Baker, please," he said when a receptionist answered the phone. "It's urgent." The doctor wasn't available, but his nurse promised he'd call right back.

Ten minutes later, after Norman had had ample time to ponder worst-case scenarios about the future of his career, Dr. Baker called from Florida and advised Norman that the treatment he had received so far was sufficient, but that he wanted to take a look at the wrist as quickly as possible. As soon as Norman hung up, Hughes Norton got on the phone and chartered Norman a private jet.

Norman walked from the locker room with Norton, his wife, and his father amidst pandemonium as dozens of camera motor-drives whirred and shutters clicked, and reporters called out questions. Norman's skin tone, which is normally deep, sun-baked brown, was nearly white, and his expression was grim. Norman patiently explained to the horde what had happened, and then said, "This is probably the lowest point of my career."

Norman told the reporters that his doctor thought the root of his problem was in his childhood. Norman said his wrist had been bothering him recently, and he had been taking medication for it, but that the doctor told him he had probably first injured his wrist as a child, and it had only been getting worse since.

As the Norman entourage moved toward their car, Norman expressed concern that time lost because of his injury might make it difficult for him to play the full fifteen American tournaments required for him to keep his tour card, given the number of over-seas, appearance-fee tournaments he had booked for later in the year.

When the mob reached Norman's car, Norman called out weakly, "See you later, fellows," and started to lower himself into the passenger seat until a reporter called out a final question.

"Greg," came the voice, "what club were you using when you hit the rock?"

"A seven-iron," he said, before being driven off.

As the Normans packed up their belongings at their hotel, Hughes Norton was wondering if there wasn't a better doctor for his prize client to see than the guy in Florida. The Florida doctor had performed a small operation on Norman's knee a few years earlier, but Norton remembered that Jack Nicklaus and a bunch of other athletes had been worked on by a man in Alabama. Norton got the doctor's telephone number from Nicklaus's office, made arrangements for Norman to see the man that evening, and altered Norman's flight plan from Florida to Alabama.

Later that evening, after reporters had filed stories worldwide on Norman's withdrawal from the tournament, word came into the media room from Alabama on the nature of Norman's injury. He had sprained his wrist.

Sarah Strange came up from Virginia to be with her husband on Friday evening, when the 1988 Open was at its halfway point. Sarah traveled with Curtis fairly frequently, but when she was on the road she felt like she was neglecting her responsibilities at home, so she and their two young boys weren't with him every minute. While Sarah and Curtis were spending a quiet evening at their hotel that night, Curtis started going over his second round in his mind.

Strange reviewed his day on the course after every competitive round. He thought about where he did and didn't make mistakes, what shots he didn't hit properly and how he might play a certain hole differently. This evening he also considered the sum of his Open play and concluded that he had gotten off two solid rounds, that he was in contention at two shots off the lead, and that if he kept plugging along he was going to be there at the end.

Strange allowed himself to anticipate only a sliver of the ex-citement and satisfaction that might be his if his hopes came to fruition and, in doing so, he triggered anxieties that would condemn him to protracted nights of fitful sleep until, one way or the other, the tournament ended. Even though Strange now earned several million dollars a year, he would suffer from the same insomnia that had troubled him during his first and most difficult days on the tour, as his decade-long grind to approach the pinnacle of golf seemed to be nearing culmination.

When Strange dropped a birdie putt on the 9th hole on Saturday, he became the leader in the U.S. Open with twenty-seven holes to play. An hour later, as he arrived at the 12th tee, there was trouble. A foreboding summer electrical storm was blowing in from the distance. Strange stood on the tee and surveyed the sky repeatedly as though he were looking for lightning, reflections of which could be seen occasionally off in the distance. Of more immediate concern to Strange was the stiff crosswind that was preceding the storm and threatening to transform an already difficult hole into one that could steal away a man's dreams when they seemed palpable.

Strange studied the trees rustling alongside the fairway, glanced up at the sky, walked around the tee, talked to his playing partner, put his hand out to feel the sporadic drops of rain and waited futilely for the siren to sound signaling a suspension of play. Strange didn't want to hit his ball into that wind. When Strange saw lightning in the distance, he exercised an option available to him and declared his own suspension of play.

Strange and his playing partner walked off the tee to a nearby open-sided shelter, as hundreds of people mobbed around the structure to stare at them. ABC employees came pushing through the crowd with cameras, microphones, cables and announcers. Marshals, who were members of neighboring country clubs, shoved through barking orders for everyone to move back, and Strange sat there trying to look as calm as if it was just another rain delay. When the worst of the storm seemed to have bypassed the course, Strange, looking claustrophobic, returned to the partial seclusion of the roped-off tee, while the marshals, the television people, and their cables snaked after him.

Meanwhile, unnoticed in all of the excitement, the two men who had been at the top of the leaderboard earlier that morning, Scott Simpson and Larry Mize, winners of the 1987 U.S. Open and the 1987 Masters respectively, had completed the 11th hole and were moving along a narrow cordoned walkway to the 12th tee. When Simpson and Mize saw Strange on the tee surrounded by hangers-on, they stopped as abruptly as grounded ships and stood there looking at each other.

Simpson and Mize, both tour Bible study members and quiet, modest men, got a lot of bad press because of, rather then in spite of, their victories in major tournaments. Both men had edged out more popular golfers—Simpson beat Tom Watson and Mize defeated Greg Norman—to win their majors and, although the pair usually finished in the money, their other tournament conquests were few. But people didn't talk and write about Simpson and Mize's wins as being flukes that frequently; mostly they focused on the men's blandness and lack of affect—other than contentment—which, on the tour at least, was associated with religious zealotry. When a Bible study golfer appeared in the media room for a press conference, sportswriters headed for the exit.

When nonevangelical golfers won major tournaments, they used their press conferences to recount their personal triumph over the adversities of the course and the game for the media. When Simpson won the 1987 Open, he told reporters he hadn't had hardship on the course because his main goal was to play a round that was pleasing to God, and God didn't care whether he won or lost, so long as he played his best. The sportswriters said, still this had to be the most exciting day of your life, winning your first major tournament. Simpson said that wasn't true, that the most important day of his life was when he accepted Jesus Christ as his Lord and Savior.

Sports Illustrated said after the 1987 Open that Simpson was slightly more thrilling than a tuna sandwich, and before the 1988 Open the senior executive director of the USGA told *Golf Digest*—on the record—that, even though the Open prided itself on producing high winning scores, they would rather have Seve Ballesteros and Tom Watson tied at eight under par than have defending champion Scott Simpson winning at even par.

At a pretournament press conference earlier in the week, Simpson had been asked how he felt about being called slightly more exciting than canned seafood, and he said it didn't bother him at all. "Don't you ever get mad?" a reporter asked.

"I don't get mad if someone cuts me off on the freeway," Simpson said, "but I get mad at myself for making bad shots on the course."

"How can someone tell when you're angry on the course?"

"I've gotten a lot better than in my amateur days, when I

would kind of let it build up, and then I'd explode and break clubs and get into profanity. If you saw my bag flying through the air with clubs flying everywhere you could tell that I was angry," Simpson said in the gentlest of voices. "I conceal it pretty well now and I don't get as angry as I used to because it doesn't do any good."

In putting his golf game in God's hands, Simpson has found a way to disassociate himself from the considerable emotional traumas of life on the road, while playing a game that is immensely fickle for imposing amounts of money. Simpson's approach lopped the deeply felt highs and lows off competition, but it also deprived galleries of their central satisfaction of watching golf—observing professionals demonstrate that they can handle one type of tribulation better than amateurs can. It also separated Simpson and other evangelical golfers from the pros on the tour who played the game without a prophylactic on their nerves.

As Simpson and Mize shyly waited in the walkway to the 12th hole, debating whether they should go up onto the tee with Strange and all the other important people, they were joined by a sprinkling of spectators, for whom the golfers pleasantly signed autographs, and by Mrs. Simpson and Mrs. Mize.

There were as many different types of wives on the tour as their were golfers, from childhood or college sweethearts who had struggled to success with their mates, to recent arrivals who were bored by golf but loved the money and the glamor, to women who had been around long enough to know their husbands were never going to make it and were sick of the whole mess, with variations in between. The wives, without golf to distract them and with other wives being the only familiar faces they saw on the road, tended to be clannish, and the code of the clan was that wives were the spouses of sports celebrities and they should dress the part. Some women flouted the precept and dressed comfortably, but those who didn't took their fashion cues from the sleek blondes in their twenties who traveled with battalions of luggage.

The archetype of the young professional golf wife was a blonde, always a blonde, in her mid-twenties with hair that was shoulder-length or longer—hair long enough to require fussing with and the time to accomplish this. She wore shorts in all but the coldest weather to highlight her nicely tanned and rounded legs, a stylish but demure top that hinted but never revealed, visibly expensive aerobic or athletic shoes, and a huge diamond ring. Every aspect of her appearance, from her hair to her makeup to her clothing to her figure, was taut, smooth, and wrinkle-free. Although she was unfailingly attractive, the net effect was a bit too lacquered and asexual—until she put her socks on. She'd pull a pair of long, heavy cotton or wool athletic socks up over the soft curve of her calves, then flop them back down to her ankles, where they would bunch up like sweaty sheets tossed from a bed in the most intense moment of passion. They were the kind of droopy socks otherwise naked women wore in photo layouts in men's magazines, and they screamed sexuality.

The wives of Bible-study golfers also followed the fashion lead of the young professional golf wife, except for one salient feature. Evangelical wives didn't go near those socks-to-be-left-on-in-bed. Nothing could be seen above their sneaks except flesh.

Scott Simpson and Larry Mize finally walked onto the 12th tee as the suspension of play dragged on past an hour, although the sky had cleared long before. The people on the tee greeted them warmly, especially the announcer Jerry Pate and the ABC crew who had long ago run out of things to say to fill up television time.

Pate grabbed Simpson and Mize, notified his production trailer that he had fresh interview material and turned to the crowd as he waited to go on the air. "Make sure you yell 'Hi, Mom,' and act like fools when we go on the air," Pate said derisively to the gallery.

"Hey, Jerry," a spectator called back, "show us how."

When play resumed, Curtis Strange's lead increased to three shots after his closest rival double-bogeyed the 15th hole. Three strokes would have been an extremely comfortable margin to take into the final day, but Strange couldn't sustain it, losing one shot each on the 16th and 17th holes.

"How do you feel about tomorrow?" a reporter asked when Strange was brought into the interview room with a one-shot lead.

"I feel good," he said. "Anytime you're leading going into the final round you have to feel good. It means you're doing something right."

"Will you be nervous tomorrow?"

"We'll all be a little nervous tomorrow morning, and rightfully so. If we weren't we wouldn't be human and we wouldn't be in that position. And it will get tight coming down the last . . . so many holes tomorrow afternoon." Strange knew that if he specified a hole where it would start getting tight, his pulse would rise at precisely that point.

"You have to have control of your emotions, control of your golf swing, keep breathing and go from there, because there is going to be pressure. No matter how big a lead you have, it seems to get tight down the stretch. It never seems to come easy at the end. Somebody always seems to make a run at you, or you make some mistakes, and it gets tight."

Curtis Strange came to the course on Sunday wearing his red shirt, and feeling tense and tired from lack of sleep, but telling himself it didn't matter because there was a job to be done. By the third hole of the day, he was no longer the leader of the tournament, having fallen into second place behind his playing partner, Englishman Nick Faldo, the only one of the ten overseas players who had entered the Open who was still in serious contention. Strange pulled back into a tie on the 7th hole, and when he birdied the 10th hole to regain a one-shot lead he was feeling like he was in control of the match, that all he had to do was hold on for eight holes and it was his.

Strange took a long time selecting a club for his second shot on the 11th hole. The wind was moving around, and it wasn't the time to make a mistake. He was trying to think his shot through completely before he hit it. As Strange stood there reviewing every plausible contingency, and his huge gallery waited silently for his next move, a low droning sound came from behind Strange's back to encroach upon the quiet. The noise grew incessantly louder and more imminent as he waited. It was a small yellow single-engine airplane, flying at low altitude, trailing an advertising banner, and the pilot, seeking the largest audience for his message, was homing in on the leader.

Strange resisted the impulse to look at the airplane. To acknowledge its presence would only make the noise more intrusive. He selected a club, took a practice swing, looked toward the green, then walked back to his caddie to exchange the club for a different one. Strange repeated his preswing routine, waited, then changed clubs again. He duplicated all his previous actions, then switched clubs a third and fourth time before he hit the ball as the airplane cruised toward the next hole and its noise began to abate.

Strange got out of the hole with a par, hit a good drive on the 12th hole, and was preparing for his second shot there when he looked over to see Charles Abdennour, AKA "Kodiak Charles," standing inside the gallery ropes, thirty feet away, in the midst of a slew of USGA officials. Abdennour was an unbalanced man who followed the golf tour around the country from time to time, somehow managing to gain admission to sold-out events so he could approach golfers to whom he had taken a fancy. Abdennour was especially drawn to Strange, whose parents were said to live near Abdennour's parents, and Jack Nicklaus, who was said to live near Abdennour in Florida.

Abdennour had last been seen three weeks earlier at Nicklaus's Memorial Tournament, where he came to Ben Crenshaw's hotel, and when Crenshaw moved, Abdennour located him at his second hotel. Abdennour was said to have made a threat against Strange at the Memorial, and police circulated photographs of the man at the golf course and provided Strange with armed plainclothes security people at the match.

Strange called for the police who were escorting him at the Open to apprehend Abdennour, and the man took off down the side of the fairway for a short distance before he was arrested. The entire affair was being televised, and two detectives who were watching the tournament in California recognized Abdennour as a man they were seeking for having skipped out on a $2,500 hotel bill during a California tournament by telling the hotel that Jack Nicklaus was picking up his tab.

Strange struggled to regain his composure, put his second shot on the 12th green and two-putted for another par. Strange was holding on, but that was all. He needed to score some birdies to buttress his slim, one-shot lead. Another banner-trailing airplane appeared as Strange was on the 13th fairway. Strange moved away from his ball to talk to his caddie until the plane passed. But this plane didn't continue down the course. It banked and returned to the 13th hole just as Strange was attempting a very makable birdie putt. The relentless buzz of the plane passed over the green as Strange missed his putt, and Strange finally glared up at it in anger.

Nick Faldo tied Strange for the lead with a birdie at the 15th hole, then returned the lead to Strange with a bogey on 16. All other possible contenders were effectively out of the tournament by now and Strange and Faldo's gallery, which had seemed to double with evey hole they played, finally pushed past the gallery ropes and poured onto the course behind the golfers as they walked down the 17th fairway. The marshals did the only thing they could, encircling the golfers, who were in the final minutes of an undecided and tremendously important tournament, as they disappeared into a sea of spectators.

Strange hit onto the rear of the 17th green, fifteen feet from the flag, needing only to two-putt the hole and par 18 to win. He was feeling pretty good about where he stood. After years of being assaulted by comments about how he had choked at the 1985 Masters, he hadn't let this major get away from him. Curtis Strange was about to show the world that he hadn't been devastated by anything—not losing a major in the closing holes, or having his father die when he was fourteen.

Strange was in a position that called for a lag putt, one that snuck up on the hole so that, if it didn't go in, it remained close. But Strange struck the ball too firmly, and it missed the hole and rolled six feet past. Stunned and worrying that he was about to blow it, he missed his second shot as well. As Strange tapped in his final putt, the spectators on the 18th hole were amusing themselves by alternately bellowing the lines of a beer commercial—"Tastes great," and "Less filling"—at maximum volume.

Strange walked to the 18th green knowing it was unlikely he could win without a playoff, but telling himself that he could not, absolutely could not under any circumstances or conditions let this goddamn tournament slip away from him now. The session in the media room following a loss, and the things that would be written and said about him for years to come—"Curtis Strange choked on the threshold of another major tournament today"—were not things that he was going to let happen to him. He simply couldn't endure it.

Strange and Faldo drove on off the 18th tee, then tens of thousands of spectators were all over the course as the golfers and marshals picked through the crowd. People were yelling and screaming at Strange, "Come on Curtis, do it man," but Strange kept his head down and his thoughts focused and his feet moving forward.

Strange put his second shot in a bunker short of the green; Faldo was long and at the rear of the green. Strange knew that he had to get it out of that bunker and close to the hole, or all the torment he had gone through to that point would be for naught. The hordes were a hundred deep in the fairway, only yards behind Strange. People were sitting on other people's shoulders, and there were mass huddles on the ground when spectators who were unable to see the green found someone with a miniature, battery-powered TV. Then, as Strange prepared to swing, everyone fell into eerie silence.

Strange bit his lower lip, blasted out of the sand to five feet from the pin, Faldo missed his first putt, and they ended in a tie. Strange had shot his worst round of the week, a one-over-par 72, but it had been just good enough to get him into an eighteen-hole playoff the next day.

Strange was the first golfer into the interview room. "You should have given me a few more minutes," he said, trying to keep eleven years of tour anguish from his face. "I played horribly and I putted just about as bad. I had the opportunity to put everybody away on the back side with some putts and I didn't do it. The seventeenth green is a hell of a lot faster than I thought it was going to be and the putt got away from me. It was one of those times I wished I could hit it again and see if I could keep it around the hole. I went six feet past the hole and three-putted."

Strange, who had been especially cordial with the media all week, went through his round, then said, "Let's keep this short."

"Were the airplanes bothering you on the course?" a reporter asked.

"No," Strange snapped.

"What happened when that guy was taken off the course at twelve?"

"Nothing."

"Did you hit the first putt on seventeen too hard?"

"I really didn't hit it very hard at all," Strange insisted, "especially for it to go six or seven feet past the hole. It's a new green and faster than the others."

"In retrospect should you have been more conservative on that putt?"

"I just said I hit the damn thing as easy as I thought I should have."

"Tonight will you think about saving par on sixteen and eighteen, or about missing par on seventeen?" a reporter asked, trying to force Strange to admit he had made a mistake.

"I wish I could get upset about myself on seventeen, but I honestly didn't hit the putt very hard. Granted, I hit an awful second putt, but I was more in shock than anything else."

"How disappointed were you on seventeen?"

"I didn't have time to think about it," Strange said and his voice dropped, echoing vulnerability for the first time. "I had one more hole to go, and I had to do my damnedest to not let it get the best of me and lose this thing outright."

"Playing against an Englishman tomorrow, do you think of yourself as the Great American Hope?" a reporter asked.

"I couldn't care less who I'm playing," Strange said. "Whoever it is and whatever I have to do, I want to win."

Nick Faldo, having been given new life by Strange in a tournament he had seemed destined to lose, followed Strange into the interview room with a rosier perspective. "I'm obviously very pleased with the way that I played," he said. "I played very solid. I got tied up with the putter and didn't let it fly away nice and freely, and I left a few short. Then I was struggling to find the pace, then struggling to find the line as well. That made life hard work, but I'm pleased."

"You won the British Open shooting par, and you had fourteen pars today, is that something you are consciously trying to do?" a reporter said, referring to Faldo's 1987 British Open victory, which he had secured by shooting exact par—no birdies, no bogeys—on every hole in the final round, and for which he was castigated widely in the British press for being a boring plodder.

"I'm trying to make birdie every hole, not par," Faldo said firmly. "I thought you guys would give me a wonderful time if I made eighteen pars and won today."

"You and Curtis didn't talk to each other on the course today, why was that?"

"In a championship like this you have to concentrate so hard. It's not like you're not sociable, but it is a day of work."

"Do you think of the playoff tomorrow in nationalistic terms?" a reporter asked.

"I think you do," Faldo said, representing the nation that had invented golf, only to have the Americans steal away their dominance of the game for years. "Yes, of course. British TV is here and there are probably twenty British press guys here, and only Sandy Lyle and me played, so it gets nationalistic."

Strange and Faldo went to the driving range and then the practice tee, where they hit balls well away from each other, without having much to say, before going back to their hotel rooms with their wives. Strange went over his putt on the 17th hole in his mind, then tried to forget it, then went over it in his mind, then tried to forget it. He didn't feel like eating much, and he wasn't able to sleep, so he waited.

*   *   *

When Curtis Strange and Nick Faldo began play at The Country Club at two o'clock on Monday, the temperature was above ninety, and humidity was almost as high, the wind was swirling, and the boisterous fans were ready for a dogfight. It didn't happen often in golf that two men dueled it out over eighteen holes without dozens of other golfers on the course to distract the spectator's attention. Everyone knew that one person was going to win—that happened every week—but now there was only one person, rather than seventy or so in a normal tournament, who was going to lose.

Neither man, given the conditions, played anything resembling precision golf. Strange hit less than half the fairways from the tee, and less than half the greens from the fairways. Faldo was straighter with his shots, but he scored bogeys on a third of the holes because of missed putts.

The golfers plowed along, Strange with a one-shot lead or tied with Faldo until he went up by three at the 13th hole. Their wives walked along the course with them, as they had done the previous day, being friendly and making chit-chat, pretending not to be aware of tension and never wishing the other's husband bad luck, but each quietly cheering for her own husband all the while.

Strange allowed himself to admit he had won when he was up by four strokes after the 17th hole. He still hit a safe two-iron off the tee at 18, rather than a wood, because you never know when something you don't anticipate is going to happen, but when he was walking up the 18th fairway, Strange allowed himself to think about his dad for the first time, and what this would have meant to him. To have him standing on the side of the fairway, heaving with pride, as his son marched down the course to claim the U.S. Open title. Strange fought against the thought and forced it from his mind.

Sarah Strange was already crying when she walked onto the 18th green with Nick Faldo's wife, Gill, after the last putt dropped. She couldn't stop her tears the way Curtis could. Sarah was so filled with happiness that she grabbed Gill Faldo and gave her a tremendous hug. Gill, whose husband had just lost, went rigid.

Curtis came over and embraced Sarah hard and buried his eyes in her neck to cover his tears. He was worried that he wasn't going to be able to get through the ceremonies that were coming, and the television cameras were already on the way across the green.

Nick Faldo, who had continued his strategy of keeping the ball in the fairway while shooting an inflated four-over-par 75, handled his press conference good-naturedly until, perhaps anticipating the stories that would be appearing in the British press the next day, he was asked about his playing style. "Was it discouraging to you that Curtis was all over the course and still scoring well?" a reporter said.

"No, that's the game," Faldo said. "If you hit it down the middle they call you a boring plodder. On a day like today it's the score that matters, it doesn't matter how."

"Now that he's won a major, how do you rank Curtis?" a reporter asked Faldo.

"He's been out here for what, ten or twelve years, and it has capped off those years. It's a great achievement. I don't think people fully appreciate how hard we work, and mentally how hard it is to win a major. People say some hurtful things just because you miss one or blow one or something happens, and they don't understand that to us majors are *the* events. We only have four a year, so it is pretty difficult. There are a lot of things you have to get right that one week. Everything from your game to health to whatever. Just hundreds of things have to jell."

A reporter asked Faldo what it was like after you won your first major. "Now," he said, "you feel as if you start again."

With all of the award ceremonies and congratulations being bestowed, an hour passed before Curtis Strange appeared in the interview room. He had almost lost control when he was dedicating the win to his father on TV, but he thought he was okay now. Yet Strange's emotions soared once again as he got to the microphone. He was facing the people he had to explain himself to after every important round of golf, and some of them had seen him through it all. They were the people who represented Strange to the public, and Strange read the stories they wrote about him carefully.

"This is going to be tough, so hold on," he began, his voice cracking and thick. "This is for my dad . . . and . . . that's all I can say. I've been waiting a long time to do this. I screwed up the 1985 Masters, and I think I was as disappointed about that as anything else. But we don't have to bring up that part of it. We're supposed to be having fun."

Strange thanked the man who had been his surrogate father when he was a teenager, and the other members of his family, stopping periodically to fight for composure. "This is the greatest thing I have ever done," he continued. "This is the greatest feeling I have ever had . . . and it was a hell of a tough day out there, Jesus. But I don't mean to be like that. I honestly waited a long time and, you see my dad started me out years ago. I just wish he could have been here. . . ."

Sarah Strange was standing in the back of the interview room with a glass of champagne in her hand, looking through the legs of the tripods from the television cameras, and crying like she did when her children were born. She kept thinking, Why is he doing this to himself? But she knew what it meant about his father, and what they had been through together. She thought the release was good for him.

"What does the win mean to you?" a reporter asked after Strange had talked about his round.

"It got me to that next level, goddamn it. It also means that it is my first one, my first major, and it'll get you all off my back about that one," he said to the reporters.

Strange talked for a long time about his thoughts on the win, then someone asked, "Does this mean you're the best golfer in the world?"

"Goddamn, what took you so long to ask the question? You all were scared to death about who was going to ask it first," Strange said. "This is just my first major. It doesn't mean that I'm any better than Seve or Greg or Sandy or anybody else. No, it doesn't mean I'm number one to answer your question. It doesn't really do much for that. I'm not going to jump to number one on the Sony World Rankings, nor would I expect to, because of one tournament."

Sandy Lyle was the hottest golfer on the PGA Tour during the early months of the 1988 season.

Bob Libby

Lee Trevino's ambivalence toward the Masters tournament tore at him every year when he received his invitation.

Bob Libby

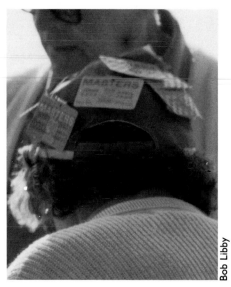

Bob Libby

Some spectators so prize their Masters tournament admission badges that they display them like heirlooms.

Davis Love III discovered that signing autographs was only one of many demands that would be put on him when he joined the tour.

Bob Libby

Bagpipers in Scottish garb signal the beginning of the MCI Heritage Classic in Hilton Head, South Carolina.

Greg Norman with Jamie Hutton (seated) on the driving range at Hilton Head

Fred Couples unwittingly found himself at the center of controversy again at Hilton Head.

Ray Floyd surfaced at the top of the leaderboard for the first time in two years at Houston.

Bob Libby

Peter Jacobsen struggled both physically and mentally in his attempt to return to the winner's circle.

Bob Libby

Steve Wilson

Gary Koch and the media wait to discover whether he would win the Panasonic Las Vegas Invitational and $250,000.

PGA Tour commissioner Deane Beman meets the golf media.

Bob Libby

Steve Wilson

Jack Nicklaus was reduced to spectator status when he missed the cut at his own tournament.

Hale Irwin moments before he made a declaration that would change Curtis Strange's life

Steve Wilson

Curtis Strange reacts to his final
putt of the Memorial Tournament.

Seve Ballesteros demonstrates his
visceral approach to golf.

Ken Green's antics on the course displeased PGA Tour officials and players frequently.

HOLE 1
YARDS 452
PAR 4

Greg Norman with his customary overflow gallery on the 1st tee of the U.S. Open

Steve Wilson

The imposing clubhouse at The
Country Club, site of the 1988
U.S. Open

Nick Faldo saw himself
as the Great European Hope
at the U.S. Open.

Steve Wilson

Curtis and Sarah Strange surrounded by the blazered men of the USGA at the awards ceremony of the U.S. Open

The course at Oak Tree Golf Club in Edmond, Oklahoma, features Pete Dye's hallmarks: water, stone walls, earthen mounds, and sloping greens.

Jack Nicklaus was not optimistic about his chances of making the cut during the second round of the PGA Championship.

Jeff Sluman throws his ball to the crowd after completing his final round of the PGA Championship.

Steve Wilson

Greg Norman's hair was nearing its normal length when he teed off at the World Series.

Tom Watson wondered if he hadn't used up his allotment of nerve during the 1988 season.

Bob Libby

Curtis Strange was in one of his special moods in Akron, Ohio.

Steve Wilson

Ian Baker-Finch had one of the worst days of his life during the final round of the World Series.

Steve Wilson

Mike Reid found his beloved adversity on the course at the World Series.

Bob Libby

The second shot on the 8th hole at Pebble Beach, one of Jack Nicklaus's favorite medium-iron shots in golf

Steve Wilson

The storied 18th hole at Pebble Beach, site of yet another encounter between Curtis Strange and photographers

Tom Kite was one of Curtis Strange's closest friends on the tour, but he became just another obstacle during the Nabisco Championship.

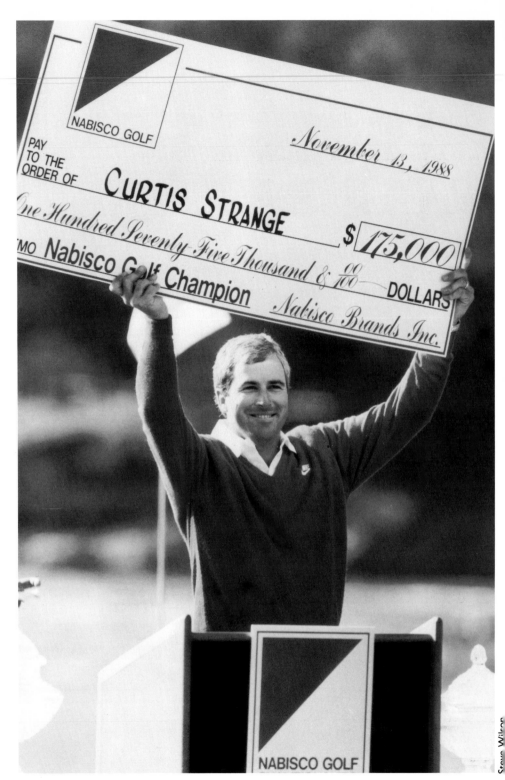

Curtis Strange raised his bonus check for the crowd at the Nabisco Championship, but only under duress.

THE BEST GOLFER IN THE WORLD

PART THREE

Immortality

Two kinds of people arrived at St. Andrews golf course on June
20th in automobiles with blacked-out windows. The first group
were plainclothes policemen, whose government-issue, four-door
Chevys were so readily identifiable as unmarked police vehicles
that, while the darkened glass might obscure the number of cops
staking out a suspect, they could not camouflage the presence of
the constabulary. The second group were the icons, celebrities, and
potentates of American golf, who swept into the golf club outside
of Yonkers in limousines with glass tinted as black as their chauf-
feurs' suits. The occasion was a variant on the pro-am, called the
hero-am, which *Golf* magazine was staging to inaugurate its day-
long celebration of the one hundredth anniversary of golf in America. St. Andrews had been organized in 1888, and the magazine
figured the club's founding to be the initiation of Yankee golf.

   The golf match was to be followed later in the day by a gala
black-tie dinner and awards ceremony at the Waldorf-Astoria Hotel in Manhattan, where people the magazine had designated as
the 100 Heroes of American Golf would be honored, and one of
them would be named Player of the Century.

   As the noon hour approached at the golf course, the policemen
went to the back door of the club's kitchen to inquire as to whether
there might be some expendable foodstuffs on hand, while the
folks from the back of the limos joined the buffet line in the dining
room. The small media contingent at the tournament would avail
themselves of the free eats in due course, but the reporters were
afraid to leave the overheated room that was serving as the press

center before learning if Ben Hogan would grant them one of his rare audiences.

Hogan was a man of seventy-five who had joined the tour in 1931 after, in the old-world tradition, having worked his way up from the caddie shack in Fort Worth, Texas. Hogan had won sixty-two official tournaments—he trailed only Sam Snead and Jack Nicklaus on the career victories list—including nine majors. Hogan's game had featured a wicked hook during the first part of his career, but Hogan had studied the golf swing and the laws of physics, and then happily pounded golf balls on the practice field, all the while experimenting with minute variations of the motions, until it went away.

Hogan's bent for research led to his becoming known as the thinking man's golfer, and his success at applying his theories brought the title "best ball-striker in the history of the game." Hogan later survived a near-fatal 1949 automobile accident and returned to win again, and he was hailed for his courage and determination. That Hogan accomplished these feats while having little to say to the press only gilded the veil of his mystique.

Hogan became reclusive after he retired from the game, but now he had come to New York for the first time in eighteen years, and the reporters were anxious to hear what the fabled man might have to say. At least they had been before a Centennial of Golf official apprised them of the stipulations for a Hogan press conference. After consulting with Hogan, the man told reporters they could submit, through him, five easy, simple, uncomplicated questions, in writing, and Hogan, if the queries met his approval, might deign to come deliver his replies, to those inquiries only, in the flesh.

The press turnout at St. Andrews was small because the 1988 U.S. Open, which had been scheduled to end the previous day, was currently being decided in a playoff, and most golf writers had remained in Brookline for the conclusion. The reporters at St. Andrews decided that a canned Hogan interview was better than no Hogan interview, and they drafted some benign questions, which the offical went off to tender to Hogan. While the reporters were awaiting Hogan's decision, the official had returned to announce that Jack Nicklaus had completed his round in the hero-am, and asked if the reporters wished to speak to him. The consensus was: Sure, why not?

Fortunately for Nicklaus, the reporters present were not aware, or were too circumspect to mention, that Nicklaus's previous visits to St. Andrews were under less than heroic circumstances. Nicklaus's multihundred-million-dollar-a-year company, Golden Bear International Inc., had been commissioned in 1982 to redesign the historic course and to construct several hundred luxury condominiums on adjacent land. The deal collapsed when the builders Golden Bear contracted with were unable to complete the intricate custom work in the units on time, and Chemical Bank of New York foreclosed on the project in 1986, leaving Nicklaus to absorb three million dollars in losses.

The St. Andrews insolvency was one of a series of financial defeats the company suffered in fields ranging from communications to education to automobiles to restaurants and oil development. Nicklaus had replaced his chief executive officer, and the corporation was said to have recovered and narrowed its scope, but, lest he forget the past, Nicklaus came to a pressroom that was sweltering in the summer heat because an electrical problem had rendered the air conditioning inoperative.

"Jack," a reporter began the session, "when did you meet Ben Hogan for the first time?"

Nicklaus shrugged. "I can't remember the first time I met him, but I played the last two rounds of the 1960 U.S. Open with him. I didn't pay too much attention to Hogan then because I was trying to win. But at every tournament I went to after that, if Ben was there he sought me out to play a practice round with him," Nicklaus said, using a phrase—"he sought me out"—that Nicklaus favored when discussing his involvements with other golfers. "I was very proud that he always wanted to play with me."

Some reporters who weren't familiar with Nicklaus's concerns about the current state of golf asked his thoughts on it, and Nicklaus slipped into his familiar litany concerning the factors—the all-exempt tour, high-technology clubs, the too-long ball—that he felt were conspiring to hinder the emergence of the next Jack Nicklaus on the tour. Then, in a casual voice, a reporter asked Nicklaus who he thought was going to be selected Player of the Century that evening.

"You're asking the wrong person," Nicklaus said, trying to find a diplomatic way to say this. "I obviously hope it would be myself. If I won it would be something extra special to me."

Golf magazine was about to give Jack Nicklaus, who as an adolescent had dedicated his life to becoming the best golfer ever, the bizarre opportunity to discover how he would be remembered while he was only forty-eight years old. In less than a dozen hours, Nicklaus would know whether or not he had achieved his life's goal, and the timing couldn't be better.

Golf excited Jack Nicklaus only when it was at the highest level: when he was playing his best game on the best courses against the best competitors. After participating—and doing well—in every sport available to him in his childhood, Nicklaus had selected golf as his game because he thought it was where he could make his mark. When he came to the tour in the era of martinis, rare steaks, and dropped-ceiling family rooms, his devotion was complete. During the first six months of the 1962 season, he was home only seventeen days. Nicklaus had vowed to his wife, Barbara, at the time of their marriage that he would never be gone more than two weeks at a stretch, but by that he hadn't meant that he would stay home long when he got there.

The first time Nicklaus was home for nine days in a row, after he had been on the tour for two and a half years, he bought a seven-passenger airplane and hired himself a pilot to expedite his constant travel. Nicklaus was twenty-four years old then. He had astounded the golf world with his debut and his budding business empire was promising to provide long-term material comfort. One component of the formula for immortality was lacking, however, and that was support from the galleries.

Nicklaus dieted (although he insisted he lost the poundage because it was affecting his game, not for crowd appeal), abandoned his military-length hair and, when he found he couldn't smile more on the course, he just kept winning. In time spectators came to believe that Nicklaus was obsessed rather than possessed, and they began to warm to him as the Vince Lombardi of golf. As Nicklaus observed these changes in the people outside the ropes, he told himself that they had come to enjoy watching his determined game because their lives were lifted momentarily when he had a successful tournament, and that gratified him.

But all of this was history now. Nicklaus hadn't played golf at its highest level in years. He was missing the cut routinely in the tournaments he entered. Nicklaus had argued at his 1988 Memorial Tournament that the lack of practice time had accounted for his being bumped on Friday there but, three weeks later, he told reporters before the start of the U.S. Open that he had spent two weeks preparing for that match, and he missed the Open cut as well. Nicklaus hadn't even been able to win the meager $2,450 he needed to pass the $5 million career earnings mark.

Most middle-age golfers point to their tendency to injure easily and heal slowly, or to their loss of fine touch and confidence to account for their dimming careers. Jack Nicklaus, of course, was not most golfers, and he had a different explanation for his deterioration. When reporters had asked Nicklaus about his game several months earlier, he had said that it wasn't so good because the person who was Jack Nicklaus, world-beater, had somehow departed him and left an impostor—a mortal—in his stead. Nicklaus said that he still loved golf, but only when he played like Jack Nicklaus, not like the impostor who had been inhabiting his bones for the past few years. Nicklaus said he didn't know that guy.

The last time Jack Nicklaus had seen the real Jack Nicklaus on the golf course had been two years earlier, during the 1986 Masters. Nicklaus told his wife then, "I think I've found that fellow out there I used to know," and then went out and won an unprecedented sixth green jacket at age forty-six by shooting seven under par over the final ten holes, as the now-admiring spectators shouted "Jack is back" at volumes that may have been unequaled in Masters competition.

Jack Nicklaus didn't know how the soul of Jack Nicklaus the colossus entered or left his body but, having become familiar with what the titan was capable of, he regarded him warily when he recognized him. The moment Nicklaus saw each of his first three children—all of whom resembled their father—after their births, Nicklaus fainted on the spot.

As Nicklaus continued talking with reporters at St. Andrews, a commotion developed in the adjacent hallway as a large, noisy mob moved toward the pressroom. When the door opened, Ben Hogan and his entourage piled into the small room, and the reporters inside jumped from their seats, depriving Nicklaus of his congregation. Nicklaus stopped in midsentence to look over in displeasure, then stood up. "Oh, is my press conference over?" he asked.

No one answered Nicklaus directly, but momentarily he witnessed the elderly Hogan being escorted to the seat Nicklaus had been warming, and Nicklaus wandered out of the pressroom unnoticed.

When the room grew quiet, an official of the event began reading off the questions that had been submitted to Hogan. "What do you think about the size of the purses on the tour today?"

"It's a lot of money," Hogan said. "But I never thought about money when I played. I knew there would be some there if I won."

"What's your daily routine like now, Mr. Hogan?" the official read out.

"I go to the office every day, then I hit some balls," Hogan said.

The insipid questions and pro forma answers continued until they reached a crescendo with an inquiry meant to probe Hogan's strength—his knowledge of the golf swing. "How did you fix your hook?" the official asked.

"That's a long story. I went home and thought about how to fix it, then I went back on the tour," Hogan said, and nodded to indicate the press conference had just concluded.

As Hogan was being led from the room, a reporter dared to call out a question. "Mr. Hogan, are there any players you especially admire?"

"I admire all the golfers," Hogan said, as the event official scowled over Hogan's shoulders at the reporter. The reporters laughed at the futility of the enterprise and went to lunch.

Nearly a thousand people in tuxedos and formal dresses poured into the ballroom of the Waldorf-Astoria that evening. Of the one hundred designated heroes of golf, only thirty-five of the sixty-three living heroes were present, and they took their places at brightly illuminated rows of tables on the stage. Half of the honored one hundred were professional golfers, the remainder being a potpourri of people with golf connections. There were entertainers, former presidents, sports agents, golf administrators, amateur golfers, and golf writers and broadcasters. To reduce the number of people who would address the assembly, the field of competitors for the Player of the Century Award had been pared to eight, and gossip gave three of those men the edge on receiving the award: Sam Snead, Ben Hogan, and Jack Nicklaus, who accounted collectively for 217 official PGA Tour wins.

After Dinah Shore sang "God Bless America" and the multitudes were fed, ABC golf commentator Jack Whitaker, the master of ceremonies, introduced Sam Snead, a man who had come from the back hills of Virginia to win eighty-four PGA Tour events over a forty-two-year period. Those were pre-Deane Beman years, however, and Snead's official take during four decades was only $620,126. But Snead was golf's equivalent of Samuel Johnson—he believed no one but a blockhead ever played golf except for money, and Snead's take as a golf hustler was thought to be many times greater. Snead had joined the tour at a time when the stature of professional golfers was so humble they weren't allowed to enter the clubhouses of the golf courses they played, and recognition seemed to be on his mind when he came to the podium.

"Why does everybody think I'm Hogan? Do I look like Hogan?" Snead blurted out, provoking sustained laughter with his unexpected remark. "Coming to the hotel today I had my straw hat on with the red band I always wear and this man said to me, 'Mr. Hogan?' I said, 'No.' He said, 'Aren't you Mr. Hogan?' I said, 'Sorry sir, I'm not Mr. Hogan.' He said, 'You're not Mr. Hogan? Well you're somebody.' I said, 'Yep, I'm somebody.' "

Snead kept his audience going by nodding toward the priest on the dais who had offered an invocation. "I played golf with a priest the other day," Snead said, "and he told me he had a twelve handicap, so I gave him twelve strokes. Then when we played, he shot par-par-par-par-par-par-par. Finally I said to him, 'Father, if you're playing golf like this you haven't been saving many souls lately.' "

Arnold Palmer, who would have been the uncontested winner had the title being awarded that evening been Most Popular Golfer of the Century, charmed the audience with brief remarks about his fondness for golf, and Ben Hogan talked, to the amazement of everyone, about the mechanics and physics of the golf swing, analyzing the swing position of a golfer that illustrated the evening's program, as people cleared their throats and looked around the audience to see if they recognized anyone who was sitting near them.

Then Jack Whitaker introduced Jack Nicklaus, recalling the remark Masters tournament founder Bobby Jones made in his later years while he watched Nicklaus dominate that tournament yet another time. "Nicklaus," Jones said, "is playing an entirely different game, a game with which I am not familiar."

As others had all evening, Nicklaus got directly to what was on his mind when he took the podium. "I've never been on a golf course and had sweaty palms before. I never had to play all these fellows and gals at once," Nicklaus said as the audience sat looking at him in silence. The audience didn't understand that to everyone else this was a dinner, but to Nicklaus it was the ultimate competition of his life. Nicklaus looked surprised at the flat reception his remarks received, then quickly adjusted his tack. "But all of the players are great players. You might say that we are all players of the century. Each one of us as we grew up had the push or something to excel."

The room went dark as a videotape highlighting the careers of the eight finalists was shown, then the editor of *Golf* magazine stepped to a second podium at the far end of the stage, next to a six-foot object that was draped with a cloth. "Ladies and gentlemen, we're not going to keep you in suspense a moment longer," he said. "On behalf of *Golf* magazine and the centennial committee, it is my privilege and pride to announce to you that the Player of the Century is . . . Jack Nicklaus."

Nicklaus walked stiffly to the far end of the stage to the accompaniment of a standing ovation, and waited as the editor pulled at the cloth and unveiled a life-size bronze statue of Jack Nicklaus twisted around in the finish of his golf swing. The power of the Nicklaus stroke was so evident in the object it seemed as though it could walk off the stage, and the piercing intensity of its eyes was such that no one would have attempted to stop it. Nicklaus stared at the statue quietly, then whistled a low sound and shook his head from side to side. There at arm's length was the person Jack Nicklaus had lost. It was Jack Nicklaus the Hun.

Nicklaus took a second to gather himself and to gauge the proper response. "I don't know what to say, George," he said to the editor. "The finalists were all asked to prepare a speech, and I said that would be presumptuous. I said that if I was chosen I would have to think of something at the time. Now I can't think of anything.

"But, ah . . ." Nicklaus attempted to continue, but each time he glanced over at the reproduction of himself he fell mute. Nicklaus studied the embodiment of the boy from Columbus, Ohio, who took on the world and won, then raised a palm to ward it off. "You have to get him away from here," he said finally. "Those eyes."

Nicklaus repeated that all of the honorees were really players of the century, and lapsed into often-told and comfortable stories about his early days in golf. He was verbally treading water, trying to get through the closing holes of this tournament that was already his without breaking down, without saying through tears of relief, "You can't even begin to imagine how hard I have had to work for this, what I had to go through, how I always had to be so strong, what I gave up." Nicklaus didn't want to say those things. Shouldering the load was part of the territory, but a man had to have an outlet somewhere.

"Through the years the game of golf has been wonderful to me, and of course . . . there is obviously somebody . . . who has shared all of those years with me," Nicklaus said, and he was losing it. Tears were stinging his eyes and his voice was heavy and thick.

"Barbara, hang on, honey . . . words . . . Barbara sitting down here. We have been married for . . . I better get this right . . . Barbara and I have been married for twenty-eight years." The audience applauded Barbara Nicklaus, and her husband tried to continue, but it was becoming impossible. After all these years of living with Jack Nicklaus, the athlete who had always needed to be the world's best, Jack Nicklaus the person was standing there with a sculpture of his talents and ambitions confronting him—accusing him, reminding him, and Jack Nicklaus lost track of who was who, as he attempted to introduce his children, now that the struggle was over.

"Of course, Steve's right there and Jackie is going to be married in about a month to Barbara. These kids . . . I've grown up . . . they've grown up watching me play, and Barbara has had to put up with me all of these years, and believe me that isn't an easy chore. Barbara's wife couldn't be here with us tonight—Michael couldn't be with us tonight because he is playing golf this week, which is a rare occasion for Michael, I think."

Nicklaus recognized the only course was retreat. "Anyway I'm delighted they are with me this evening to share this moment. I guess there's really not a whole lot more to say, except it is quite an honor and quite a privilege to be in the company of all these great golfers and quite a privilege to be selected. Thank you and good golfing."

"Thank you, Jack, and thank all of you for coming here tonight," Jack Whitaker said to close the ceremony. "We can now go to the bar and start the arguments."

People clustered around Nicklaus to shake his hand and take his picture, and drifted out to the lobby bar, or up to a reception the magazine was throwing on the next floor. People talked about what a nice evening it had been, and how delicious the food was, and about where they were going on vacation, and wasn't the heat terrible. The one thing they didn't do was quarrel. Most everyone agreed that Jack Nicklaus was the best golfer in the history of the world. But no one said they envied him.

JUST HAVING FUN

Angst

Anyone who saw Peter Jacobsen crying on his July 3rd flight
out of Chicago for Virginia might have thought he was shed-
ding tears of joy. Jacobsen had just won $97,200—slightly more
than the cost of the average American home—for playing golf
for four days at the Beatrice Western Open, bringing his earnings
for the year to $311,412. Jacobsen's friend Bill Murray, the ac-
tor and comedian, had even visited him at the tournament, and
they had done some well-received clowning together—Jacobsen's
great love—on the golf course during a celebrity pretournament event, so he should have been in an especially buoyant
mood.

But Jacobsen, a hulking, six-feet-three-inch, 210-pound, thirty-
four-year-old father of three, was crying tears of pain and humiliation. He had come to the 72nd hole of the Western with a
one-stroke lead, needing only a par to secure his first tournament
win in four years and, with thirty thousand spectators and several
million TV viewers watching, he had sent his second shot flying
completely over the 18th green and into the pond that lay beyond
it. In a situation in which pros routinely choose a weaker club than
the distance to the flag seems to dictate, because their adrenaline
level will cause them to hit the ball farther, Jacobsen had felt the
need for a stronger club.

Jacobsen had double-bogeyed the hole, presenting the tournament win to a twenty-four-year-old kid who was competing, on a
sponsor exemption, in his first tournament on the PGA Tour. All
the money in the world and all of the adulation of the crowd

couldn't prevent Jacobsen from feeling like he had failed himself again, as his airplane closed in on the East Coast.

Jacobsen had seen his second-place finish in Las Vegas in May as a sign of renewal: Peter Jacobsen had returned from his back injury and was ready to earn some respect. Next he claimed a strong sixth-place finish at the Memorial against a difficult field. Jacobsen didn't do much over the first three days of the U.S. Open, and when he got to the first tee for his final round he was resigned to a poor showing at the tournament. It didn't matter to him at that point what he shot on Sunday. Suddenly the fairways seemed a lot wider and the greens flatter, and Jacobsen shot a 64, tieing a U.S. Open record by taking only three strokes on seven consecutive holes.

Jacobsen was at his comedic best in the pressroom after that round. "I've played a lot of pro-ams with guys who didn't make a four until the ninth hole, but it wasn't preceded by a string of threes." Then, "Am I boring you," he quipped to a reporter, "I know I'm not one of the leaders here, but please don't yawn in front of me." But he ended his session in a serious tone: "I'm getting out of town on a good note. It's always good to leave on a high. I'm going into the summer with a positive attitude and maybe I can win a few tournaments." But, when a tournament had been his for the taking two weeks later in Chicago, he had given it away.

Jacobsen's wife, Jan, tried to cheer him up on the plane, his oldest daughter, Amy, told him that he had, after all, finished second, and to perk up because he would have a lot more chances to win, and his sports psychologist, Chuck Hogan, had told him the loss was history, and to go out there the following week and have some fun. A friend from home in Portland was writing him a letter that would begin by listing the names of all the golfing greats who had had disastrous finishes in tournaments during their careers, to lift his spirits.

Once Jacobsen got over the initial disappointment, he knew that he couldn't allow his mind to linger on the double bogey on the 72nd hole. If he fixated on the double bogey, he told himself, every time he had a good round he would begin to tremble on the 18th tee. He had to remember only the other seventy-one holes in Chicago, the ones that got him to eleven under par to lead most of the tournament. And, he had to get right back out there on the course. He was going to concentrate on the things that he had done right, and he was going to go out there and play the Anheuser-Busch Golf Classic in Williamsburg like nothing untoward had happened in Chicago.

Mark Wiebe was thankful to be the hell out of Chicago and on his way to Virginia on Monday morning. Wiebe had finished tied for eighty-third at the Western Open, after shooting a mortifying final round of 82, including forty-five strokes on the final nine holes. Wiebe, his wife, and twenty-month-old daughter had been sick all week and, when Wiebe couldn't get his putts to drop on the final nine on Sunday, he had given up. He resolved that he wasn't going to get mad or disgusted during his final round, and he wasn't going to embarrass himself by throwing clubs or swearing or yelling. He was going to keep hitting the ball until he finished the seventy-second hole, then he was going to flee.

Wiebe had struggled for years trying to get on, and stay on, the tour. He had been through five of the PGA Tour's national qualifying tournaments, gaining and then losing his playing privileges, before he earned a two-year exemption by winning his first tournament, the 1985 Anheuser-Busch Golf Classic, when he was twenty-seven. Wiebe won another tournament the following year, and he thought his travails were over. He had earned $260,180 in 1986, placing twenty-fifth on the money list. Wiebe and his new wife built a house in Colorado, started a family, and settled in for the life of considerable prosperity that Deane Beman made possible for players who won a tournament per annum.

Wiebe told himself that, according to the money list, he was the twenty-fifth best golfer on the PGA Tour, and that continuing to win the occasional tournament was manifest destiny. Halfway into the 1988 season, however, he hadn't won since 1986 and he began to fret. Was it mental, physical, or both? Was he playing too much or not enough? Wiebe started changing his swing and consulting his teacher more frequently. He tried not trying so hard, and he tried being more confident, but neither of those was really possible when he wasn't winning. Wiebe knew he had to act like he was going to win every tournament he entered, but he didn't have enough of the thespian in him.

Wiebe's wife, Cathy, wanted him to see a sports psychologist, but he absolutely refused. He didn't understand how it worked that you went to somebody you had never met before and spilled your guts out. So Wiebe made a deal with Cathy in which she would become his sports psychologist. He would talk to her about his game, and she would give him feedback. Cathy had proven to be a stern taskmaster of her husband's golfing psyche. She had been pretty hard on him at times, and she always made it very clear when she thought his attitude was bad. After a difficult day on the course, Wiebe got to spend the night with his most vocal critic.

Wiebe's view of sport psychologists was a common misperception, one stemming from the shrinklike title they embrace. Most sports psychologists are actually attitude coaches and motivators, with little or no training in clinical psychology, who work with their clients on the telephone and on the playing field, rather than on the couch. If Wiebe had volunteered information about some conflict in his life to sports psychologist Bob Rotella, Rotella would have told Wiebe he was glad to hear the story because it helped him understand Wiebe better as a person, but that he couldn't do anything about Wiebe's past. The golfing future was what Rotella dealt with, and he'd ask Wiebe if he wanted to do something about his.

Rotella had worked with a multitude of athletes like Wiebe, young guys who wanted to win so much, and who were so afraid they weren't going to win, that they couldn't win. Mired in this Catch-22, the golfer would start breaking down the game he had spent several decades building, and before long he was back to scratch, constructing a new swing out of advice coaches and other golfers gave him.

Rotella would counsel these golfers, who had already substantiated their talent by making it onto the tour, that they had to learn to trust themselves. He would tell them to abandon perfectionism and accept that they would make mistakes on the golf course. All they had to do on the course, he would say, was to have their minds so totally absorbed in where they wanted the ball to go that, when they hit it, they were convinced it was going to land at that spot. They were not allowed to begin any shot until their heads were in that zone. Then, wherever the ball went, they were to accept it with a nonjudgmental response, and duplicate the procedure on each shot. It was as simple, and as impossible, as that.

Mark Wiebe had known where he wanted his putts to go when he stroked them in Chicago, but they seldom complied. Wiebe was convinced that it didn't have anything to do with mental discipline. It was more like something was wrong with his eyes. They seemed to be misaligned in his head or something. Wiebe believed that when he directed his putter so that it appeared to him to be square to the hole, it was actually aimed left of the hole. Wiebe had been working with his coach in California on this, and was sending him videotapes of his putting from the road. When Wiebe got to Virginia, he would spend many hours on the putting green Monday evening and Tuesday, trying to get his eyes accustomed to what his putter looked like when it was straight.

Wiebe would be able to conduct these exercises in what, for a little-known player such as himself, would be friendly surroundings. Since Wiebe had won the Anheuser-Busch tournament three years earlier, it was one of the few stops on the tour in which people in the gallery actually knew how to pronounce his name.

The Western Open had been something of an occasion for Tom Sieckmann. It was the first time in a string of thirteen consecutive tournaments, spread over five months, that he had survived the Friday cut and earned a paycheck. Sieckmann's recent performance hadn't been atypical of his four-year stint on the tour, but he always kept at it, even in the continued absence of financial rewards, because he believed that one of these days he was going to get everything right. Along the way, one of Sieckmann's primary—and not insignificant—sources of pleasure in life had been the act of working at improving his game.

Sieckmann had spent the better part of the last fifteen of his thirty-three years relentlessly trying to fashion a winning game. He studied books, consulted teachers, changed equipment, and pounded practice balls because, well, everyone wanted to be good at something, and Sieckmann had decided that golf was what he was going to be good at.

Sieckmann was a big guy, six feet five and 220 pounds, who had grown up as a roughneck on the plains of Nebraska, thinking only sissies who were afraid to get bloody in real sports played golf, while developing an appetite for the mysteries of the remote world that lay beyond the wheat fields. Sieckmann thought there were some fine people in Nebraska, but he also couldn't wait to get out of town, and professional athletics seemed to be the path that would take him there. Sieckmann tried a year of basketball at the University of Nebraska, where his angry outbursts at players, coaches, and referees engendered a steady supply of technical fouls, while competitors who were less thickset outleapt him by a foot. That left golf, which Sieckmann had played with his father on a nine-hole, par-three course, during the four months a year the midwestern elements permitted.

Sieckmann put in a few years on the Oklahoma State University golf team, then turned pro—which required no more than a declaration of that intent—even though he couldn't play professional-level golf, and the courses the pros were playing intimidated the hell out of him. Golf courses in Nebraska had been short, flat, dry, and treeless. Sieckmann had never played long courses overlaid with water hazards, trees, and out-of-bounds areas. When he got on them he felt like an acrophobic in an ascending glass elevator, and he couldn't play golf if he looked around.

Sieckmann also had some serious swing flaws, but he was determined to address them somewhere other than Nebraska, so he took his clubs to the airport and left for Europe and the Orient. He took lessons from so many people he couldn't remember their names anymore, and sometimes the teaching was ill informed enough to cause him to regress. But Sieckmann was on the road: adrift in an ever-changing world of cultures, languages, foods, and experiences while working on his game, and he was happier than he had ever been. His golf came along slowly as he learned on the run. After having been nurtured as an athlete on the pandemonium of basketball tournaments, Sieckmann played golf with Asians and witnessed the equanimity the game requires. When he returned to the States on visits in the late 1970s and told his friends about the great young international golfers who were developing overseas, people scoffed at him and said that only an American could be the best golfer in the world.

By 1984, Sieckmann had won seven tournaments in Asia, Europe, and South America after a seven-year sojourn, and he decided it was time to return to the plains and to the PGA Tour, where he wanted to become the first golfer from Omaha, Nebraska, to make a name for his town on the circuit. Sportsconscious folks at home agreed to continue his sponsorship arrangement—normally a syndicate of several dozen people who stake a golfer $50–$60,000 a year for expenses, taking all of his annual winnings up to that figure and a percentage of each dollar above it—and Sieckmann returned home as he had left: still working on his game.

Sieckmann did miserably in the States, losing his playing privileges two out of his three years back, and the pressure mounted.

He spent thirty-five weeks of 1987 whacking balls, missing twenty-five cuts, and sitting in motel rooms, wondering whether he was pissing his life away. He was well aware that people back home thought he was a bum because he didn't have a job and a life full of responsibilities like everyone else. And his sponsors were beginning to make remarks like, "Well, maybe just one more year." To make matters worse, Sieckmann didn't have many close friends among the other players, or a wife to shore him up on the road, and it got lonely and draining as the season progressed.

Sieckmann thought about getting a job—so he would have the money to go skiing for a month when he wanted to—and he might have been able to admit to himself that he wasn't going to make it if it weren't for one thing. He kept getting better. People couldn't see how much he had improved since college, or they wouldn't be so disparaging. Every year he was better than he had been the year before. He was so close, and he had something he loved to give him satisfaction: working at his golf game.

Sieckmann came to Virginia having earned money on the golf course for the first time in months and, perhaps more important, to a tournament he had played well in for three rounds the previous year. In addition, the field wouldn't be the most difficult, with only eight of the top thirty money winners present. It was the week before the British Open, and many top players would be heading across the pond to acclimate themselves to the wind, rain, and cool weather, and the vastly different links-type courses that were characteristic of that tournament.

"All right," Curtis Strange said, walking into a pretournament press conference in Williamsburg, "my pro-am round took forty-five minutes longer than it was supposed to, so let's make this quick."

Strange's shirt was so soggy with sweat that he appeared to have been playing under a hose with his kids. The temperature was in the nineties, and the humidity wasn't far behind. The occasional dense breeze that crept off the James River at the southern boundary of the course seemed to cloak rather than cool the skin. But Strange was used to the July weather. This region of Virginia was his lifelong home, and local folks always remarked that the arrival of tournament week seemed to occasion the sultriest days of summer.

Strange both represented the posh Kingsmill resort and conference center where the Anheuser-Busch tournament was staged, and lived in a home he had built near the course after he and Sarah had sketched it out on scratch paper one night on the road. As resident pro, Strange was the tournament's host, and tour decorum dictated that he invite some of the golfers he was closest with to stay at his home during the match. But Kingsmill adjoined Colonial Williamsburg and several immense amusement parks, which, like the Kingsmill resort, were owned by Anheuser-Busch, and that meant every pro who had children was accompanied by them. Strange wanted to be hospitable, but having squadrons of kids screaming through the house was not his idea of a fun time.

It was Strange's first meeting with the local media since he had won the U.S. Open. The reporters were curious about the aftereffects of the local hero's victory, but Strange was wearing his Open crown self-consciously.

"Do you have a different sense of yourself since you've won?" a reporter asked.

"No."

"Even though people were always talking about your never having won a major before?"

"They've only been talking about that since the Memorial Tournament. Hale Irwin said his piece there, and it brought me into the spotlight. Then when I got to the Open it started that Curtis is maybe the best player who hasn't won a major, and it snowballed. But I never heard much of that before, and I haven't done anything different."

"Jack Nicklaus picked up on Irwin's remark too, didn't he?" a reporter who wasn't familiar with the story said.

"Well, Hale was the one who said it. Jack was very political in what he said . . . but . . . ah . . . Jack just kind of said the same thing Hale did . . . but . . . ah . . . and then different writers went around to different people and they said basically the same thing." Strange hadn't been present for Nicklaus's early remarks at the Memorial, but he had ascertained them nonetheless.

"As far as my own self-esteem or satisfaction, yeah, it is satisfying, but you have to go on. I'm not going to downplay it. It was the most exciting thing I've ever done. But me as a person, no. I'm still going to go out on the river on my boat and drink beer. Those who know me know it won't change me."

"Do you think people will say, 'Oh, he's gone big-time now?'" someone asked.

"I sure hope it is never said. If you ever sense that in me I hope you tell me," Strange said earnestly. "I don't think I'll ever be that way or have that said of me, but if it is, or if I am getting that way, I hope somebody tells me. I really hope that is never said, because we are in somewhat of a small town here, and gosh, I've always been so conscious of that. I try hard to be just the opposite."

Strange was so concerned that his friends and neighbors might think him haughty after his victory that, when a local paper told Strange they wanted to run a short item on his best hole each day as part of their tournament coverage, Strange consented only after the paper agreed to write about his worst hole of the day as well.

"Curtis, what surprised you the most about winning the Open?"

"The response from people from all over the world. I played in the French Open the following week and the people there had stayed up all night to watch it on live television. And the telegrams and letters. The people you never heard of before who picked up a pen or pencil to write a letter to you. A lot of it was the excitement of the Open and the playoff, but every one of those letters mentioned the ending with Sarah on the green and the things I said about my dad, which was awful nice of them.

"I didn't think people would sit down and write letters. I have a roomful. I don't know what a roomful means. I have a bunch and it is still coming in every day. It took me three or four days of three or four hours a day to get through it. I read every piece."

"Are you going to respond to them?"

"Somebody asked me that seriously," Strange said, then noticed that his questioner wasn't smiling. "I don't think it is the kind of thing you respond to, it's congratulatory. The people who did ask for a response one way or the other I'll try to. I don't think most of them need responses, thank goodness."

"Were the letters gratifying?"

"They just surprised me," Strange repeated. "To take the time and the effort, and I'm not just talking about 'Congratulations, Curtis, Sincerely, John Doe.' I'm talking two- and three-page letters really saying what they felt after the playoff, and after the emotional finish. About family and that kind of stuff. People were really awfully nice, and yeah, it did kind of surprise me a little bit." Strange had been touched by the letters but, just as he wasn't going to act superior over his victory, he wasn't going to become Mr. Softee every time he walked into a media room just because he had cried on international TV once. Strange was now the U.S. Open champ, he was at the next level of the game, and vast new challenges, which Strange wasn't certain how to handle, lay before him.

"Are you upping your schedule now?" a reporter asked.

"No, all of my foreign appearances were already booked, and I've added only one tournament in Japan. I have offers to go all over every week, but I don't have to and I don't want to."

"Will winning the Open make a lot more money for you?"

"No, it won't change drastically. If a young upstart player won the Open it might be worth the one million dollars everybody says an Open victory is worth, but to somebody who has been on the tour for twelve years and done well, it doesn't mean that much. To put it bluntly, my price tag was already up there," Strange said, and then immediately regretted it.

"That is something I hate to say because people take it the wrong way. Not you all, but the people who read that in the paper. It's something I'd hate to even have mentioned ever because people take it the wrong way. They'd rather read about how you're playing. They don't want to read about the money stuff, that turns them off." Strange made a valiant try at defining for the writers what readers wanted to read, but it didn't work. The quote was too irresistible, and it would appear, in context, in most of the local papers the next day.

"Don't you have more offers now?"

"Yes, I can be more selective. I'm not going to be jumping from here to there. I've got my loyalties to people I've been with over the years and they've been with me. That's what sponsors bank on, they hope that you're going to win the Open." Although Strange would remain with his existing sponsors, those contracts were up for renewal at the end of 1988, and Strange's agent, Hughes Norton of IMG, would negotiate a substantial increase in Strange's fees.

"Have you adjusted your goals for the year upward now?"

"I'd like to win another golf tournament. I've never won four in one year. Without getting too crazy, the money title is right there. Anything after that is really getting the cart before the horse. In the past I have had a tendency to slack off or relax a little bit, but I'm not going to do that this time," Strange said emphatically. "I will have a lot of big tournaments to play."

One of the tournaments Strange had to play was the upcoming one before his hometown fans, a tournament he wanted dearly to win—to show his stuff locally—but never had. "Is there any emotional difference between this tournament and others?" a reporter asked.

"You always see your friends out there. When you play well it really helps the momentum to have the people behind you, but when you play bad it works just the opposite and you feel even worse. You want to dig a hole and jump in it."

The Anheuser-Busch Golf Classic was Fuzzy Zoeller's kind of tournament. Whereas marshals at other events held up signs that read "Quiet" as golfers were addressing their balls—except at the Masters and the Memorial, which considered their galleries too sophisticated to require such prompting—in Virginia the signs read "Hush y'all" and "Ssshhh y'all." The crowds were not as massive as in larger metropolitan areas, but they were supplemented on the weekend by Curtis Strange's Navy, a flotilla of everyday people in pedestrian boats who dropped anchor in the James River off the 17th hole, where they partied and visited in the dusky water until Curtis Strange appeared on the tee, whereupon they blasted their air horns in salute. Strange sometimes joined the boat people after his round and, a few years earlier, he had spent the night on the river with them after the vessel he was on ran out of gas, and Strange insisted his fellow communicants not radio the Coast Guard for a potentially embarrassing, and sure to be publicized, rescue mission.

Zoeller, who lived in Indiana but represented the neighboring Ford's Crossing development on the tour, and Strange had each finished their second rounds on Friday at seven under par, three shots off the lead. They were scheduled to be paired in a local-favorites twosome on Saturday, one that held the promise of great entertainment, which the duo previewed in the interview room Friday evening. Zoeller had won the tournament in 1986, but both he and Strange had missed the cut in recent years, and when Zoeller walked in to find Strange concluding his interview he called out, "I'm proud of you neighbor, you made the cut. When you live here and don't make the cut it's embarrassing."

"I'm sure Mr. Ford was happy with you last year, too," Strange retorted.

"Curtis, how do you feel about your game going into the weekend," a reporter asked.

"I'm playing well," Strange said.

"But how's your putting?" Zoeller called from the back of the room.

"Bad," Strange said.

"I don't believe that," Zoeller countered, "but if that's your story you better stick with it. These guys are writing down everything you say."

A reporter told the pair they would be playing together on Saturday and Strange said, "Oh, shit."

"Curtis, do you like playing with guys who talk a lot on the course?" someone asked.

"I guess there isn't much you can do about it, is there?" Strange said.

"Sit back and listen, that's all you can do," Zoeller said.

Strange joined in the fun on the first few holes on Saturday, giving Zoeller a comic hat on the first tee and passing the occasional remark, but it didn't last long. Strange had a tournament to win, and an impressive year he wanted to make extraordinary. He was capable of doing it only one way: soberly.

Zoeller whistled his way down the fairways, smiling and winking at the crowd, slipping into a brief trance of acute concentration when he pulled a club from the bag and quickly struck his ball, snapping out of it moments afterward. Zoeller had compiled a succession of ten victories, including two majors, during his fourteen years on the tour, before his back went out and the surgeons reworked his disks. Zoeller still had pain, and his game was fickle, but none of this appeared to touch him deeply. He tried to win when he could, he talked to NBC about a commentator's job in case he couldn't, and he whistled and smoked and played golf. Golfers, seeking to disassociate themselves from bad rounds, frequently said, "Who I am is not my golf score," but Zoeller was the only player who appeared to have internalized the thought.

Zoeller and Strange each bogeyed the 16th hole on Saturday to fall to three and four shots off the lead respectively, and Strange was furious with himself as they walked to the 17th tee. As they waited on the tee for the group in front of them to finish, Strange dropped a ball to the ground and intensely practiced his putting stroke, before cramming his putter back into his bag, muttering, "Goddamn bogey." Zoeller stood sedately off to the side, having a smoke.

Strange would finish the day tied with Zoeller once again, but trailing four players, three of whom were Peter Jacobsen, Mark

Wiebe, and Tom Sieckmann. Sieckmann had overcome an unusual tour nemesis—unfortunate third rounds—to sit at the top of the leaderboard. Sieckmann had an explanation for this. He thought he had found the right guru at the right time.

Sieckmann, deep in despair during the height of his dry spell in May, had checked the extensive book of statistics the PGA Tour keeps on all of its players and learned he was ranked dead last in putting proficiency. Sieckmann, who had owned more than a hundred different putting implements in his career, was long off the tee, but he was two-putting, or worse, virtually every green. Sieckmann went to visit a scholar of the short game, Dave Pelz, a former NASA physicist who, after years of intense statistical analysis and observation, had developed an unusual putter that resembled a plumbing fixture rather than a golf club.

Pelz tutored players in the use of his putter and other aspects of the short game, and he and Sieckmann had clicked well enough that Sieckmann thought he saw an immediate, dramatic improvement in his putting. After his own decade-long hunt for the perfect golf swing, Sieckmann had found a soul mate in Pelz, and he respected Pelz's application of scientific method to the game.

Sieckmann was soft-spoken, calm, and reserved when he came to the interview room on Saturday evening. "Tomorrow I'm going to be thankful that I have an opportunity to be in contention, and I'm going to go out there and have fun doing it," he said. "It took me a long time to learn that golf isn't like basketball, where you have to go out psyched up and thinking about winning. In golf you have to keep your concentration under pressure. I'm just going to have fun and stay relaxed."

"Is having fun just being out here on the tour, or is it being out here and in contention on Sunday?" a reporter asked.

It was a question Sieckmann wasn't prepared to answer directly. "When I go home and watch tournaments on TV," he said, "I'm proud to be out here with the greatest players in the world."

The pressroom at televised golf tournaments always contains several television sets that are tuned to the broadcast of the match while it is in progress. Sportswriters and radio reporters can't observe all of the action on the course firsthand, since it extends over the entire course simultaneously, and if they are doing "hard news" coverage of the competition they are forced to follow at least the closing holes of the day on television. The reporters, if they are so inclined, are able to follow a golfer who interests them on the course for part of the day, and a sportswriter's waistline is usually a good indicator of his inclinations, but the basic dependency on television by reporters from other mediums is not one that sits well with the press.

Televised golf is entertainment first and sports journalism second, yet everyone who covers a tournament is in the information business, and those who work in the newspaper end of the game often harbor considerable disdain for their television counterparts. There are two reasons for this: money and glamor. The electronic boys are paid far more handsomely than their print colleagues— $5,000–$20,000 per tournament versus $400–$1,200 a week on the average, and the basic nature of their tasks differs considerably. Broadcast commentators prepare for their work before the tournament, talk on camera while it is under way, and leave when it is over. Print reporters follow the tournament, interview the competitors after the fact, and begin their work when everyone else has deserted the premises, except for the clean-up crew, which is purging the grounds of trash. Print journalism might be more intellectually satisfying, but it is comparatively dirty work.

Sportswriters retaliate for this imbalance by either watching the television coverage with the sound turned off, or by gathering around a set with the volume up and denigrating much of what is said. And thus it was that when NBC began its final-round coverage of the Anheuser-Busch Golf Classic by zeroing in on Peter Jacobsen, the tournament's Sunday leader at midround, and NBC commentator Bob Goalby said, "The pressure is on Jacobsen after his *tragic* loss last week," the pressroom went into hysterics.

"Tragic," someone called out. "What happened, did someone die?"

"Yeah," came another voice, "Jacobsen almost choked to death."

Jacobsen had been among the leaders in Williamsburg for the previous two rounds, earning trips to the interview room for questioning both days. During those visits, Jacobsen's examiners had introduced the inevitable inquiries about the seventy-second hole in Chicago, and Jacobsen had done his public-relations best to answer them. He downplayed the impact of his crash, retreated to confess some misery, and flashed forward to project optimism about the tournament at hand. The reporters wrote hopeful paragraphs in their stories—everyone thought Jacobsen was a decent

enough fellow and a good golfer, but the writers inevitably reserved their final judgment for Sunday night. The only way Jacobsen could truly refurbish his image was to substantiate that he had
broken the hex.

Jacobsen retained his one-shot lead through the 12th hole on
Sunday, before the looming final holes did him in. The end was
miserably slow in coming. Jacobsen was battling with Mark Wiebe
and Tom Sieckmann—Curtis Strange and Fuzzy Zoeller were out
of the running—and each of them would reach fourteen under par
on the back nine. Then Jacobsen bogeyed the 13th, 14th, 16th,
and 17th holes while the others held steady, and Jacobsen was
forced to endure the caustic reality of his impending loss one long
hole at a time, over the span of an hour and a half. Jacobsen sped
from the scorer's tent after his round, calling out to his wife to
gather their children and meet him at the locker room with the car
immediately, as a large assembly of spectators at the 18th green
looked on silently.

If Jacobsen's struggle on Sunday was with the apparition of
Chicago, Tom Sieckmann's was with the reality of his life. Sieckmann had won only forty-two thousand dollars coming into Virginia, and that was less than half of what he would need to finish
in the top 125 and retain his exemption for the next year. It would
be a shame if Sieckmann didn't win in Virginia, but it would be a
catastrophe if he didn't finish high enough on the leaderboard to
secure a big check.

Those kinds of thoughts could make a man play too conservative a game on the PGA Tour. While he was being overly cautious, any one of the dozen players who were always lurking a few
shots off the pace could trample him right off the leaderboard. Jeff
Sluman, for example, the player who had fascinated reporters in
Dallas with his stories of theft and murderous assault at the Byron
Nelson tournament, and who hadn't been in contention on the
tour since, had bolted from the also-rans to shoot a 64, vaulting
past Peter Jacobsen.

Sieckmann fought to keep the reality of the top-125 list from
his mind and remain patient, failing only occasionally, until he got
to the 16th hole and bogeyed to fall one stroke behind. The bogey
jolted Sieckmann. He recognized then that he was close enough to
win, and he began to think about the hardships of the past eleven
years. The scrounging for money, the tramping around the world,
the sheer work on his game that was enough to have earned him

two Ph.D.'s, and the humiliating explanations to the folks in Nebraska about why it was taking him so long to succeed. Sieckmann looked at the leaderboard and told himself, *You deserve to win this. You've worked your butt off.*

Sieckmann birdied the 17th to pull even with Mark Wiebe, and defeated him in the second hole of the playoff. Sieckmann came to the interview room in a daze, the implications of the victory just beginning to seep in. He talked about his game, and especially his putting, before a reporter asked what he was going to do with the $117,000 he had just won.

"I'll pay off my creditors," he said, "and I've had a group of sponsors for a long time who will get some. I don't really care about the money. It will be spent some day, but I've got this for the rest of my life. I've just won a tournament on the PGA Tour."

"But over all these years," someone said, "haven't you been telling yourself that when you finally won a tournament you were going to buy a BMW or something?"

"No," Sieckmann said quietly, "what I'm looking forward to more than anything is going home to work on my game. I have a couple of little things that I need to get ironed out of my swing, and this will allow me to spend a little more time at home, working on my game."

The Meek
Inherit the Tour

EDMOND, OKLAHOMA.
The weekend after Greg Norman injured his wrist during the second round of the U.S. Open, ABC dispatched a television crew to Norman's house in Florida. The network wanted to include a shot of Norman lounging by his pool with his arm bandaged as part of their Open coverage, and Norman was happy to oblige. The crew recorded the footage, and the network aired the shots for a few moments. The technicians packed up their gear and left Norman alone with his family, while ABC filled the airwaves with images of other golfers in Norman's absence.

The PGA Tour rolled into Atlanta and Chicago during the following two weeks, but all Norman could do was mope temperamentally around the house in Florida. Norman was an impulsive man of action, someone who could hardly conceive of a risk without simultaneously feeling the need to take it, yet he was shackled. Norman grew restless and began searching for an outlet. He made daily visits to the new house he was having built, he repeatedly washed his collection of exotic cars and, when neither took the edge off his impatience, he decided to alter his appearance.

Norman's most conspicuous feature was his longish, flaxen locks, which balanced his otherwise pronounced facial features nicely. But in an attempt to do something—anything—to mitigate his agitation, Norman engaged a hairdressr to shear his tresses close to his skull. The ritual clipping might have reflected Norman's Samson-like loss of golf virility, but it did nothing for his appearance. Norman left the shop looking as underplumed as a chick fresh from the egg. Norman immediately regretted the haircut, only to embark on another adventure. He sailed off on a fishing trip to the Bahamas. Then, still unsatiated, he returned home and went for his golf clubs two weeks from the date of his injury.

Initial reports had targeted Norman's recovery time as two weeks, but his agent, his doctor, and a fellow pro who had suffered a similar injury all urged Norman to remain inactive longer. Golfer Andy Bean had damaged his wrist when he struck a tree root with a club in 1981, and he warned Norman not to test his wrist prematurely. Bean predicted, based on his own experience, that Norman would be able to hit some balls without discomfort, but that continued practice would obliterate the healing that had taken place and Norman would be back to ground zero.

Nonetheless, Norman began a four-day test of his wrist under the supervision of his Florida orthopedic surgeon on the first day of July, in the hopes that he would be able to compete in the British Open two weeks hence. Everything went fine, and Norman was ecstatic with his miraculous recuperation, until the final nine holes of a practice round he played on July 4 when, true to Andy Bean's predictions, Norman's wrist became as painful as it had been at the moment of first damage.

Norman was still unconvinced that he would have to sit out the British Open. He went home, mulled the situation with his wife and advisors for a day, then ultimately told Larry Guest of the *Orlando Sentinel,* whose report numerous other American newspapers picked up, that his practice rounds had convinced him that going to England would be career suicide.

When the starting times for golfers in the British Open—the only major Norman had ever won—was published a week later and Norman saw that his name was not included, he fully accepted for the first time that he would not be competing. Norman returned to the Bahamas to go scuba diving, to avoid further news of the British Open until it was over and to decide, at some point during his hiatus, what would be the most advantageous things to tell the press about the activities of his forced vacation when he returned to action at the PGA Championship in mid-August.

"It's been a long frustrating seven and a half weeks for me, missing out on the British Open and the U.S. Open," Greg Norman told reporters when he was brought to the media room before the start of the PGA Championship. "I handled it pretty good. I didn't try to practice during that period. I knew I had to keep away from it. I think it has done me a world of good not only in healing the wrist, but in refueling the fire inside of me, and I am really ready to go."

"How many rounds have you played since the U.S. Open?" a reporter asked Norman, as a bolt of lightning from a summer electrical storm cracked through the sky outside of the press tent.

"I hope this thing has lightning rods," Norman said anxiously about the microphone he was holding. "I played a round of golf every day for the last five days, once before that, so six rounds. I was supposed to keep away from it. I didn't even pull the clubs out of the closet until last Friday."

"How many tournaments on your schedule did you miss?"

"Three," Norman said, although he had made formal commitments to play in only two, the Western Open and the British Open, the latter one not being part of the PGA Tour.

"Since you missed tournaments, are you going to add any in the U.S.?" a reporter asked, wondering if Norman, who had previously said he would make only three more appearances in the States during 1988, was going to make his required fifteen U.S. tournaments.

"No. I have a very heavy schedule from now on in anyway. Rather than play next week, I figure I've been away from the game for eight weeks, so one week on and one week off is a good routine to come back. Then I play very, very heavily overseas right through December 8th. I'll probably have only two weeks off in that time."

Norman was implying that he was going to skip the next week's tournament, the International in Castle Pines, Colorado, as part of his rehabilitation plan. Actually Norman had insisted earlier in the press conference that he was now fully recovered from his injury, and he had gone on the record a year earlier as saying that, after two tries, he would not play in the Colorado tournament again because it employed a unique format that was not to his liking. Ordinarily, that would have been Norman's prerogative. But, as his remarks about his heavy, appearance-fee-based schedule hinted, foregoing the International meant that Norman wouldn't fulfill his fifteen-tournament commitment to Deane Beman.

"I just spoke to Deane Beman in there with a query on the fifteen-tournament rule," Norman continued, "because I doubt whether I can fit in another tournament in the United States. So I have to write to him and see if we can get a waiver."

"Did Beman give you any indication that you would be treated sympathetically?"

"I don't know whether you would call it sympathetic or not, but I think the rule is that he can give a dispensation if there is an injury. I would be in a tough situation if I didn't get one. I don't know where I would go. I might have to go back overseas." Norman didn't want it to appear that, as the premier crowd-pleaser on the American tour, and as a normally loyal member of Team Beman, he might be receiving favored treatment. But, at the same time, he didn't want anyone to overlook the potential consquences if he didn't obtain such special consideration.

Landing the PGA Championship—the season's final major and, like the U.S. Open, one that is played on a different course each year—was the most blessed thing that had happened to the folks in Oklahoma in some time. The state's economy was heavily dependent on oil exploration and production, and they had been hit hard during 1988 by deflated oil prices and the crises of insolvent savings and loans. Undercapitalized Oklahoma financial institutions had found themselves holding uncollectible energy and real estate notes, and seventy-nine banks had gone under in the state during the previous two years. Former University of Oklahoma football player Brian Bosworth had just published a book in which he charged that everything about the locally revered championship college football team was not what it seemed. And *The Last Temptation of Christ,* Martin Scorsese's new film, which some residents of the state that housed Oral Roberts University considered to be damnably sacrilegious, was about to open in the area.

Neighbors argued about, and newspapers reported on, whether the financial difficulties in Oklahoma had bottomed out, but everyone acknowledged that if the state was going to recover its prosperity people were going to have to make it happen themselves. The focal point of that effort for communities in the environs of Oklahoma City was the PGA Championship, which would contribute about twenty million dollars to the local economy, as well as provide hours of international TV exposure to an investment-starved region that was seldom a topic of conversation in other parts of the world. Oklahoma wasn't going to allow this opportunity to slip by unexploited. People knew it wasn't likely to reoccur soon.

The first order of the day was to lure corporate executives to the tournament, so that they might be touched by the friendly, down-home nature of the local citizens and be impressed by the area's vast undeveloped acres of land, while experiencing how expertly the town could stage a major sporting event. The economic realities of 1988 being what they were, when the people of Oklahoma thought about the location of investors they would like to woo, the town that was mentioned most frequently was not New York or Los Angeles, but Tokyo. Japanese manufacturers had been investing in neighboring states and, as tournament time approached, Oklahoma officials flew to Japan to extend personal invitations to top Japanese officials to visit the PGA Championship at the state's expense.

Several dozen executives accepted and they, along with 1,250 Japanese tourists, crossed the Pacific Ocean to find an Oklahoma that wasn't at all like the parched wasteland they remembered from John Steinbeck's *Grapes of Wrath*. Oklahoma City, and its northern neighbor Edmond, were green places with impossibly wide, numbered streets that ran into three digits, and with broad spaces between even the most modest of homes. It was a flat, unpretentious, midwestern kind of place that seemed to have slipped out of the corn belt and down onto the saddle of northern Texas. The local Edmond newspaper unabashedly printed letters to the editor like the one from a resident who had twenty dollars stolen from her shopping cart at the supermarket and wrote to ask for its return.

An image-minded Tulsa newspaper editorialized before the tournament that, given the anticipated 100-degree temperatures, the state legislature should pass a bill making it a felony to stage an internationally televised, outdoor, daytime sporting event in Oklahoma during July and August, but no one else really complained. The golfers said it had been hotter in Memphis the week before, and the tens of thousands of civilian visitors to the tournament were too stunned by the irrepressible friendliness of the local residents to notice the heat during a summer in which sweltering days had become conventional.

The congeniality of the folks in Edmond was partially a ritual of economic courting, but there was more to it than that. It was also part of a sensibility that caused residents to tie ribbons on their mailboxes when a local postal worker had gone berserk at work in 1986 and murdered fourteen postal employees before killing himself. The second anniversary of the tragedy would fall during the PGA tournament, and people still talked of it as though they were deeply ashamed something like that could have happened in their town. But residents were putting the past behind them now, for golf's preeminent professionals were coming to play a major tournament on their jewel: a twelve-year-old course designed by Pete Dye. It was a layout the golf magazines were calling the most difficult and terrifying par-71 course in the world.

Pete Dye was a slight, eccentric, sixty-two-year-old course designer who was managing to go bald on his dome without his remaining hair turning gray. He was a descendant of a long line of Ohio insurance brokers and state Democratic party officials who tinkered with golf courses. Dye's father had built a nine-hole course on farmland Dye's mother owned, and the boy became the course superintendent when the maintenance man who held the job was drafted during the early 1940s. Dye became a good enough golfer to compete in national amateur championships, but in college he met and later married a woman who would win more amateur golf titles then he did. Dye's wife, Alice, then got him a job in the insurance business—a field in which she was already successful—in Indianapolis, and it was there that Dye had an experience that would influence all his future work in golf course design.

Dye was playing golf at the Indianapolis Country Club one day in 1947 with a German man who had a fourteen handicap. It was a friendly enough game in which the stakes were less than five dollars. The German was not having a good day, and he put his drive on the 14th hole into a deep ditch 220 yards from the flag. Dye stood in the 14th fairway waiting for the German to take an eight-iron and bump the ball a short distance out of the ravine, to a place where he could shoot for the green. But to Dye's astonishment, the German went into the ditch with a two-iron. The man intended to go for the green from an impossible lie.

Dye called out to the man and asked if he was crazy. Didn't he realize he had no chance of reaching the green, and would only hit into more trouble if he attempted such a shot? The German waved Dye off, carefully addressed the ball with his two-iron, and sent it flying for the flag. The ball rolled to a stop just short of the green as the German jumped in elation. Dye had never seen anyone so delighted on a golf course, and he told the man that Sam Snead would have paid him a thousand dollars to have that shot. The man said he wouldn't sell it for any price.

For weeks, all the German could talk about was that two-iron from a ditch. Dye thought the man's fixation on one shot from an otherwise undistinguished round would pass in time, but it didn't. Every time Dye heard the man talking golf around the club he would work the two-iron shot into the conversation. That was when Dye decided that what avid golfers really wanted was to play courses so treacherous that 90 percent of their shots would have them shrieking in agony, while the remaining 10 percent that were well played would have them crying in relief and satisfaction.

Dye's early designs followed this precept in relatively conventional ways, with two exceptions: He employed smaller-than-average, tiered greens, and he introduced British influences such as heavily bunkered fairways and the use of railroad ties as shoring around hazards. Dye won enough acclaim for his courses by the mid-1960s to leave the insurance business, and he parlayed his success into demands for complete artistic freedom in his design work, refusing to submit course sketches for approval or to deal with committees at the country clubs that commissioned him.

For all his apparent achievement, however, Dye failed in one important aspect of his work. When the pros played his courses they usually slaughtered par just as they did everywhere else. Dye resented the low scores. But what really frosted his nuts was that the pros, using the high-tech equipment Dye loathed, were hitting the ball so far they could tee off with a safer club than the difficult-to-control driver, and they were still getting the distance they needed for a manageable second shot to the green. Sometimes they even used irons off the tee!

Dye was convinced the modern pro wasn't really stronger, better coached and conditioned than his predecessor. It was that damn equipment. So when Dye received the commission to create the first Tournament Players Club course—at the PGA Tour's own headquarters in Ponte Vedra, Florida—in 1979, he upped the design ante by creating a layout that resembled a sprawling outdoor pinball machine with water hazards. It was a course where balls ricocheted rather than rolled. Dye said he was ushering in an era of target golf, a game that would require precision placement of every shot by severely punishing long but errant hits through a combination of massive bunkers in the ground, mounds that heaved above the fairways, and water, water everywhere on each of the eighteen holes. Then he finished it off by severely contouring the greens. The myriad obstructions required such extensive hand-mowing that Dye fantasized about bringing in sheep to maintain the course.

Deane Beman initially thought the distinctive course was wonderful. Beman had hopes that the annual match that would be played on the course, The Tournament Players Championship—the only tournament conducted solely by the PGA Tour—would become golf's fifth major. And, since the course was to be a model for future Tournament Players Clubs around the country, he thought it set a high-profile precedent for attracting additional spectators, and their money, to tournaments. Galleries, Beman told reporters, came to tournaments to see the game's top professionals struggle through adversity on the links.

But Beman's rank and file detested the course, with its inherent potential for humiliation, the moment they saw it. They began hollering during the practice rounds, and the winner of the first tournament held on the course, Jerry Pate, shoved Pete Dye and Deane Beman into a lake off the 18th green during the awards ceremony to make their point. Beman's boys continued screeching about the course so intently that the commissioner ordered an immediate and extensive neutering of the layout, and the scores—and the design of future Tournament Players Clubs—declined accordingly in the following years.

Now the pros were in Oklahoma for the first major to be played on a Dye design, and it was one over which the PGA Tour had no control. The PGA Championship was sponsored by the PGA of America, the association of golf-club teaching professionals—out of which the separate PGA Tour had sprung—and the club pros had selected Dye's Oak Tree Golf Club for their tournament. Oak Tree, as a 1976 course, didn't embody the golf surrealism of Dye's more recent work. But it was plenty tough, and when those prevailing 30-mph Oklahoma southeasterlies blew, it was supposed to be murder.

Jack Nicklaus thought he had played reasonably well in the two tournaments he had entered since being selected Player of the Century in June. He made the cut at the British Open in July—his first since the Masters three months earlier—and finished the tournament tied for twenty-fifth. Nicklaus had won the British Open three times, placing second on seven other occasions, and he was as well received by galleries in the United Kingdom as he was in the United States. Nicklaus had suffered a minor slight in England when, after shooting a 75 in the first round, the press officer of the sponsoring body, the Royal and Ancient Golf Club of St. Andrews, refused reporters' requests to invite Nicklaus to the pressroom. "Others might hang on Nicklaus's every word," the man said, "but I find his seventy-five makes him immaterial to the conduct of the Open Championship."

Reporters didn't want to talk to Nicklaus as a contender, which no one thought him to be, but in his role as senior statesman of the tour, a position that sat much more comfortably with Nicklaus since he had been immortalized by his bronze statue. When reporters later tracked Nicklaus down during the Open it was to solicit his opinion on the latest salvo in the American versus European golfers controversy, one that had been fired by the world's foremost agitators, the inimitable British tabloids.

The tabloids had discovered golf as a new vehicle for inflaming British working-class sensibilities when the European team was victorious in the Ryder Cup, and when a Scotsman and then a Brit won the British Open in 1985 and 1987 for the first native-son wins in a decade and a half. The newspapers, between informing readers about a member of Parliament who hadn't had sex in forty years, and about a doctor who had had sex with one of his patients every day for six years, devoted heavy, if exaggerated, coverage to the Open. One tabloid, *The Sun,* even posed one of the nude models in its daily, tits-on-page-three photos with a golf glove, club, and ball in honor of the prestigious, 117-year-old event.

It was not easy to sensationalize the most fussbudget tournament in golf, but the tabloids found a way. Tony Jacklin, a noted forty-four-year-old English golfer who had captained the victorious European Ryder cup teams, told the tabloid press that he thought a European would win the tournament. "We'll Tank the Yanks Again," the resulting *Sun* headline read, followed by the lead, "Tony Jacklin last night warned the invading Yanks: the Europeans are going to give you another thrashing in the Open."

A number of American golfers reacted harshly to the story, leading, of course, to further inflammatory headlines, but Nicklaus remained stoic. "I can't believe Tony would say that even if he believed it," Nicklaus told reporters who repeated the headline to him. Nicklaus wasn't going to get drawn into the shouting but, in truth, he didn't mind if the others did. Needling was all part of the competitive experience that Nicklaus lived for, but which his advancing age increasingly denied him. Nicklaus also relished the thought that the provocation of the tabloids might jolt the Americans out of their complacency before the 1989 Ryder Cup.

Nicklaus had also played well at the Jerry Ford Invitational, a small, non-tour-sanctioned, two-day event the former president threw in Vail, Colorado, each August. Nicklaus earned money in Colorado, as he had in England, but, because it was "unofficial" money, he came to the PGA still not having broken the $5 million career earnings barrier.

Nicklaus shot a decent one-over-par round at the PGA on Thursday, but his second round wasn't going well. He lost two shots to par on the front nine, and when he double-bogeyed the 15th hole he was several shots above the projected cut level. Nicklaus came to the 16th tee needing to birdie the short par-five hole—at the minimum—to stay in the running, and that was when Pete Dye, who believed that golfers should be penalized for errant shots, got to demonstrate his design skills.

Nicklaus sliced his drive on 16 into tall grass off the side of the fairway. He tramped into the weeds like some Sunday hacker—only Nicklaus was assisted by dozens of eager spectators and marshals—looking for the ball so he could hit it back into the fairway. Nicklaus and his galleries carefully explored the foliage, pushing aside the brush with their feet and peering into bushes with squinting eyes, but to no avail. It had been two years since Nicklaus had lost a ball in competition but, with the alloted five minutes' searching time about to expire, Nicklaus had to declare the ball gone.

Under the rules of golf, a player who loses a ball is required to play another ball, with a penalty of one stroke, as near as possible to the spot from which the original ball was struck. For Jack Nicklaus, that meant a humbling 250-yard walk back up the fairway to the tee, while his two playing partners waited and hundreds of concerned fans looked on. Once at the tee, he would encounter the threesome following his group, which Nicklaus was delaying, who would make nervous jokes about Nicklaus having lost his ball, before watching as he tried again. Then there would be the dreadful stroll back down the fairway.

At some point as he emerged from the weeds, Nicklaus decided that he simply could not endure the walk back to the tee. Instead, he walked a nominal distance back up the fairway, illegally dropped a ball at a random spot and played it from there. Nicklaus's infraction would incur an additional two-stroke penalty if he were called on it, but at that point he didn't care. He had admitted to himself that he was going to miss the cut anyway, and all that he wanted to do was get off the course with his dignity intact.

Nicklaus let loose with a three-wood, and the ball sliced to the right again. Only this time the curve was far more severe, and his ball hurtled deep into a heavily wooded hillside. Nicklaus and an expanded entourage, who knew nothing of Nicklaus's resignation, stomped through the rough again. Hundreds of worried eyes tried to help Nicklaus find his ball so he could extricate himself from this mess. Nicklaus declared the situation hopeless after a short time, and hiked another nominal distance up the fairway to hit his third ball—also illegally. Without the penalty strokes for disregarding the rules, Nicklaus would be taking his fifth stroke on the par-five hole, and he still wasn't close to the green.

Nicklaus's third ball landed on the top of a thinly-grassed hill, close to the gallery rope and still to the right side of the course, but finally in play. Nicklaus grimaced as he walked to the ball, his face shaded against the Oklahoma sun by a straw hat. "Come on, Jack," people along the ropes called out as they applauded Nicklaus's arrival. Nicklaus nodded in acknowledgement, but he wasn't gratified. He had been around long enough to know that these were ceremonial cheers, ones that drew on the past as a way of obscuring the present.

The fans near Nicklaus's ball were staring at it and discussing its lie, the way galleries do when a shot hit by a professional golfer lands near them. The ball was resting on hardpan—grass in that spot was scarce—and people were predicting that Jack would use a thin sand wedge to minimize the bounce of the club off the firm earth.

An adolescent boy carrying a placard that displayed the scores of Nicklaus's threesome hurried along in front of Nicklaus as the golfer approached his ball. The sign bearer was at that gaunt, gawky age where boys seem to be all feet, and his biggest concern appeared to be staying out of Nicklaus's way. The gallery watched as the boy approached quickly, then moaned in horror as the tip of his right sneaker caught Nicklaus's ball squarely, sending it skidding down the hill. The kid knew from the impact on his shoe and the pained noises from the crowd that he had done something dreadful, but he didn't stop to discover what it was. Instead, he broke into a run.

Nicklaus arrived at the spot where his ball had been and encountered twenty people who were anxious to explain what had happened, and to point gravely in the direction in which the boy had disappeared. "Get a marshal over here so you won't be penalized, Jack," an elderly man said. "I'll be a witness for you. That kid wasn't watching where he was headed."

Nicklaus suddenly began laughing gently to himself as he looked at his third ball—his third ball!—resting at the bottom of the hill. He sent his caddie to retrieve the ball, as people looked quizzically at each other, trying to understand why Nicklaus was amused when they had been so concerned. This was, after all, a major championship. Nicklaus decided to let them know that he had switched to hacker rules when he bent to replace his ball. "Let's see," he said in an exaggerated voice, while scanning the near-barren dirt, "I'll bet that ball was resting on this tuft of grass right here before that boy kicked it, wasn't it?"

"Yeah, that's right, Jack," people said and laughed.

Nicklaus began to address the ball, then stopped to look up at the crowd. He was unable to play the shot without offering them an explanation for his unorthodox behavior. "It doesn't really matter now anyway," he said softly.

Nicklaus pitched his ball onto the green and, prolonging the misery, took three putts to get down. The crowd cheered loudly when his ball finally found the hole. Nicklaus raised his hand to acknowledge the applause, and he smiled. Ignoring the penalty strokes for his rules infractions, Nicklaus had just carded a nine on a par-five hole. But, uncharacteristically, he was able to smile without a trace of a smirk. Nicklaus's fans were telling him by their applause that it was enough for them that he was Jack Nicklaus. Nicklaus heard them. And, at least for today, he had found a way for it to be enough for himself as well.

Seve Ballesteros once said that, because of the abundance of water hazards on PGA Tour courses, you had to be able to swim to play golf in America. Ballesteros wasn't pleased when he arrived in Edmond and discovered that two thirds of the holes at Oak Tree had water, and he thought the par-threes Pete Dye had designed there were especially difficult. Each was highly exacting, with an abundance of water and sand hazards often all but replacing the fairways between the tiny tees and the small greens. Each of the par-threes required pinpoint shots from the tee, and heavily penalized those who were unable to deploy one.

The par-three 13th that Ballesteros came to on Friday afternoon, at a time when he also was in danger of missing the cut, was classic Pete Dye. The tee overlooked a fairway that was sand for the final third of its length, ending just short of a small green, which sloped off to the left. There was a four-foot drop off the left edge of the green, to the bank of a small stream. Ballesteros put his tee shot onto that bank, requiring that he chip off the bank and up onto the green, while shooting over the stone wall that Dye had installed to shore the edge of the green.

Ballesteros was having one of his best seasons in four years. In addition to his victory at Westchester in June, he had won four tournaments in Europe, including an impressive eleven-under-par victory in the British Open, his third win there and his fifth major. Ballesteros had managed his low score in the Open despite horrendous English weather—heavy rains, driving winds, and chilly temperatures—and without the usual erratic play that had become part of his game. Ballesteros's victory precipitated a slew of articles insisting that now, without question, *he* was the best golfer in the world.

Ballesteros was jubilant about his victory in the Open, and it seemed to clear the last bit of uncertainty from his life by boosting his ever-wavering self-confidence. Ballesteros's long-planned wedding was said to be in the works, he had rid himself of a business manager he detested—Ed Barner, an American—by buying out his contract for an amount that Ballesteros intimated was several million dollars, and he had broken his jinx in the majors. Ballesteros seemed to have received everything he wanted, except for a phone call from Deane Beman.

Part of Ballesteros's charm is a streak of boyishness that coexists with the fervent determination that propelled him and his golf clubs from a Spanish fishing village to the capitals of the world. It is not naïveté, for Ballesteros is too sophisticated for that, but more an indefatigable hopefulness that the world will turn out to be as pleasing a place as a boy would like it to be.

When Ballesteros mentioned to the media in Westchester that he would like to play in the States more frequently than the eight times he was permitted, but less than the fifteen times currently required, he actually believed that Deane Beman, upon hearing the news, was going to pick up the phone and say, "Seve, why don't we have a beer and work this thing out?" He really thought that the pit bull of golf—the man who had retroactively banished Ballesteros's name from the tour's 1985 money list—would make a call like that. Ballesteros believed Beman would discover altruism, and overlook Ballesteros's having reneged on a done deal, simply because everyone but Beman would probably benefit from having Ballesteros play more in the States. Ballesteros was so convinced of this he was astonished when Beman didn't call.

Ballesteros hadn't lost his craftiness, however, and when reporters asked him before the PGA about his plans for the States for the coming year, he said, "I have been looking at the schedule just about every day, every week, and it seems to me that I would really like to play eleven or twelve tournaments over here."

Ballesteros said that he loved playing in America, that golfers were treated like kings here, and the American galleries had even learned that his name was Seve, not Steve, but that he couldn't play fifteen because of commitments on his home tour in Europe and in Japan. When the reporters asked Ballesteros what he was going to do about his situation, the Spaniard pulled a Bemanism out of his sleeve.

"I think it would be a good thing to have a referendum between the players and the sponsors," Ballesteros said, "to see if they would be in favor of keeping the rule at fifteen, or putting it back to twelve. It would be nice to have a referendum instead of just having Deane Beman and his tour policy committee decide." Ballesteros made a nice try, but no one jumped up to start passing around a petition. The next day Ballesteros said that he had resigned himself to playing eight U.S. tournaments the following year.

Now Ballesteros was gazing over a bit of Pete Dye's handiwork, a stone wall on a golf course, while studying the flag on the elevated 13th green in front of him. Ballesteros swung at his ball with a wedge, then realized a microsecond after striking it that the ball was going to bounce off the wall in front of him and come caroming straight at his head. Ballesteros yanked his face out of the way at the last possible moment, just as the ball flew by.

It would take Ballesteros six strokes to get off of Dye's parthree 13th hole. He would miss the cut in the tournament, and leave town the next day to begin a twenty-three-hour sequence of flights that would take him from Oklahoma City to Dallas to New

York to Madrid to Santander, where his neighbors had renamed the main street of the town after him. Ballesteros wouldn't play golf again in the United States for six months.

While a number of top players missed the cut at the PGA, they did it on a course that, although still favoring precision over distance, was far tamer than tournament organizers had intended. The course had been set up with relatively slow greens and relatively short rough—for a major—because everyone had expected the brisk Oklahoma winds would make the course too difficult otherwise. The wind hadn't blown on Thursday and Friday, and when the leaders came to Oak Tree on Saturday morning the members of the host club, who had taken so much pride in all the talk about the terrors of their course, were starting to get defensive about scores that ran as low as nine under par.

Among the leaders was Jay Overton, who had shot a 66 on Friday. Overton was a thirty-seven-year-old golf club professional who had gained a berth in the tournament as one of the top forty finishers in the PGA of America's 1987 club-pro championship. He was one of five club pros who had survived the cut, and the only one who was in contention.

Overton had turned to golf after he was injured playing college football, but his early attempts at the pro game made him think he didn't have the makings of a tour professional. When he was offered a club-pro job in North Carolina after college, Overton jumped at it. Curtis Strange, who was preparing to enter the PGA Tour at the time, used to come by the course Overton worked at, and they hit a lot of balls together and went out on the course at times.

In June of 1988, Overton had watched Strange on TV as he was winning the U.S. Open, and it got Overton to thinking. Overton had learned to live with his decision to reject the tour life. He still played in the occasional pro match and got his ego stroked that way, and he had done well in the club-pro business. Overton was head of golf operations at two resorts, where he oversaw the work of twenty-one other club pros. Hell, the man had been PGA Merchandiser of the Year in 1982. But sitting there watching his old practice-range buddy winning his first major got Overton to wondering about what might have been.

Overton started talking to his wife about the old days, and he dragged out some films and snapshots of himself and Curtis playing together back then. Overton recalled aspects of his game he used to work on with Strange, and thought about how they talked about making it in the big time. The next day Overton went out and shot a 64 in a local tournament, and that really got him thinking. Overton knew that the PGA Championship was two months away, and he upped his daily ration of balls on the practice range from fifty to one hundred.

Overton said in the interview room after his second round at the PGA Championship that he was delighted to have made the cut, having missed it in the six majors in which he had previously competed, and that he was just going to go out on Saturday and have some more fun. He said it wouldn't matter now if he hit six balls in the water on the first hole. But when Overton's wife and thirty of his friends flew in from Florida at the last minute on Friday night, it wasn't because they had been wondering what Oklahoma was like in August.

Overton's being one shot off the lead on Saturday created a number of unusual situations. People in the gallery, pulling for the underdog, would call out encouragements to Overton, and he would go over to the ropes to chat with them. Overton would get fired if he wasn't nice to the resort guests where he worked, and it was hard to block that reflex now that he was in a major tournament.

Saturday's round also meant national television, and Overton had to devise a way to work around an alignment problem he had been having with his swing. When he was playing at home, Overton would drop his club on the ground before he swung to check that he was square to his target. Overton didn't think something as inelegant as that would be palatable on TV, so he had his caddie stand behind him to watch. As it was, Overton would be on the course and he would hear the people working the TV cameras in the towers calling into their headsets, "Which one is Overton? What color is his shirt?"

Overton started his round more relaxed than he expected, but that was still pretty tight. His swing was less than fluid, and the situation deteriorated quickly. On the 2nd hole it started to look like Overton was going to birdie and his playing partner, Paul Azinger, the one-shot leader, was going to bogey, giving Overton the lead, and the prospect of that terrified him. Both golfers parred the hole, but when Overton bogeyed the next hole he flipped in the other direction and began to fear that he would shoot 100. Azinger scored a hole in one on the 4th hole, increasing his lead to four shots, and Overton came back to his senses. He told Azinger the tournament was his, and went back to just having fun. Overton shot a 76 on Saturday and a 74 on Sunday to finish tied for seventeenth.

Jeff Sluman was one of only seven golfers who broke 70 at Oak Tree on Saturday, when the wind came up and the course began to live up to its reputation, and he came into the final round at three shots off the lead. Sluman hadn't been in contention since his final-round 64 in Virginia a month earlier, but as a nonwinner on the PGA Tour, he was playing at a time that seemed to favor young, lesser-known golfers such as himself. The past six consecutive tournaments, since the Western Open in July, had been won by golfers who were recording their first professional victories on the American tour.

The thirty-year-old Sluman was atypical of the young pro in that he grew up in the Snowbelt in Rochester, New York, and played golf only infrequently as a child. He was an average, non-scholarship golfer at Florida State, and he couldn't touch the opponents he met who had torn up the junior golf circuits as teenagers. Sluman took to the novelty of being in the sun all year, and he spent a great deal of time pounding balls, trying to catch up with his more seasoned opponents. Sluman saw progress in his game from month to month, and it gave him hope.

After college, Sluman qualified for the U.S. Open as an amateur, and he went off to see what golf in major tournaments was all about. Small and shy, he went through the first two days of the match, until he was cut, with his head down, afraid to look up at anybody. Although Sluman missed the cut, he hadn't embarrassed himself, and he resolved to keep practicing until he was good enough for the tour. Sluman knew that a little guy like himself was never going to be Jack Nicklaus, but a lot of professional golfers weren't Jack Nicklaus.

It took Sluman two years to qualify for the tour, and he lost his card for a year once he got on, but he persevered and, like another short man who went on to become commissioner of the PGA Tour, he learned how to play exacting golf. Sluman, who majored in finance in college, plotted his game like an actuarial table. When he was done, he knew definitively how far he could hit the ball with every club in his bag, and that played right into the designs of the man who had created the course he was playing on. Jeff Sluman didn't hit the ball a mile, but when he hit it he knew where it was going to stop.

Sluman had been one shot off the lead after two rounds of the 1987 PGA, and had self-destructed on the weekend. He had thought he was experienced enough to handle the pressure of the closing rounds of a major, and had learned he wasn't. This year, Sluman formulated a new game plan. When reporters asked Sluman how he was going to handle the final round of the 1988 PGA, Sluman said that he wasn't going to look at the leaderboard or pay attention to anyone else's game during his round. He was going to play as well as he could, he said, "and just have fun."

"Just having fun" was an old tour cliché that had reentered the golfer's pressroom vernacular in recent years as more young players began consulting sports psychologists and coaches in an attempt to find any edge that would help them win amidst the intense competition on the tour. A player had to have a tremendous desire to win in order to be able to do so, but the long odds against winning could transform the ache to win into panic about not winning faster than tinder burned. The coaches and gurus advised the players to escape the psychological double-bind about winning by rising above it. Just go out there and have some fun, they counseled, and let the winning take care of itself. It was a doctrine that Sluman was going to attempt to embody on Sunday.

Sluman birdied the 2nd hole of his final round, then put a spectacular 115-yard sand-wedge shot in the cup for an eagle three on the 5th. Sluman didn't know it, but that shot tied him for the lead. He birdied the 7th and 10th, and then on the 11th, a hole on which he had been having trouble with his driver all week, he hit a great drive and a six-iron to the fringe at the rear of the green. When Sluman got to his ball, he discovered there was a bug on it. Sluman didn't want to lose this thing because of an insect interfering with his putt but, since the ball wasn't on the green, the rules prohibited him from lifting his ball. The bug was all over the ball, but Sluman's hands were shaking and he didn't want to try to knock the bug off, because if he moved his ball he would incur a penalty. Finally, after what seemed like twenty minutes to Sluman, he just putted the ball and the insect flew away.

After two more birdies and a bogey, Sluman allowed himself a peek at the scoreboard on the 15th hole. That's when he learned he had a four-shot lead in the tournament with three holes to play.

Sluman put his head back down, as he had at his first U.S. Open, but this time it was out of determination rather than shyness. At 18, Sluman saw that his lead had been cut to three, but didn't allow himself to think that, if he parred this hole, he would win his first tournament and his first major simultaneously. Sluman blocked out the noise and the sight of the tens of thousands of people lining the 18th hole, and then he went out and did it.

The reporters in the interview room afterward told Sluman they had to know more about him for their stories.

"I'm low-key, shy, and laid-back," Sluman said quietly. "I like the tour and being out here, but I'm not afraid to take time off to have a good time."

While other golfers wore visors touting the products of major corporations, Sluman's read "Paycheck," and the reporters asked about that.

"Paycheck does payroll systems work for small companies in Rochester, and I used to work for a small company in Rochester, so they said they'd be my sponsor," Sluman said.

Sluman told the reporters that winning a major wasn't going to change him, but maybe it would shut down those people who had been telling him he couldn't keep it together on the weekend. The reporters knew that Sluman had spent the week at the home of Willie Wood, a fellow five-seven golfer—Sluman and Wood amused themselves during practice rounds by standing back-to-back and asking spectators who was taller—who lived in Edmond, and they asked Sluman if he would celebrate with Wood.

"Yeah," Sluman said, as calmly and quietly as if he were discussing his plans for any unremarkable evening in his life. "We'll probably have a couple of beers tonight and talk about it. Maybe I'll even change his kid's diaper."

Nostalgia

It would have seemed like the late 1970s in Akron if the smoke-stacks on the tire factories had been pushing out soot. Restaurants with blond wood and fern plants were scarce, bowling alleys remained an entertainment staple, and Curtis Strange, the ogre, was back on the golf course. Strange was playing in the pro-am at the NEC World Series of Golf on August 24, and he was as visibly overwrought as he had often been during his first years on the tour a decade earlier.

Strange was the defending champion of the tournament, and that meant his pro-am partners included the VIPs: the president of NEC and a vice president of Firestone, a secondary tournament sponsor. Strange shook hands with his partners on the first tee, but the tight set of his lips and the rigid erectness of his shoulders informed the others there wasn't going too be a lot of schmoozing taking place. Strange was in the kind of mood where he wouldn't mind pissing some people off, and if those folks happened to be from the upper reaches of the socioeconomic strata, that would only be a bonus.

The amateurs in Strange's fivesome were stuck with their draw, but the fans in the gallery, who could sense his tension, weren't. Hundreds of people had crowded around when Strange—brushing by as many autograph requests as he honored—arrived at the first tee, but fewer than seventy-five spectators accompanied the U.S. Open champion down the fairway.

Strange huddled frequently on the course with his caddie, as though they were lifelong friends, while barely exchanging a word with the corporate chiefs. Strange passed his waiting time between shots—none of which pleased him—alternately practicing his swing or staring off into the distance with his arms crossed tightly on his chest. When he hit an errant shot that landed outside the gallery ropes on the 7th hole, Strange cursed it and then hurried up the course ahead of his partners. He forcefully yanked a gallery-rope stake that was blocking his path from the ground, then threw it down, as his followers, who had dwindled to thirty, looked on.

Strange was sulking because he felt he had been snubbed recently by the International Golf Association, a group that conducted an annual tournament called the World Cup. The World Cup pitted twosomes from numerous countries against each other, including such non-golf powers as Tunisia and Yugoslavia. The 1988 U.S. team was selected randomly, but Strange figured one of the invitations belonged to him. He had, after all, won three tournaments during 1988, and one of them had been a major. Yet the association had invited Ben Crenshaw instead. Crenshaw was a deft putter and a talented and likable golfer, but his career peak seemed to have passed in recent years.

The rebuff caused Strange to remember that, as a kid, the World Cup had been something special to him. He associated it with Jack Nicklaus and Arnold Palmer—guys like that. The World Cup match had become less visible in the United States since then, and when Strange was invited to play in the tournament in recent years he declined because the locations and purses involved hadn't interested him. Now that he was the reigning U.S. Open champion, Strange felt a 1988 invitation was an entitlement—regardless of his refusals to participate in the past.

Strange had previously disdained sentimentality about golf, having skipped the historic British Open a number of times because, he said, some smart son of a bitch was always telling him he *had* to play it. Yet, with a major to his credit, Strange was becoming concerned with his place in the annals of the game. Strange had played in the Walker Cup, the Ryder Cup, and the World Amateur—three other international competitions—and now the idea of playing in the World Cup, and becoming one of the few golfers to participate in all four matches, struck Strange as having a certain cachet.

Strange had caused a ruckus in the pressroom about the World Cup earlier in the week, but his vile mood on Wednesday was also precipitated by the failure of his game to hold up in the aftermath of the Open. Strange had finished tied for fourteenth in front of his neighbors in Virginia, tied for thirty-first at the PGA Championship, and he had placed outside the top ten at two tournaments he had played in Europe, the most recent being at the Irish Open, the week before Akron. Strange had gone to Ireland for an appearance fee and to give the folks a look at the new U.S. Open champ, then he played badly. Later, when he caught his connecting flight between Ireland and Ohio in New York, they lost his goddamn luggage and golf clubs. Strange knew he could get another set of clubs, but the prospect of wearing the same underwear until they found his bags set the tone for his visit to Akron.

Strange had told himself, as he struggled to improve his game over the past ten years, that winning his first major would take him to the next level in golf, where he would be widely acknowledged as a force to be reckoned with. People in the game would be more deferential, and he would expect himself to be a factor in most of the tournaments he entered. Neither of those prophecies were coming true immediately—to the extent Strange had imagined—and, amidst the anger, Strange was wondering where he'd gone wrong.

The NEC and Firestone executives in the pro-am gave Strange a wide berth on the course, socializing amongst themselves, but Strange's behavior wasn't doing any good for a tournament that was already in trouble. Ford Motor Company had hired Jack Nicklaus to build a golf course near their headquarters in Dearborn, Michigan, and, after Nicklaus told Ford officials the easiest way to secure a stop on the PGA Tour was to sign on as a Tournament Players Club, they had cut a deal with Deane Beman as well. Now there were serious rumors that the World Series might be relocated to Dearborn when the tour's contract with Akron expired in 1989.

The people in Akron were distressed that the PGA Tour was going to join the ever-growing parade of income producers that were marching out of the aging and colorless industrial town. The glory days of Rubber City were history, with both Goodyear and Firestone having long since gone. The town was trying to find some new beginnings. They converted the old Quaker Oats cereal factory into a hotel, and they had landed the National Inventors Hall of Fame. But life in Akron remained such that when an idling, driverless automobile jumped out of park and into reverse and began spinning in circles on a downtown street, the *Akron Beacon Journal* covered the event—with a map—in a box on page one.

Some of the gloom Curtis Strange was engendering on the golf course was being offset by Greg Norman, who was delighting in the attention of hundreds, while playing before his first pro-am audience in eleven weeks. The sharpness was missing from Norman's game after his layoff, but that didn't trouble his fans, who applauded him at every turn. And any concerns that Norman had about his wrist or his competitiveness were temporarily eased by the cheers and attention, which could be taken as reaffirmation of his standing on the tour.

When Norman arrived at the 5th green, where his shot from the fairway had struck a spectator, Norman asked whom the ball had hit. The crowd pointed to a thin, freckle-faced teenager whose hair gleamed with styling gel. "It hit me," the boy said, stepping forward proudly.

Norman asked the boy if he was okay and, when he said that he was, Norman added, "The next time my ball hits you, kick it onto the green." Norman signed an autograph for the boy, then asked where the ball had struck him. "In the rear end," the boy said shyly. "Oh," Norman responded loudly, "I hit you in the tush, did I?"

Norman signaled his caddie to fetch a ball from his golf bag so that Norman could present it the boy, while hundreds of eager fans pushed toward the gallery rope, wanting a picture, an autograph, a word, anything they could get from the Shark. Norman stood there and gave them as much as he was able.

The World Series of Golf was an invitational tournament that originated in 1962 as a made-for-TV, two-day event among the men who had won the year's four major tournaments. That format evolved over the years into a standard, four-day tournament that featured the winners, during the preceding twelve months, of all the tournaments on the PGA Tour, plus the winners of eighteen select events from the more than 120 tournaments that were played on the five other professional circuits around the world.

Half of the thirty Americans who were participating in the 1988 World Series were doing so for the first time, after having become first-time tournament winners during the preceding twelve months. In the rush of new winners on the tour in recent years, half of the World Series field was composed of men with names and faces that were unfamiliar to golf fans, while many tour golfers with higher recognition factors had failed to qualify. Sixty

percent of 1987's top twenty-five money winners were absent from
the World Series, as were 70 percent of the top twenty-five active
players on the all-time money list.

Mike Reid was one of the better-known of the lesser-known
golfers at the tournament, at least among the golf media, for the
infamy he had won in 1986. That was the date when, after ten
years on the tour, Reid's career earnings passed the one-million-
dollar mark without Reid's ever having won a golf tournament.
Whenever someone wanted to make a point about the dearth of
the killer instinct or the monetary excesses on the all-exempt tour,
Mike Reid was one of the guys whose names always followed the
words "for instance."

In addition to the notoriety Reid attracted with his winlessness,
he was also a born victim of scorn. Tall but extremely thin, the
thirty-four-year-old Reid was so soft-spoken he made the typical
seminarian seem gregarious. Reid was the adult version of the kid
in school that everyone picked on.

Reid had played in the Jerry Ford Invitational in early August
where, being a nontour event, the golfers were allowed to use golf
carts. Two holes from the end of the match, a local caddie Reid
had engaged for the tournament drove Reid's cart under a gallery
rope, while momentarily pushing up the rope for clearance. The
caddie released the rope too quickly, and it snapped back and
decapitated the three woods in Reid's golf bag, which was strapped
to the rear of the cart.

Two weeks later at the International tournament, Reid told
reporters that the experience was "heartrending, like losing a member of the family. It was like getting punched in the midsection by
Mike Tyson. I sat down on the cart and cried. The clubs had
served me well for five years, and in one swoop all three of them
were gone."

Reid said that he wanted to wring the caddie's neck, but when
he found him in the woods, where the caddie had run after the
incident, Reid discovered that the caddie was crying as well. "I
realized then," Reid said, "that anything I could say couldn't make
him feel any worse. I just went over and put my arm around him
and told him maybe the accident would force me to learn something about my swing by using new clubs. Sometimes you have to
look for opportunities behind the adversity."

Reid gave the clubs to a repairman, who was able to reshaft
two of them, but the third, his four-wood, was beyond repair. Reid

went home and gathered up a selection of four-woods from the dozens of clubs he kept in his basement, then went to a practice field near Brigham Young University, where he had attended school. Reid pounded balls until he narrowed the field to a handful of candidates he would take on the road with him, but he was still traumatized.

After a decade of winlessness on the tour, Reid had finally won a tournament in late 1987, only to have his lucky woods, which had helped him accomplish what, to him, seemed like a monumental task—prevailing over 150 other golfers—destroyed ten months later. Reid had, to his mind, failed about every way a man can fail on the golf course, and then he had managed to succeed once. He had found a set of woods that enabled him to ignore the voice that echoed in his head, "What are you going to do wrong this time, Mikey?" every time he was in contention, and then they were taken away.

Reid had played well for two days at the 1988 PGA Championship before crashing to sixty-fourth place in the final rounds. The next week he had rebounded to tie for eleventh at the International. Now he was tied for the lead after two rounds in the World Series, earning himself a trip to the interview room. Reid talked about his round, then a reporter asked how he was making out with his new clubs. Reid looked at the reporter suspiciously for a moment, remembering the mocking stories that had been written about his pained confession at the International, before answering.

"I changed drivers this week," Reid said. "The reshafted driver looks too much like my old one. I'm sure the reshafted club is a fine club in its own right, but I still have too many memories of the old one to use it."

The people of Akron who attended the World Series engaged in an annual ritual that was derivative of one practiced by row house residents in ethnic neighborhoods of large eastern cities. When city people wanted to reserve their precious parking spots in front of their homes, they dragged their trash cans into the street whenever they moved their cars. When Akron residents wanted to secure a prime tournament-finale viewing spot near the 18th green, they would stake a claim to the site by positioning their aluminum folding chairs there hours before the first golfers were due to arrive. The residents would then go off to watch the golfers play the holes prior to the 18th, before returning hours later to claim an unobstructed view from their chairs at the now-crowded final green.

When Tom Knoll, the president of Akron Golf Charities, the nonprofit administrator of the World Series, began to hear the persistent rumors about Dearborn stealing Akron's golf tournament, he followed the same approach. Knoll told Deane Beman he wanted to save Akron's spot on the PGA Tour schedule by signing a multiyear agreement that would reserve the World Series for Akron beyond the existing 1989 contract expiration. Beman, who exulted in the leverage he gained from annual contract renegotiations, came to Akron to talk, but he did so without enthusiasm. Speculation about the tournament continued until Beman brought Knoll and other tournament officials to the media room for an announcement and press conference on Friday of World Series week.

Beman had suffered a rare defeat recently when the United States Golf Association resisted Beman's attempts to get the USGA to reverse itself on the square-groove issue. Beman's announcement at the Memorial Tournament that the tour was considering breaking from the USGA by issuing a ban on square-grooved clubs in 1989 had not prompted the USGA to change its opinion that the clubs were acceptable. The only concession Beman won was a USGA promise to reconsider its position, and Beman said he would not act until he heard from the organization. As the USGA's reply was not expected until late 1988, Beman then had to abandon any hopes he had of banning the clubs during early 1989, regardless of the USGA's decision. The tour players would require at least six months' advance notice of any equipment changes to give them time to secure and become comfortable with clubs of a new design.

Nonetheless, Beman strode into the interview area of the pressroom with confidence in his step. It was Tom Knoll, the president of Akron Golf Charities, who looked beleaguered. Knoll took his seat before the reporters with the put-upon demeanor of a suspect who had been forced to participate in a police lineup.

Beman took command of the meeting, saying that the tour had reached a multiyear agreement with Akron Golf Charities, then asking Knoll to explain the details. Knoll did his best to make it sound cheerful, but the gist of his announcement was that Akron had received a one-year extension of its existing contract into 1990. Knoll didn't mention that 1990 was the anticipated completion date of the course in Dearborn.

Other officials made appropriately positive comments, then Beman interjected that, before he opened the meeting up to questions, there was a point he wanted to make. Beman said that although the contract with Akron had only been extended one year, the tour had successfully completed negotiations with NEC to continue its sponsorship of the World Series until 1992. "We are having continuing discussions with Akron Golf Charities about holding the tournament here beyond 1990," Beman said, "but as of this moment we haven't reached a specific agreement with Tom Knoll on anything other than the two years."

"Are there difficulties in reaching a longer-term agreement?" a reporter asked Knoll.

"There are things we need to discuss. We would obviously like to see as long an agreement as possible, but a shorter one gives us a chance to go back to the table once in a while. I also think Deane likes to keep me on edge," Knoll said without a trace of humor in his voice, "and I suppose that's part of the deal."

Beman was not pleased by Knoll's remark. He argued that few tournaments had long-term contracts, and insisted it wasn't anything to be alarmed about. "It's just the way the tour has run its business," Beman said. "And Akron Golf Charities doesn't want to stay with the one-year agreement they were happy with a year ago."

"Do you think the tournament has been hurt by the speculation?" a reporter asked Beman.

"I think there was a good basis for the speculation. But I don't think there is any reason for concern," Beman said. The commissioner answered a few more questions, stopping far short of guaranteeing Akron Golf Charities they could have the tournament as long as they wanted it, then summarily dismissed the other panelists from the press conference. Tom Knoll, who had spent a good part of the proceedings examining the ceiling, left quickly.

Beman excused the other speakers because he had an additional controversy to address, one that had started at the PGA Championship when Greg Norman said that, although he wasn't playing at the International, he didn't think he would be fulfilling his fifteen-tournament commitment to the tour. Reporters had asked other golfers how they felt about the Norman situation, and the resultant stories said none of them were pleased at the prospect of Norman receiving an exemption. Beman was going to have to do some verbal high-wire work on this one.

"I have been asked a number of questions about Greg Norman over the last few days," Beman began, "and I want to make the tour's position clear. Greg Norman committed to play in fifteen events in 1988, and I feel absolutely confident that he has fulfilled every intention of obligation possible. It is possible that Greg might only play in fourteen events. It is also possible he might be able to pick up the fifteenth before the end of the year. I know what Greg's schedule is for next year, and it is more than fifteen events. I told Greg I would give him flexibility this year, based on the circumstances."

A reporter noted that Beman's decision seemed to be based on Norman's having committed to more than fifteen tournaments during 1989, and asked if the system was such that you could build up credits from one year to the next.

"Not at all," Beman said. "I have a number of options under the rule. I could say, 'You scheduled fifteen but, because of an injury, you're only going to make fourteen. That's good enough for me. Next case.'"

"Did you go over Norman's fall schedule with him to see if he has any openings?" someone asked.

"I know generally what his fall schedule is, but I didn't go over it tournament by tournament."

"Greg said earlier this week that he had one week free between now and December 8th. Do you know what that week is?" a reporter asked.

"Yes I do, but I won't say any more than that."

"Are you aware that a lot of players are upset over this?"

"I know that some people are concerned," Beman said, deftly transforming the reporter's words, "and it is my job to make a decision. Frankly, I think they are wrong, and I don't know how they can be unhappy since the year is not over yet. He may pick up the fifteenth. But I am not basing my decision on whether they are unhappy."

"Is the fifteen-tournament rule under review?" someone asked.

"No, it is not," Beman said curtly.

"Will Greg have to apply officially for a waiver if he doesn't play a fifteenth tournament?"

"No," Beman said, "I've already taken care of that administratively."

Since Beman was being so accommodating to Norman, a reporter asked Beman if he was aware that Seve Ballesteros, who was playing in Germany that week after having declined a World Series invitation, wanted to play more frequently on the American tour during 1989.

"I have not specifically heard from him on that issue," Beman said. "I have seen some press reports about that, but if Seve wants to come back, I'm sure he will let us know."

When Ian Baker-Finch was a thirteen-year-old Australian farm boy, he decided he wanted to become a professional golfer. Baker-Finch quit school at fifteen, when his handicap fell to three, and began a three-year apprenticeship under the tutelage of a local teaching professional. There were no college golf scholarships in Australia, and even fewer people who wanted to bankroll a young hopeful while he learned the game on the road. That meant Baker-Finch—his grandmother had married twice and kept the names of both of her husbands—was going to have to leave Australia one day to pay his dues around the globe, while living on very little money, but he wasn't put off.

Baker-Finch played in his first Australian professional matches in late 1979, just after his nineteenth birthday. His winnings were slim, and when Christmas presents for his family and five siblings left him broke, Baker-Finch went to work pumping gas until the Australian tour resumed in March. Over the next three years, Baker-Finch, six feet four inches tall and strikingly handsome, traveled and partied with the boys on the Australian golf circuit, squeaking by on $10,000–$15,000 a year in golf winnings, supplemented by his earnings from the seven months a year he spent picking tobacco and pineapples.

Baker-Finch made his first breakthrough in 1983, placing second in the Australian Open, then winning the New Zealand Open, and a $50,000 stake to put him on the road, shortly afterward. The New Zealand win precipitated invitations from Europe, where, at the 1984 British Open, one of those illusions that prompts teenage boys to consign their lives to golf almost materialized. After three rounds, twenty-three-year-old Ian Baker-Finch found his name at the top of the leaderboard in the British Open. It is often said that major tournaments aren't won by the champion as much as they are lost by the contenders, and when Baker-Finch acknowledged to himself the magnitude of what he was caught up in, he shot a final-round 79.

Baker-Finch was disheartened, but not dissuaded, because he

was learning. He learned that an unattached golfer who hung around with the boys and lived on the edge couldn't compete in the professional game, so he teamed up with a young woman from home named Jennie, who was perhaps even more comely than himself, and set off to find his niche in the international game. In 1985 he parlayed an invitation to the Masters tournament into enough sponsor exemptions in other PGA Tour events to learn, after earning only $4,825 in nine tournaments, that he wasn't ready for golf in the States.

Baker-Finch upped the pressure on himself and began playing a murderous schedule of thirty-seven-plus tournaments in Europe, Australia, and Japan, flying from the Orient to Europe and back again the way other people take a crosstown bus. His income climbed into six figures as he began earning top-ten finishes in a third of the tournaments he entered, with the occasional win. Then, during the early months of 1988, he won once in Australia and twice in Japan while playing fifteen tournaments in a sixteen-week stretch. Baker-Finch's victory in the Australian Masters earned him an invitation to the World Series and, when he got an invitation to the preceding week's tournament, the International, he decided it was time to earn his American tour card.

Baker-Finch felt he was playing better, and was more mature and confident, than during his last visit. His goal had always been to play in the States, and now the time seemed right. His game was ready and he and Jennie—they had gotten married in 1987—were expecting a child. He wanted to end the international travel and have a proper family life in a country where he could speak the language, but Baker-Finch had no taste for the expense and hassles of participating in the PGA Tour's series of qualifying tournaments where he might earn American playing privileges. Baker-Finch's recent success had convinced him he could earn his tour card in a most unconventional way.

Baker-Finch had two invitations to American tournaments, and he figured he could wrangle a few more. He decided that he would earn enough money in these events to place in the top 125 of the money list and earn his tour card for the following year, something few golfers have ever accomplished while playing in only three or four events. Baker-Finch finished in seventy-eighth position at the International, earning $1,840 of the $75,000 or so he would need to finish in the 125th spot, and no other invitations to American tournaments were forthcoming at the moment. That gave him two options. He could either win the World Series and immediately earn the special ten-year PGA Tour exemption that went to the victor of that event, or he could finish second and probably earn his card at the end of the year with the $97,200 second prize. Nothing less would be good enough.

Baker-Finch and Mike Reid were tied for the lead, and waiting to tee off in the day's final twosome early Saturday afternoon, when they heard an escalating series of roars emanating from further down the course, and saw their gallery dissipate as people went stampeding toward the noise. Baker-Finch studied the leaderboard and understood the commotion. Tom Watson, who had won the World Series in 1980 at the height of Watson's and Akron's strength, but who, like Akron, had accomplished little in recent years, had just birdied four of the first five holes to move into striking distance of the lead.

Watson had seemed destined to rival Jack Nicklaus as the greatest golfer of all time when he began a ten-year tear on the tour in 1974. Over the next decade, Watson won thirty-one tour events, including three American majors, plus five British Opens. He was player of the year six times, leading money winner five times, and the winner of four showdowns with Jack Nicklaus in the closing holes of major championships. Then in 1985, when Watson was only thirty-six, the enchantment simply vanished from his clubs.

Everybody pointed to Watson's loss of touch on the putting green as the culprit, but Watson himself wondered if he hadn't simply used up the reserve of competitive stamina he had been rationed at birth. Watson didn't win again for three years until, after losing the 1987 U.S. Open to Scott Simpson by a stroke, he captured the season-ending Nabisco Championship four months later. Watson continued to play enough passable golf in tournaments with large purses to put him within $125,000 of Nicklaus on the all-time money list, although Watson had only half of Nicklaus's victories to his credit, but, at thirty-nine, Watson seldom turned up on anybody's pretournament forecasts of likely winners.

Only a few years before, Watson could walk to the first tee telling himself that, at that moment, he was the best golfer in the world. Now he spent his winters in Mission Hills, Kansas, discontentedly working on an article attacking every aspect of modern golf course design, which had reached forty pages. But today, Watson was out on the links feeling those long-absent sparks of greatness. He birdied six of the first eleven holes on Saturday, pulling within a few shots of the lead, as the golf fans of Akron became drunk with excitement.

"Come on, Tom," "You can do it, Tom," thousands of people called out as they burned their hands red with applause. Each birdie drew additional people from around the course, as older fans who had come to see only the closing holes abandoned their aluminum chairs and hurried to witness Watson's resurrection. He was putting the ball in every one of the tight, tree-lined fairways on the course, and the putts were rolling in as if by remote control—some from twenty-five feet. Watson finished the day with a 64, putting him one shot off the lead shared by Baker-Finch and Reid, both of whom had shot one-over-par 71's, and a third golfer, Larry Nelson.

When Mike Reid got up on Sunday morning and saw it was teeming rain, and heard that intermittent precipitation was expected throughout the day, he wanted to do handsprings across his hotel room in his pajamas. Most pros hated to play golf in foul weather, but not Reid. His fondest childhood golf memories involved playing alone in the rain. Reid could get out there on the spongy turf and act out his golf fantasies, and no one would be able to observe him and run back and tell the other kids how queer Mike Reid had been acting on the course.

Reid would play two balls and pretend they belonged to Nicklaus and Palmer, rather than himself, and that it was the closing holes of the U.S. Open or the Masters, instead of a deserted neighborhood course. Reid could hear the galleries urging him on, and imagine the announcers using admiring words in their voice-overs, and he could feel like the greatest golfer of all time, even if no one else believed that was his destiny.

There was another aspect of the inclement weather that fed into Reid's psyche as well. Reid was known for his accuracy with his clubs—his nickname was Radar—but not for his length. Firestone Country Club, the site of the World Series, was a long course to start with. The rain would soften the fairways and make the 7,136-yard layout play more like 7,500 yards, which was disastrous for a short hitter like Reid. And that's why he loved it: It meant additional adversity.

No one would be taking Reid seriously as a contender anyway—especially against Watson—but in the rain most people

would completely write him off. Reid loved it. He thrived on
adversity the way other people flourished on good fortune. Standing in his hotel room, looking out at the water pooling in the
parking lot, Reid wanted to yell out, "Yes, give me more adversity," but he didn't. Reid only did things like that when he was out
on a rainy course alone, where no one could overhear the dialogue
of his secret life.

Reid had worked with his coach in the field near Brigham
Young University before he left for the World Series and, as the
session was breaking up, his coach had told him, "You're a champ,
Mike. Hold that picture in your mind. Go out there and believe."
Mike Reid hadn't heard that kind of high praise frequently in his
life, but he had managed to repeat the words to himself before
every one of the swings he had taken through three rounds of the
tournament. Today, in the rain, with thousands of people watching, he had to intone them sixty-some times more. It couldn't be
"And Arnie drops the putt to win the championship" anymore.
This time it had to be Mike Reid.

Ian Baker-Finch wasn't as delirious about the rain as Reid.
Actually, he was too worried about his pairing for the day to
notice the weather much. After years of preparation, Baker-Finch
was within eighteen holes of a ten-year exemption on the PGA
Tour, and who had they given him as a playing partner but Tom
Watson? Baker-Finch had heard all the commotion up ahead as he
was playing bad golf on Saturday; now he would be surrounded
by it like an atheist who had stumbled into a revival tent.

Watson didn't have to prove anything to anybody. He'd won
five British Opens. But Baker-Finch was a nobody over here. He
was one of the favorites in the tournaments he played in Australia,
and he couldn't walk through a train station in Japan, where his
height made him stand out like a beacon, without having to sign
a hundred autographs. But who'd ever heard of him in the States,
and who was going to root for him against Watson in Akron,
where Baker-Finch was just another new foreigner who was dis-
rupting settled-in lives?

Baker-Finch believed that he would never be able to call himself a great player until he had won in the States. But it wasn't that
he was obsessed with having the premiere victory come against an
icon like Watson. Baker-Finch only wanted to get his tour card
and move on to the next season of his life. Now Watson was
standing in his way. It was either beat Watson, or look forward to

another year of twenty-nine-hour commuter flights, with a new baby at home, wherever home might be.

Baker-Finch and Mike Reid managed to increase their shared lead over Watson to two strokes at the end of nine holes, only to have Watson pick up a stroke on them on the 11th hole, just as play was suspended. The drizzle that had been falling on and off since the start of play turned into a downpour that flooded the course. The hour-and-ten-minute halt in the action gave Baker-Finch unneeded time to mull over the implications of the match he was engaged in. He couldn't get that ten-year exemption—or the name "Tom"—out of his mind.

Baker-Finch must have heard the crowd call out Watson's name a thousand times already that day, and the closing holes would certainly be worse. It wasn't that the fans were actively rooting against him, but they weren't encouraging him either. Baker-Finch would hit a second shot to within five feet of the pin and receive polite applause, then Watson would hit to twenty feet and the throngs would erupt with their chants of "Come on, Tom" and it was getting on Baker-Finch's nerves.

Watson birdied the 16th hole when play resumed, pulling him even with the others, and it was like VJ day again in Akron. Baker-Finch ignored the noise as best he could but, by the time he reached the 17th hole, that Sunday was beginning to seem like the most difficult day of his life. The pressure was taking its toll. Baker-Finch couldn't keep his eyes off the scoreboard, which showed that Reid had dropped a stroke off the pace, and he couldn't decide on a strategy. Should he play the final two par-fours conservatively and let the others make the mistakes, or should he try to earn the win himself?

Baker-Finch decided to follow the path he had been pursuing for a decade and go for it, and he ripped a driver off the 17th tee. His ball faded right and found a fairway bunker. Baker-Finch shot for the green and missed. With his chip and two putts, he bogeyed and fell from the lead. He missed the green on the 18th hole as well, and the bogey he eventually recorded there dropped him into second place, where he collected $52,200 for his week's work, $25,000 short of what he would need to earn his way onto the top 125 of the money list.

Mike Reid birdied the 17th, moving into a tie with Watson, and they both parred the final hole to force a playoff between a golfer who was astounded to find himself in position to win his second tournament in twelve years on the tour, and one who was intimate with victory, but who wondered if it could still be a part of his life.

Reid and Watson were both on the green of the first playoff hole in two, Reid a long thirty-five feet from the cup and Watson closer at twenty feet. Reid lagged his putt up close to the hole; Watson blew three feet by. Watson stood over that three-footer as all Akron seemed to hold its breath. These close shots that became missed putts were exactly what had banished Akron's best hope to relic status over the past four years. Watson looked inside himself to discover if he still had the nerves to keep his blade straight through the stroke—only to learn that he didn't. Watson's ball rolled past the hole, Reid holed his putt, and the fans went home disappointed.

Reid's hands were trembling as he held the microphone in the interview room later. He tried to talk but didn't have the composure, so he sat there shaking his head from side to side. Mike Reid couldn't believe that Mike Reid had won another golf tournament. He had defeated adversity again—or at least some of it. The task of talking to the media still lay before him and, thinking back to the press conference after his first victory last year, Reid finally cried out in disgust, "Oh, no, I'm going to mess this up again."

Reid managed to get through the ordeal in time, then a man from Akron came to lead him off to the winner's reception with the folks who ran the tournament. "I'm sorry," Reid apologized to the man, "I messed it up again."

"Everything's okay, Mike," the man said reassuringly. "You did just fine, and the people of Akron are looking forward to meeting their new champion at the party."

Money Between Friends

PEBBLE BEACH, CALIFORNIA.
It was early November, eleven months into the 1988 season, and
Curtis Strange was getting sick of golf. He had played twenty-three
events on the PGA Tour, six more in Europe, Japan, and Australia,
and a host of one-day corporate junkets. Strange wanted to get out
of California and go home. He hadn't seen his family in two
weeks, and a new fifty-five-foot boat, which he had just taken
delivery of at the beginning of the month, was awaiting him in the
James River.

Strange was weary even though he had reduced his tournament
schedule since the U.S. Open in June, playing only seven times in
twenty weeks. Golfers who transformed exceptional years, such as
the one Strange was having, into successive seasons of accomplishment became known as champions, while the majority who didn't
were soon forgotten. Strange wanted to avoid the plunge to obscurity at all cost, so he paced himself through the second half of
the season to ensure that he would come out fresh the next year.
Strange did, however, make daily visits to the practice range during his respites. He had pushed himself long and hard to get his
game to its current level, which, even if he hadn't won since the
Open, was still better than it had been in previous years. Strange
went to the practice tee because he was worried that, without
vigilance, he might wake up one morning to discover his game was
gone.

Strange knew that any November tedium he was feeling would
be replaced by purposefulness on the first tee at Pebble Beach, for
he would be competing in a most significant event. It was the

Nabisco Championship of Golf, a tournament that Deane Beman and RJR Nabisco, the tobacco and food products conglomerate that was the major benefactor of the PGA Tour, had fashioned into a season-ending orgasm of cash. Nabisco invited only the year's top money winners to Pebble Beach, where it would unleash three million dollars in corporate funds, an amount greater than the sum of all tournament purses during 1965. The favored golfers would compete for a two-million-dollar purse and, through a variation on the double-indemnity clause, an additional one million dollars in bonus money, which would be awarded to the golfers for having won enough money during the year to qualify for the tournament in the first place.

RJR Nabisco had entered golf sponsorship modestly enough by attaching its name to tournament scoreboards in 1981. Over the next seven years, the company increased its involvement until the level of expenditures reached twenty-five million dollars annually among the men's, women's, and senior tours. In addition to sponsoring tournaments and buying substantial amounts of commercial time on golf broadcasts, RJR Nabisco contracted with Jack Nicklaus, Fuzzy Zoeller, Ben Crenshaw, and other golfers, at up to $250,000 a year, to be corporate spokespersons; they bestowed $25,000 annually on each of the leaders in ten statistical categories on the men's tour; they financed a two-million-dollar charity competition; and they supplied hordes of tournament paraphernalia to local tournament operators.

Deane Beman had nurtured RJR Nabisco's comfort level with golf during the early 1980s, before approaching them in 1985 for assistance in solving a problem he was facing. Beman's campaign to increase tour purses was meeting with unprecedented success, except for the fall segment of the tour schedule, when practically everyone involved, except the people who operated fall tournaments, lost interest in the PGA Tour. The television networks turned their attention to more lucrative football games, damning fall tournaments to obscurity; corporations that could afford to underwrite large golf purses wouldn't fund untelevised events, leaving tournaments with diminished purses; and most golfers with name recognition departed for foreign shores where the fall purses plus appearance fees eclipsed the purses in the States, resulting in American tournaments with fields of anonymous competitors. Beman couldn't very well demand larger purses for tournaments that his top players routinely avoided.

The remedy Beman devised, with RJR Nabisco's money, was the grand finale Nabisco Championship, where only the year's top thirty money winners, as of the conclusion of the penultimate tournament, would be eligible to compete. They would be eligible to compete, that is, if they were members of the PGA Tour. Beman wasn't going to let Seve Ballesteros horn in on this whether he made the top thirty or not.

The idea was to make the tournament so lucrative—first place was worth $374,000 to $535,000 depending upon the bonus earned—that top golfers would play themselves into a froth throughout the fall to maintain their top-thirty position and qualify for a chunk of the bonanza. And to RJR Nabisco, Beman offered the marketing distinction of title sponsorship in golf's richest event.

While some golfers—none of them superstars—began playing more frequently in the fall in response to Beman's financial bait, many didn't. Tom Watson, who had earned $384,000—or 8 percent of his total career winnings—as the winner of the 1987 Nabisco Championship, and who was hovering in the mid-thirties on the 1988 money list during the fall, made no attempt to improve his position on the money list. Nor did twenty-four-year-old Scott Verplank who, while in thirtieth place the week before Nabisco, with only five thousand dollars separating him from the golfer in thirty-first place, chose to attend a college football game at his alma mater rather than participate in that week's tournament, leaving his invitation to hinge on whether the man behind him won more than five thousand dollars during that week.

Deane Beman's dilemma was that he had succeeded so well in his quest to increase tournament purses that anybody who played decently during the core of the season didn't really need—or, in some cases, have any concept of—the money by the time the Nabisco Championship rolled around. Chip Beck, a thirty-two-year-old golfer who had won $1.25 million during nine winless years on the tour before winning twice during 1988, came into Nabisco at the top of the 1988 money list with $776,016. Beck was one of thirteen golfers at Nabisco who, if they won the tournament, would become the first golfer to pull in one million dollars in official earnings during a single PGA Tour season. Reporters asked Beck at a pretournament press conference how the money would change his life. "It is a lot of money," Beck said. "It's probably more money than a lot of people make in five years."

Curtis Strange came to the Nabisco Championship determined to do everything he could to downplay the monetary immoderation that was the essence of the event. He was concerned that golf fans were beginning to think the pros cared more about money than golf, what with all the publicity being churned out about RJR Nabisco's largess. Strange had had the chance to become the tour's first million-dollar man at the 1987 Nabisco, and he believed the excessive money talk at last year's tournament had distracted him and contributed to his last-place finish in the match. Strange was also mindful that when people were discussing bankrolls, they wouldn't be attending to his now considerable prowess with a golf club.

Strange had won the 1987 money title, and the Arnold Palmer Award that accompanies it, despite his poor Nabisco play. But he had lost the PGA Player of the Year award at that tournament, which was based equally on earnings and average number of strokes per round, and Strange had sorely wanted it. Strange was currently in second place in the 1988 Player of the Year race behind Scotsman Sandy Lyle, who had played infrequently, and had only one top-ten finish in the States since he had capped his three-victory streak by winning the 1988 Masters.

Strange occupied seventh place on the 1988 money list coming into Pebble Beach. If he were to win the Nabisco, he could take both the Player of the Year and Arnold Palmer awards, he would become the tour's first million-dollar man, and he would achieve his first four-victory season on the PGA Tour. It would be difficult for even Jack Nicklaus not to respect a man with accomplishments like that.

Strange had pounded enough golf balls to know that any musings about winning a tournament were academic until a golfer found himself in contention on the back nine on Sunday. That's when Strange, should he find himself near the top of the leaderboard, would walk through fire naked to get it done. Until then, he would be patient, playing his own game and staying in the hunt. He wasn't going to arrive at the first tee on Thursday morning telling himself he was determined to win the tournament and everything that went with it. But then again, Curtis Strange hadn't come all this way to lose.

A light rain fell on the Monterey Peninsula on Thursday morning, dampening the arid foothills of the California coastal mountains and the towering trees of the Del Monte forest, and softening the greens of the Pebble Beach Golf Links, which the dusky brown hills and the closely bunched trees overlooked. The clouds began to lift at noon, as sea otters played on the rock-strewn beach beneath the plateau where the course was situated, at the intersection of the western edge of the continent and the Pacific Ocean. Pebble Beach was a classic, 1920s golf course, where the design of the holes fitted the terrain so subtly it was a surprise to turn a corner and happen upon sand traps and putting greens, rather than an uninterrupted flow of the emerald grass. The topography was rich with the optical illusions of unseen dips and rolls. Pebble Beach was a course of great difficulty, in a setting of truly astounding natural beauty, but when the skies cleared on Thursday and the wind abated, it was at its most vulnerable.

Curtis Strange hit his first drive on Thursday and watched as it rolled to a stop in the middle of the fairway, precisely where he had planned. His second shot was a nine-iron that quit four inches from the hole. Strange birdied the 1st hole, as he did the 2nd, 5th, and 6th. He parred the difficult 7th through 10th holes, which adjoin the Pacific Ocean, before finding himself 131 yards from the flag on his second shot on the 11th. As spectators who were so inclined sipped champagne they had purchased at concession stands, and as a maid in a blue smock peered out the picture window of a luxurious courseside villa, Strange holed his second shot on the 11th for an eagle two.

Strange had come to Pebble Beach feeling something was missing from his swing, but he didn't know what it was. Then he had spoken with Jimmy Ballard, a Florida golf instructor, on the phone, and as they talked about the golf swing something clicked for Strange. He realized what he had been feeling was a weakness in his right leg, which meant that he wasn't bracing his weight against it properly on the backswing. Strange came out on Thursday morning feeling he was in total control—a feeling that was essential to Strange's well-being—and he completed the day's round in 64 strokes, giving him sole possession of the lead in the Nabisco at eight under par. It was as good a round of golf, on an intricate course, as Strange was capable of playing, and he was elated.

Strange returned on Friday wanting to continue his assault on Pebble Beach, but it was a new day and magic often wasn't transferable. Strange birdied the 2nd hole, but by the time he came to the 18th, he was only one under for the day. Strange hadn't been able to get it going and, even though he knew better, he was getting impatient with himself. After five months of mediocre play, he thought he had his game back on Thursday. Now a pack of golfers was closing in on his lead, and Strange blamed himself for that.

Strange came to his second shot on the scenic, par-five 18th wanting to finish the day with a birdie, so he could return to his hotel room in a more confident frame of mind. Strange pushed his drive over to the right side of the fairway, near the gallery ropes, where hundreds of people stood watching. As Strange was in the middle of his backswing on his second shot, the piercing whine of a motor drive on a professional camera shattered the silence, destroying Strange's concentration. Strange managed to complete his shot, but his anger wasn't directed at himself any longer. There were strict and normally respected tour regulations that forbade photojournalists from taking pictures while a golfer was making his swing. Strange was furious, but he controlled his reaction. He knew the national TV cameras were focused tightly on him.

Strange turned to hand his club to his caddie, and was shocked to discover there were two hundred people, who had ducked under the ropes, standing behind him in the fairway. What the hell did these people think this was? Didn't they have any concept of what Strange had at stake here? Strange sprayed the crowd with his death-look but the rope crashers, recognizing it wasn't likely that Strange would interrupt his game to shoo them off the course, kept marching down the fairway. The gallery seemed destined to follow Strange to the green until a tournament official came speeding over in a golf cart and herded them off the course.

Strange composed himself as he stood over his third shot, a difficult pitch over a large tree that guarded the green, then, right in the middle of his backswing, the camera went off again. "Come on now, let me swing before you take the picture, okay?" Strange exploded, glaring over at the photographers at the ropes, the instant after his club struck his ball. Strange looked hard at the group, trying to identify the offending photographer, when his eyes made contact with those of a photographer he knew. The photographer waved his hands frantically in a negating motion. "It wasn't me," he called out emphatically. "It wasn't me."

Strange wanted to charge over to the ropes to find the photographer who was responsible, and it only intensified his anger that he knew he couldn't. Strange was aware that his televised shouting on the course had made him look bad already—when he felt he was only defending himself—but storming the ropes would be a public-relations catastrophe. Here he was, on the verge of recovering that feeling of control from Thursday, and a photographer comes along and takes it away from him. God, did he want to tear somebody's head off.

Strange was still reeling when he reached the 18th green and discovered—he hadn't heard the applause his third shot had produced—that his ball was quite close to the hole. Strange tried to take his time over the putt, but he didn't have a chance of making it, given his agitation. Strange parred out and, after refusing to do a live TV interview, headed to the relative safety of the pressroom, where the stories that would be produced, Strange believed, would couch his anger more in the context of the provocation he had endured than the broadcasted stories would.

"I just wish we could stop this," Strange began, struggling to control the harshness of his voice. "It's tough enough to play out there without the cameras going off and people running in the fairways. We're a professional tour—instead of patting ourselves on the back we ought to solve these problems. I'm still fuming."

Tom Place, the tour's director of information, fidgeted in his chair beside Strange, and looked nervously around the room as the golfer unloaded on the highly receptive reporters. At the first break in Strange's monologue, Place asked Strange to go over his round. "Tom's trying to get me off this," Strange said with a smirk, before continuing his complaint.

A reporter asked Strange if he thought the crowds at golf tournaments had changed since golf had moved into the mainstream of big-bucks spectator sports, where the sale of alcoholic beverages became an important component in meeting the substantial overhead. "It's like a goddamn baseball game out there," Strange said. "I don't mean to be putting down baseball; I scream at baseball games. But we've always been different, and it's changing."

Strange eventually exhausted his anger and the chummy camaraderie he had developed with the press began to creep back into his voice. Strange seemed to remember that, at the midpoint of the tournament, he was still at the top of the leaderboard. A slew of glory, and another half a million dollars, was within reach with thirty-six holes to go.

Strange left the pressroom feeling relieved, but Tom Place was still a bit nervous. Ken Green, the plain-talking golfer who had wanted to win the Westchester Classic so desperately, was heading into the interview area to replace Strange, and Place never knew what Green was going to say. Green's fortunes had improved considerably in the aftermath of his Westchester loss and, after a two-year drought, he had won two tournaments in consecutive weeks in September. Now Green was two shots off Strange's lead in the Nabisco.

Green's newfound success had both enhanced his irreverence on the golf course and drawn more attention to it, to the extent that Green was becoming the target of ill will among tour officials and fellow players. Green had developed a repertoire of snappy ways of tossing his club to his caddie, often over considerable distance, after he completed his shot. The throws were showmanship, not displays of anger. Green's caddie—a role currently filled by his cousin, who had replaced his sister—always caught the club, and the routine had become a favored target of TV cameras during lulls in tournaments. But a lot of people didn't like it.

Indignant television viewers sent letters of complaint to the tour's office about Green's conduct, which the tour always forwarded to Green, and other golfers complained privately to reporters that Green was grandstanding. The tour office couldn't do much about Green's club flinging, other than mildly disapprove, but when Green missed too many putts and took to chucking his putter into water hazards on the course, he was fined five hundred dollars a toss.

Green had incurred such a fine at the Canadian Open, a tournament he won, as well as an additional $250 fine that resulted from the sharp eyes and assiduous efforts of a high-minded TV viewer, who had caught an infraction of decorum everyone else had missed. Green had been displeased with an iron shot he made at the Canadian, and he indicated that by giving his ball the finger as it flew over the green. A woman caught Green's gesture while watching the tournament on videotape, and was spurred to take action. She studied the tape to isolate the offending passage, carefully copied the three seconds of abhorrent material onto a blank cassette, packaged the tape along with a letter of outrage, then shipped it off to Deane Beman so that Beman might properly punish the crime.

A reporter at Nabisco asked Green what he thought of his chances on the weekend, after Green had talked about his round.

"My wife is flying out here tonight," Green said. "I haven't seen her in two weeks, and I'm horny, so that should help."

Everyone in the pressroom howled at Green's remark—save Tom Place—more out of shock at hearing a sexual reference on the PGA Tour than anything. But Place didn't get overly concerned about Green's bawdiness. He knew that most newspaper editors would never allow their reporters to repeat Green's remarks in print anyway.

In addition to the three million dollars RJR Nabisco would be awarding to the contestants in the Nabisco Championship, the corporation would also be dispensing an additional two million dollars as the payoff for the Nabisco Team Charity Competition. Under this program, the organizations that conducted each of the local tournaments on the tour "drafted" four players to be their representatives during the season. At the conclusion of the Nabisco tournament, the dollar earnings of each four-player team were calculated, and the teams were ranked according to the total earnings of their members. Nabisco then awarded grants that ranged from $6,000 to $500,000 to the tournaments, which the tournaments passed on to charities in their localities, courtesy of RJR Nabisco.

Deane Beman was so thrilled with the five-million-dollar package when it was assembled that he said it was "the biggest, most important promotion in sports history," and he dubbed the program Nabisco Golf. RJR Nabisco was sophisticated in its subsequent tournament promotions, confining potentially troublesome cigarette sponsorship to the senior tour and never engaging in blatant oversell. But the cumulative effect of the Nabisco scoreboards, signs, trash containers, and myriad other golf artifacts made it impossible to attend a golf tournament without multiple exposures to RJR Nabisco trademarks.

Yet, when R. John Greeniaus, the bearded CEO of the Nabisco Brands Inc. subsidiary of the parent company, appeared on ESPN during the Nabisco Championship broadcast—the tournament had been unable to obtain network TV coverage for the November event—he confessed to the announcer that he had no idea how the team charity competition worked. And, when the announcer misquoted the amount of the prize as $2.5 million rather than $2 million, Greeniaus did not correct him.

Greeniaus's distraction during the crowning event of Nabisco

Golf was understandable for, as the head of the food products division of RJR Nabisco, he couldn't be certain whom he would be reporting to a few months down the road, or even if he would have a job. Three weeks prior to the tournament, RJR Nabisco's chief officer, F. Ross Johnson, had proposed taking the company private, offering a $21.16 billion bid for the corporation. Other potential buyers thought Johnson's offer was low, and a bidding war continued as the tournament unfolded.

Greeniaus's dilemma was mild, however, compared with the one Deane Beman was potentially facing. It would be far easier for Greeniaus to find another job, or to develop rapport with a new boss, than it would be for Beman to find a replacement sponsor with the pockets and enthusiasm for golf RJR Nabisco had. Rumors had been rampant all week in the Nabisco Championship media room as news reports on the leveraged buyout appeared. The stories were far from conclusive, but virtually all of them quoted experts as saying that, whoever the new owners were, they would have to sell off parts of the company to finance the transaction. This raised serious questions about whether such a heavily indebted, scaled-down enterprise could afford the marketing tab that was being run up on the links.

Beman finally appeared in the interview room, with his public relations director in tow, for a press conference on Saturday. With the RJR Nabisco battle still being waged, nothing newsworthy would come from the meeting. It was an important appearance for Beman to make nonetheless; although everyone involved in the tour was happy to take Nabisco's money, Beman had been criticized frequently for linking the fortunes of the tour so closely with a single entity. RJR Nabisco was a rare chink in Beman's armor. His dealings with the corporation were one of the few battles Beman entered without having the upper hand—although he needed to make it appear that wasn't the case in this moment of crisis.

Beman led off the meeting with a bluff, talking at length about how strong and successful the tour was, and how bright the future looked, without a single mention of Nabisco. After Beman completed his statement, a reporter said, "With Nabisco's current situation, I'm sure you're watching that rather closely . . ."

"We have a passing interest in it," Beman interrupted with a mild laugh.

"Do you have an alternative plan if the new owners don't want to make the same contribution?"

"We are not afraid of what may or may not happen," Beman said dismissively. "We think golf is strong, and we have an extended commitment from RJR Nabisco."

"But it looks like every one of the food companies may be sold off separately," someone countered.

"I have no reason to speculate about that, but frankly we feel pretty secure about the long-term contract we have for this program," Beman insisted. "RJR Nabisco recognized they would not get full value out of their program during the first couple of years. They made a huge investment, and they are just getting the first benefits from that. It would not be a good business decision to cut that off."

Beman had extracted from RJR Nabisco precisely the kind of multiyear contract he refused to give his tournaments and, should the new owners waver on meeting its terms, the commissioner had already prepared his presentation for the new board: They couldn't afford to discontinue their golf sponsorship. It was vintage Beman, never giving an inch, never acknowledging an area of vulnerability, never allowing anything to stick. When a reporter quoted Curtis Strange's remarks about the tour being unable to control tournament crowds, Beman took the same tack. He said that crowd control was the responsibility of local tournament organizers.

Local tournament organizers also bore a large responsibility for another aspect of tour operations—charitable contributions—but Beman wasn't as quick to point that out. After putting together the Nabisco jackpot, Beman was becoming as concerned as Curtis Strange that too much attention was being focused on the money the players would be earning at the tournament. "Charity is the leading winner on the PGA Tour," Beman said at the press conference, in an attempt to persuade reporters to write more on that topic. "In this age of a huge amount of dollars going to athletes, we always like to pause and remember that golf gives more money to charity than all other sports combined."

In saying that "golf" contributed to charity, Beman was using semantics to sidestep a slippery point. It was local tournament organizers, donating their net tournament proceeds, and tournament sponsors, making charitable grants, who contributed the great bulk of the money given to charity in the name of golf. Individual golfers, of their own accord, also appeared at special charity functions gratis, and some of them donated one percent of their earnings to golf programs for youngsters. But the PGA Tour, with seventy million dollars in assets, did not assign its real estate and marketing profits to charities. It plowed them back into player benefits and the expansion of Beman's empire, while seeming to don the cloak of the philanthropist.

Beman handled the press conference deftly, defusing RJR Nabisco questions by labeling them conjecture, except to say that the tour would merely be "less successful" without a major sponsor. Beman was so satisfied with himself that he yielded to the urge to vent some righteous indignation as the meeting drew to a close. RJR Nabisco and Pebble Beach had announced in early 1988 that the Nabisco Championship would be staged at the Pebble Beach course for at least three years. A few months later, however, the announcement was rescinded and replaced by one that said the tournament would rotate to a new course each year. A reporter asked Beman what had provoked the change.

Beman said the tour's policy board had decided that, in future years, they wanted the season to end in October rather than November, so players could avail themselves of lucrative overseas opportunities in November and December. Pebble Beach, which is a public-access course and resort, where anyone who can afford the $150 green fee can play one of the best courses in the world, told Beman their course wasn't available for the tournament in October.

"Does that mean the tournament won't be back here?" someone asked.

"They made a financial decision here. They can fill the course in October and their slack time is in November. If their bottom line is more important than having the event, then frankly we would be happy to give it to someone who would be more concerned about the event than the bottom line," Beman said irately, without a hint of irony in his voice.

Beman left Pebble Beach to fly to Hawaii, where a meeting of tournament sponsors would be held the next week. Among the announcements that would result from that convocation would be one noting that nineteen events on the 1989 tour schedule would offer purses of one million dollars or more.

Greg Norman trudged down the 18th fairway at Pebble Beach on Friday, trailing well behind his playing partner and their caddies. His gait was lethargic as he forced one leaden foot in front of the other. Norman's eyes were locked on the ground as he moved,

and his expression was lifeless. Norman hit his second shot
quickly, then resumed his somber march toward the green without
pausing to watch the flight of his ball. Norman's gallery was mi-
nuscule by his standards—a few dozen people—and silent. There
were no calls of "Go, Shark," or "Come on, Greg"; no Australian
flags.

Norman received polite applause from the knot of people in
the grandstands when he holed his par putt, but he didn't acknowledge it. He walked off the green, where ten kids with pens
and visors, and Norman's own two children, waited with his wife.
Norman's kids called out "Daddy," and ran over. Norman managed a smile as he bent and talked earnestly to his children. The
autograph seekers watched the scene for a moment, and when
Norman didn't acknowledge their presence, they thought better of
their mission and turned away.

Norman went to the scorer's tent to total and sign his score
card. The computations told him he had shot a 76, one shot worse
than his previous day's 75. That put Norman at seven over par for
the tournament, and in sole possession of last place by four strokes.
There was no cut at the Nabisco, and the last place finishers were
first off the tee the next morning—so they could vacate the course
to the leaders before the television coverage began—and that
meant Norman was due back at a most unglamorous 8:04 A.M.

Norman had flown in from Australia at the beginning of the
week, after playing a string of tournaments on the international
circuit—Nabisco would be his fourteenth and final U.S. tournament, the issue of Norman failing to play fifteen having become
moot after the World Series—and he was tired. But it was more
than fatigue. Norman had been beset by bouts of frustration and
futility in the States since May, and no matter how hard he
smashed a golf ball, or how fast he drove a Ferrari, they kept
coming back.

This was to have been the year Norman would finally dominate the American tour, as he had begun to in 1986, and what
happened? He shot a final-round 64 to finish tied for fifth at the
Masters, turned around the next week and won at Hilton Head,
and then lost two playoffs—making him 1–6 in these contests—
before injuring his wrist at the U.S. Open. He was not in serious
contention again in the States. Norman knew something was
wrong, but he couldn't understand what it was. He had worked
with a coach before returning from his injury, so his mechanics

were good, and his proclaimed confidence ranked second only to his fabled aggressiveness on the course. Looking back at the year, Norman could only attribute it to another string of bad breaks, which, oddly, Norman seemed to suffer more frequently than Job.

Norman had won three times in Australia, once in Europe, and once in the States, and he had earned $461,854 in thirteen appearances here, with seven top-ten finishes. He had the lowest stroke average of anyone on the tour. But this credible record was small change to the man who, although other golfers were closing in on him, had been at the top of the Sony World Rankings for twenty-six months. By definition and mindset, Norman was supposed to be the best golfer in the world, someone who could—at least periodically—dispose of his opponents at will. Norman had played some good golf in 1988, but he had not lived up to what he and other people had expected—especially in the crunch.

What was Norman going to tell Jack Nicklaus, who had all but handed him the scepter and slid over to make room on the throne? And what about the reporters and broadcasters, who had spiced their dispatches with Norman's own words of forceful certainty, and added a few admiring ones of their own? What about his parents, who filled scrapbooks back at home, and his adoring fans?

During his first appearance at the Masters tournament in 1981, Norman had found himself in contention in the final rounds, trailing Jack Nicklaus and Tom Watson by only a few strokes. Norman was a twenty-six-year-old unknown to the American media and, with his good looks and catchy accent, they swarmed him when he materialized on the leaderboard with the potentates of the game. Norman developed an instant taste for the notebooks, cameras, and recorders, and he had a gift for constructing quotable remarks. Reporters asked Norman about his hobbies, and Norman meant to answer that he loved fishing but hated sharks. Somehow Norman's presentation acquired a different spin, however, and he left the reporters with the impression that one of his recreations was shooting sharks while fishing. The reporters, eyeing Norman's peroxide hair, anointed him the Great White Shark in their articles.

The trouble was, Norman had never actually shot a shark. The stories read so nicely though that Norman couldn't bring himself to rectify them, and the moniker, and the image, stuck. The idea of being an imposter gnawed at Norman for months until, on his next trip home, he set out to certify the myth. Norman cast off in his boat and went patrolling for dorsal fins. When he found one several hours later, he shouldered his rifle and blew a hammerhead away. Norman whipped the boat back toward the coast, satisfied that he had lived up to his billing.

Norman shot a 74 on Saturday at the Nabisco Championship, putting him twenty shots off the lead, and a minimum of five shots behind everyone else in the field. Norman was in danger of becoming a nonentity at the tournament. He hadn't been invited to the pressroom all week and, on Saturday, his gallery was smaller than the average extended family. Norman had been playing his rounds quickly, and the consensus at the tournament was that he wanted to get it over with, collect his $32,000 consolation prize—plus bonus—and go home.

Norman got to sleep late on Sunday morning because of the television schedule, and by the time he arrived at the practice range to loosen up for his 9:50 A.M. round he had devised a plan to salvage the tournament. Norman didn't confidently propose to shoot a score in the high 50s, as he had suggested he might do when he was out of contention in Las Vegas. Rather, he concocted a bizarre scheme to set a new record for the fastest round of golf ever played on the PGA Tour. "Fastest round ever" might have been something Guinness recorded, but the tour didn't. Legend had it, however, that the time was just under two hours, and Norman enlisted his playing partner, Mark O'Meara, the caddies, and the volunteer lady scorers who walked with the golfers, in his enterprise.

News of Norman's scheme traveled over the sprawling acres of Pebble Beach quickly, and fans went hurtling over the otherwise vacant course in search of the Shark. New arrivals to the gallery were brought up-to-date on the race, and they joined in the cheering as Norman and his entourage went jogging from shot to shot, with the golfers' clubs banging up and down rhythmically in their bags and the middle-aged scorers struggling to keep up.

Norman's traveling gallery grew to three hundred as he reached the closing holes. People were calling out the elapsed time as the golfers completed each hole, and yelling words of support as passionately as if Norman were approaching his fourth consecutive victory in a major. Norman was smiling broadly inside the ropes as he stopped to align and execute each shot before jogging after his ball. All of the melancholy and discontentment of the season were gone. Norman was back in his realm again, and it was bliss.

Norman and O'Meara figured their round at an hour and twenty-six minutes as they trooped into the scorer's tent to compute their scores. "All right," Norman sang out when they were done, "we both broke eighty." Each of the golfers had shot 79. Norman and O'Meara emerged from the tent to talk to the reporters who were waiting for them, as a huge crowd of mostly youthful admirers hovered nearby. "Give me your name and address and I'll send you a little something," Norman called out to the scorer who had followed him, as she walked off the course. An adjacent scoreboard flashed a message that their official time had been an hour and twenty-four minutes, triggering another roar.

Norman maneuvered through the crowd of fans, accepting their congratulations and doing walk-and-signs as he moved toward the practice putting green, where the golfers who were at the top of the leaderboard were preparing to begin their rounds. "Now it's time for a beer," a young fan called out to Norman. "Well, go get me one," Norman replied, and the man ran off to find a concession stand.

The golfers on the putting green looked up, and more reporters came out of the media room as Norman arrived at the green, looking buoyant and surrounded by a happy, noisy mob. Norman slipped behind the protective gallery ropes to talk with Curtis Strange, who was diligently stroking putts. Strange had led the tournament since the opening gun, and he emitted an aura of intensity as he prepared for the final round. Strange interrupted his work to chat with Norman, and the man who had gone to the concession stand called out excitedly, but futilely, from outside the ropes, "Hey, Greg, here's your beer."

Strange headed for the first tee to begin his final assault, leaving the putting green vacant. Norman drifted back into the crowd, signing autographs, accepting the beer that was thrust at him, and giving quotes as more reporters appeared. A reporter asked Norman if the fans had trouble keeping up with him on the course. "Hell, no," Norman said, gesturing at his flock, "they're still here, look at this. I don't know what they're waiting around for, I've got to go."

But Norman didn't leave. He stood on the walkway of the shopping arcade that surrounded the putting green, surveying the scene and glancing in the windows of the expensive shops. The crowd was thinning as people moved toward the course to join

Curtis Strange's gallery. "Greg," a reporter asked Norman as he lingered there, "what motivated you to run the course today?"

"It was fun and the people loved it," Norman said quickly. It was the first serious question Norman had been asked since leaving the course, and he looked over to judge the reporter's reaction. Seeing that a puzzled look lingered on the reporter's face, Norman tried again. "Look," Norman said quietly, "it's not like we did any harm to anybody."

Norman walked off to his car, where his family and caddie were waiting. Norman did a final interview through the open window of the car, as his caddie kissed a young woman goodbye and told her he would see her again next year, before the car pulled away. Norman would learn later that, on the opposite shore of the Pacific Ocean that day, Seve Ballesteros had won a tournament in Japan. It was Ballesteros's seventh victory of the year, and with it he toppled Norman from the summit of the Sony rankings.

Pebble Beach was Jack Nicklaus's favorite tournament course in the world. He had won five matches there over the past twenty-seven years, including a U.S. Amateur and a U.S. Open. Nicklaus especially liked the second shot on the 8th hole. A golfer had to fly his ball from the jutting edge of the coastline, over a yawning gorge in the plateau where the waters of the bay rolled into a cove, and land it on a tiny, canted green that was encircled with bunkers. Arching a crisp iron shot into that green was like playing darts with the dart board floating on water instead of hanging on a wall. When the Pacific was roaring in the background and a huge gallery was cheering in the foreground, there wasn't a medium-iron shot like it in golf.

Memories like that were uncomfortably vivid for Nicklaus when he returned to Pebble Beach on Sunday of Nabisco week, for Nicklaus established an unsought precedent upon his arrival. Nicklaus came to his beloved course for the first time in his life as a golf eunuch—a man without clubs. Nicklaus was not there to be a ferocious competitor seeking yet another victory; he was there to be a flack.

Nicklaus's personal-service contract with RJR Nabisco provided that, should he not be a contestant, and Nicklaus had not seen the top thirty of the money list in four years, he would participate in the 1988 tournament award ceremony as a Nabisco emissary. The only thing Nicklaus hated more than losing was being excluded from competition. His sole consolation would be telling himself, as he stood at the ceremony on the 18th green in his little red Nabisco blazer, that this was the Jack Nicklaus he didn't know.

Nicklaus had broken the five-million-dollar barrier at the International in August, finishing tied for thirty-fourth, while looking at times like he might make the top ten—until his game got sloppy. That's what always happened now. Nicklaus would play brilliantly for a while and then he would get wild off the tee or clumsy on the greens. There would always be a mob there to witness it, too, and Nicklaus would get angry at himself and embarrassed.

Nicklaus had been in a reflective mood that week after breaking what was virtually certain to be his last record of consequence on the regular tour, and he spent a lot of time ruminating over what he was going to do about his game in the pressroom. Nicklaus vacillated between cutting back on his other commitments to practice more in an attempt to win new glories, and reducing his tournament participation below the limited schedule he currently played and learning to live with the facts. It was the continuation of a monologue Nicklaus had been engaging in before the media since the first real slump in his career, when he was about to turn forty.

Nicklaus was forty-eight years old and, even though he seldom said it publicly, he knew the past was the past. "I don't enjoy shooting 75 any more than you do," Nicklaus told the reporters at the International, while trying to explain why he thought about going further into retirement.

The reporters had laughed and told Nicklaus they'd love to shoot 75—even once. Nicklaus had chuckled gently at them—a bunch of wonderful little amateur golfers—and said, "I guess that would be from the front tees too, wouldn't it?"

Nicklaus knew the media people would never be able to understand what it meant to be Jack Nicklaus, to have your native state name a highway after you while you were still in your prime, and to have people at your own tournament search for you by calling into their two-way radios, "Has anybody seen God?" It was okay if the reporters didn't comprehend, Nicklaus just wanted them to keep asking their questions. As far as Nicklaus was concerned, as long as the sportswriters cared whether he played or not, he could consider himself to be a contender.

Outsiders sometimes asked Nicklaus if he was going to play on the senior tour when he turned fifty, and Nicklaus thought that, in asking the question, they were only displaying their own ignorance. The senior tour was where wonderful older golfers went when they couldn't hack it in the center ring anymore. Nicklaus told the questioners, sure, he'd play a few senior events to help repay his obligations to the game, but he was contemptuous that people thought he should be longing to be there. Christ, his hair wasn't even gray yet.

If Jack Nicklaus were to remove himself from the regular PGA Tour it would be the death of hope. Nicklaus didn't expect to accomplish a lot in the tournaments he played, but, still, you never knew. He could wake up one morning and find the old Jack Nicklaus standing in his cleats, and by the back nine on Sunday afternoon everyone within five miles of the tournament site would be jamming the gallery ropes twenty deep and chanting in unison: "Jack is back. Jack is back. Jack is back." There would be pandemonium as strangers kissed and hugged. The goddamn President of the United States would probably call the pressroom during Nicklaus's victory interview. People all over the country would talk about it for weeks: "Did you see what Jack did?" And he was supposed to want to give up this birthright, this commission? He had assigned his life to golf, and now he was supposed to go gently to the Pepsi Senior Challenge?

Nicklaus finished his regular 1988 season play by making his second consecutive cut, at the Canadian Open, before disappearing into the obscurity of golf course design and business deals—the activities that kept him busy, wealthy and, except for commercials, out of the public eye. Nicklaus was coasting along like another middle-aged mogul and family man until, the week before he had to get his Nabisco red blazer out of the closet for the trip to Pebble Beach, the reporters started calling again.

Nicklaus was looking at some property in Concord, New Hampshire, for a course-development deal in early November. The developers, having paid their million bucks to procure a Nicklaus layout, called the traditional press conference while they had the Golden Bear in town. And the reporters who came asked the customary question: How's your game, Jack? Only this time, instead of saying he was thinking of reducing his schedule because he didn't have time to practice, Nicklaus said he was consulting doctors about his back again, and the doctors might tell him he had to stop playing golf forever.

Stories from the press conference went out over the wire services warning that Nicklaus might never play competitive golf
again. Newspapers across the country ran the wire copy, and writers began calling Nicklaus for follow-up details. Nicklaus told
them he knew he had disk problems, and he was seeing a doctor
in Florida on Monday of Nabisco week for tests and an assessment. The doctor issued a prepared statement on Tuesday saying
Nicklaus had the degenerative back problems that were epidemic
among professional golfers, and that the only time it would trouble Nicklaus was when he played golf.

The reporters called Nicklaus again and he told them the doctor confirmed what he already knew, and that he was going to
consult with a series of doctors—as he had done before over the
years—about the advisability of surgery. Nicklaus said he didn't
know if he would be able to play in the three non-PGA Tour events
he had scheduled for the end of the year. "My body just won't let
me practice enough to be competitive," Nicklaus said, "but I
wouldn't be going through all of this if I didn't think I could play
again."

And so it was that when Nicklaus came to Pebble Beach on
Sunday, he got to spend his time not only in the Nabisco hospitality tent, but also in the interview area of the media room and in
the television announcer's booth. The reporters and broadcasters
wanted a definitive answer about Nicklaus's future in golf and,
once again, Nicklaus was a contender. "Instead of deciding about
the operation," Nicklaus told them, "last Thursday I underwent
six cortisone injections in my back. I feel better in the morning
than I have in years. Maybe this will last a few days, maybe six to
nine months."

"Are you going to play in the Skins Game at the end of the
month?" a reporter asked.

"As of right now, I'm planning to play in it," Nicklaus said,
and then paused to correct himself. There was no point in closing
off the possibility of future questions. "I'm ninety-five percent sure
I'll be there," Nicklaus concluded.

Curtis Strange wore his lucky red shirt on Sunday, but no one
could see it. Strange had the shirt sandwiched over a white turtle-
neck and under a red long-sleeve sweater. A reporter had asked
Strange at the end of his press conference on Saturday night if, as
the tournament leader, he had any superstitious things he did

going into the final round. "If I could do something to make more putts tomorrow I would," Strange said, "but I haven't figured out what it would be." Another reporter asked Strange if he had forgotten about the red shirt he had worn on Sundays for the last year and a half when he was in contention. Strange's face flushed scarlet with embarrassment, and he called out, "See you tomorrow," before hurrying from the room.

Strange had been pleasant but cool in the media room on Saturday, after his lead had diminished three strokes to two to one over the past three days. Strange continually underplayed the importance of the tournament, and the awards that went with it, in his interview. Strange was only trying to keep control. He knew he was going to pull out the red shirt on Sunday, and he knew that he was hungering for the win, but those were going to be his secrets.

In order for Strange to talk to the reporters about anything more than how he had played that day, he would have to think about the long, slow process of winning. And if Strange allowed his mind to wander over that treacherous path, the first thing he would be reminded of was how quickly life can go wrong. A man could be sauntering along happily, doing everything he was supposed to do, when—bam—something he thought was his could be taken away.

After three days of pleasant weather with temperatures in the 60s and mild winds—during which three players shot 64, equaling the number of rounds that had been shot at that score or below in all previous tournament play at Pebble Beach—a powerful storm crept in off the ocean on Sunday afternoon. The temperature dropped as the sky went dark and the winds gusted past thirty miles per hour. Curtis Strange lost his first stroke to par when a tap-in putt on the 4th hole was blown six feet from the cup before Strange could stroke it. The rain reached the course as Strange was arriving at the coastal holes and, within minutes, it was pelting him from what seemed to be ten directions simultaneously, in tremendous sheets. Visibility was reduced to less than one hundred yards and water spurted from under Strange's feet as he walked down the fairways, struggling with an umbrella that was useless against the squall, but that threatened to make him airborne. Strange lost his second stroke to par when, despite his patient and tenacious efforts, his putt skidded just past the hole on the sopping 9th green, his ball throwing up water like a rain tire as it rolled.

Strange was still clinging to his one-shot margin when the

water began pooling heavily on the course and play was suspended finally. Strange birdied the 13th hole when play resumed an hour and a half later, increasing his lead to two. But then on the 17th, Strange dropped a stroke just as Tom Kite was birdieing 18 to tie Strange for the lead. Strange arrived at the 18th green in near-darkness because of the storm delay. His ball was thirty-five feet from the cup. Strange had to drop the putt in one stroke to win. If he could snake the ball over the breaks of the green and make it disappear, incomprehensible things would happen. Strange would become Player of the Year, he would win the Arnold Palmer Award, he would earn the $360,000 grand prize, he would receive a $175,000 bonus for topping the money list, and the tournament he represented in the Nabisco charity competition, the Independent Insurance Agent Open in Houston, would win a $500,000 charity grant. That totaled $1,035,000, plus glory, all riding on one thirty-five-foot putt.

Strange studied the putt for a full minute, from three angles, took a final breath, and approached the ball with his putter in his hand, with the precise gait of a diver stalking out onto the high board. His thoughts were in order; his concentration was pure. Strange was two paces from the ball when he broke stride as a burst of brilliant light suddenly assailed his eyes. A spectator had slipped out a pocket camera, with flash cube attached, and snapped his picture. Strange's shoulders jerked up and his eyes flew to the gallery, but he didn't say a word.

Strange returned to a spot five paces behind the ball, steadied himself, walked his approach, placed his putter behind the ball, looked up to fix the line to the hole in his mind's eye, and—pow—the flash went off again. Strange's mouth fell open before he could set his jaw, and he burned his eyes at the sidelines for an extended moment. Strange turned quickly back to his ball, marked its position and lifted it, before beginning his routine anew.

Strange forced the camera and the anger from his mind. No one was going to take this away from him now. Strange stroked the ball solidly and it rolled thirty feet on line before angling two inches right of the hole. Strange tapped the ball in, setting the stage for a sudden-death playoff, which, because of darkness, would be delayed until Monday morning.

Strange went to his hotel room and tried to watch a movie. He tried to keep busy by packing. He tried doing anything he could to avoid thinking about what was dangling before him, still just out of reach. When it was time to go to bed, Strange crawled between the sheets and pretended not to notice that he was doing more tossing and turning than sleeping. Strange made it through the night, and everything improved instantly when he got to the practice tee in the morning. Strange was back in his element, and he became lost in the task. He didn't think the playoff would last more than a few holes but, like a boxer, he prepared himself to go the distance on the driving range.

Both golfers parred the first playoff hole, the 16th, before coming to the long par-three 17th, a hole on which the backdrop to the green was the Pacific Ocean. The 17th was where Strange had lost his opportunity to win the tournament outright on Sunday, but that was Sunday. Strange dropped his tee shot on Monday eighteen inches from the hole, while Tom Kite put his in a bunker off to the right. Everyone in the gallery conceded the tournament to Strange.

When Strange walked onto the green, he thought, "Okay, I'm going to have to make this." Strange wasn't thinking "I'm going to have to make this to win the jackpot," he was thinking "I'm going to have to make this to prevent Kite from holing his bunker shot and beating me." Kite would hit first, and Strange was worried that if Kite improbably put his ball in the hole, Strange might go into shock, miss his short putt, and lose everything after his decade-long grind. Kite didn't sink his second shot, but Strange did. Strange won everything he wanted, but he had anesthetized himself so thoroughly against the possibility of loss that he walked around the green as numb as though he had just crawled out of a car wreck.

Strange looked off toward the gallery to find someone to hug and be happy with, but Sarah was in Virginia. Then Strange found Duke Butler, the tournament director from Houston who had struggled through difficult times for his tournament in the bad Texas economy. Strange had just won a $500,000 grant for Houston charities, and Butler came charging out onto the course as though the half million was going to him personally. Butler grabbed Strange in a bear hug as Butler struggled to catch his breath. "Lord Almighty," Butler panted, on the verge of tears, and hugged Strange tighter.

Strange began to smile a bit as he and Butler walked down to the 18th green for the awards ceremony—which Jack Nicklaus had managed to escape when the tournament carried over into

Monday. Strange and Butler had to collect their booty and participate in RJR Nabisco's moment before the cameras, which their money had bought them.

Jack Manning, the president of golf marketing at Nabisco, had his oversized checks prepared when Strange and Butler arrived and, after the TV people positioned everyone and checked the sound, Manning stepped to the microphone.

"Well, Curtis, a little overtime, but I think it was worth it. We have a bunch here for you. First, a check for three hundred sixty thousand dollars for winning the Nabisco Championship," Manning said, pushing one end of the four-foot cardboard check facsimile toward Strange, while raising his end up to his chest. As Manning stood there smiling at the camera he could see in his peripheral vision that something was wrong. The outsized red and white check with all those zeros to exemplify Nabisco's prosperity and beneficence to all those upscale viewers at home seemed to be angling down toward the ground. Manning looked left and saw that Strange was balancing his end of the check down by his waist—like his arm was too heavy to raise after all that golf. This wouldn't do at all, the check was obscured from the cameras by the podium in front of the men.

Manning didn't understand why Strange wasn't raising his end of the check—didn't Strange understand that this was the *pièce de résistance* of the biggest, most important promotion in sports history? Manning couldn't holler to Strange, "Hey, Curtis, let's get with the program, will you?" on live television, so he turned toward the camera operators,and called out, "Is that high enough guys? Do you need it up a little more?"

Manning's remarks only nudged Strange, who had a strained smile on his lips, into raising the check slightly. The maneuver had prodded Strange into moving the check incrementally, however, so Manning hollered across the 18th green again, "How's that?" The camera operators motioned that they needed the check to be higher still, and Strange, recognizing that even golf champions have to do a tap dance for the man who doles out the money sometimes, finally relented. He took the check from Manning's hands and raised it over his head.

After Manning gave Strange the oversized $175,000 bonus check, which Strange immediately raised over his head, Manning concluded his presentation by mentioning in passing that there were also some trophies sitting over there on the table for Strange.

"I'm pleased to have played so well that I'm able to go home with the trophies," Strange said when he stepped to the microphone. "I'm kind of speechless. Here it is nine-thirty in the morning and you're giving me all of this . . . trophies and money and stuff."

Strange posed for still photographers with the trophies and went to the interview room. What he really wanted to do was go home. Strange had kept everything under control, and he pulled it off—he had won a new kind of respect for Curtis Strange, 1988's Player of the Year. Now Strange wanted to go find Sarah and let out a whoop. Strange breezed through his press conference, soft-pedaling the fact that he had won $1,147,644 in twenty-four golf tournaments since January, and saying that he couldn't understand why he wasn't more excited. Surely, someone said, it had to affect you that you beat Tom Kite to win this, and Tom Kite is one of your closest friends on the tour.

Strange's shoulders squared off the way they are wont to do when he gets serious about something, and a familiar spark appeared in his eyes. The reporters had finally gotten to a topic that penetrated Curtis Strange to the essence, even when he was tired, distracted, and lonely. "There are some friends you go out to dinner with and some you don't," Strange said. "Tom and I and Christy and Sarah go out to dinner a lot. But when it comes down to Tom standing in the way of me winning a golf tournament," Strange continued as the fearsome half-smile he usually reserves for the closing holes on Sunday appeared on his lips, "it doesn't bother me a bit. He's just one more guy standing between me and winning."

EPILOGUE

Plus Ça Change, Plus C'est la Même Chose

Lee Trevino had another change of heart about the Masters tournament during 1989; he was the first player to accept his 1989 invitation after receiving it. Trevino shot a 67 during his first round to lead the tournament, and he was tied for the lead after the second round before shooting an 81 on Saturday. He finished the tournament in twenty-fourth place, and said that he was looking forward to returning in 1990.

Fuzzy Zoeller's 1988 outburst about the speed of the greens at Augusta prompted the tournament to slow them down slightly in 1989. Zoeller had only four top-ten finishes during 1988, and his game continued to deteriorate in 1989, as his chronic back problems affected his play. He announced at the 1989 Memorial Tournament, where he had a rare second-place finish, that he would reduce his playing schedule in 1990 to accommodate his new vocation as a golf broadcaster for NBC.

Jack Nicklaus made the cut at the 1989 Masters, but he was not able to prevent Tom Watson from displacing him from first place on the career money list at the conclusion of the tournament. Nicklaus had been at the top of the money list for seventeen years.

Greg Norman won two tournaments in Australia in early 1989 and placed second, fourth, and fourth in tournaments in the States that fell before the Masters. Norman shot five over par during the first two rounds of the Masters, then made another final-round charge, moving into a tie for the lead on the 17th hole on Sunday before, as the possibility of victory loomed before him, hitting a poor second shot on the 18th that left him short of the green. Norman bogeyed the 18th to fall into a tie for third.

Sandy Lyle, the 1988 Masters Champion, had a prolonged slump in the States in 1989. After finishing second, second, and third in January and February tournaments, he missed the cut in eight of his next nine U.S. tournaments, including the Masters. The streak of British champions at the Masters was kept alive, however, by Lyle's countryman Nick Faldo. Faldo, who lost the 1988 U.S. Open to Curtis Strange in a playoff, won the 1989 Masters on the second playoff hole. Faldo fanned the flames of the growing U.S.-British rivalry by bringing a cap with a Union Jack on the dome—which he hadn't worn on the course—to the televised awards ceremony and draping it conspicuously over his knee. Masters chairman Horn Hardin did not commit a single faux pas during the winner's 1989 TV interview—he announced prior to the 1989 tournament that he would not take part in any future television proceedings.

Davis Love III, the winner of the 1987 Hilton Head tournament, became a father in June of 1988 when his wife gave birth to a daughter. Love was not in serious contention on the tour over the remainder of 1988. At the end of the 1988 season, Love's father, golf teacher Davis Love, Jr., died at age fifty-three in a tragic airplane crash in Florida. The accident also killed the pilot and two other golf instructors who were accompanying Love's father to a golf school. During 1989, Love finished second in two tournaments, including one that was dedicated to his late father, while also missing a number of cuts, as he remained extremely long, but inaccurate, off the tee.

Fred Couples, the golfer Jack Nicklaus accused of sloth, had ten top-ten finishes in 1988, earning $489,822 but failing to win a tournament. He was quoted in the official 1989 PGA Tour media guide as saying, "I need to practice and play harder," but despite another string of high finishes, he collected no 1989 trophies.

Duke Butler, the director of the tournament held outside of Houston, became a celebrity in PGA Tour TV commercials about RJR Nabisco's charity competition, in which his tournament won $500,000 during 1988. Butler attracted fifteen overseas players to his new tournament time slot of the week before the Masters, a good showing.

The Las Vegas pro-am tournament lost its corporate sponsor— and thus its network television contract—and many of the top players who used to be contestants as well in 1989. The Las Vegas Convention Bureau assumed sponsorship of the match and lowered the tournament's purse to $1.25 million. The Las Vegas purse was once one of the biggest on the tour, but in 1989 the event became just another million-dollar tournament, and many top players avoided it. Without network TV, the tournament was moved to October on the 1990 tour schedule, two weeks before the Nabisco Championship, and Las Vegas tournament organizers hope to attract more name players, who are attempting to make the top thirty on the money list to qualify for the Nabisco jackpot, in 1990. The duration of the tournament was reduced from five days to four for the 1990 event.

Gary Koch, winner of the 1988 Las Vegas tournament, finished fourth at the 1988 British Open, but otherwise had only three top-ten finishes during 1988. His fortunes did not improve during 1989.

The 1989 Dallas tournament was again decided in a playoff, and the participants were again ferried to the first playoff hole in Cadillacs with a police motorcycle escort.

The beginning of TV coverage of Jack Nicklaus's Memorial Tournament was not delayed by the Indianapolis 500 auto race for the first time in years, due to the tournament's new, early May date. The weather for the tournament, as Nicklaus predicted, was not perfect, during a season in which rain replaced intense heat as the dominant weather condition in cities visited by the tour. The vast majority of tournaments during the first half of 1989 had precipitation during at least one round.

Jack Nicklaus played well during the 1989 tournaments he entered, and was in contention during the early rounds of several. As the year progressed and Nicklaus's fiftieth birthday approached, numerous stories were published about how many, and which, Senior PGA Tour events he would participate in.

Deane Beman held a press conference at the 1989 Memorial Tournament, where he was asked again about Seve Ballesteros's drive to reduce the number of tournaments overseas golfers were required to play in the States if they wanted to have open access to the PGA Tour. Beman remained adamant in his protectionism, saying he would not allow Ballesteros to "cherry-pick" the American tour, where Beman had so painstakingly and forcefully created tournaments that were played on fairways overlaid with gold.

Beman was also asked about the new PGA Tour ban on all clubs with U-shaped grooves, effective January 1990. In early 1989, the Royal and Ancient Golf Club of St. Andrews, and the European PGA Tour, issued rulings that conformed with the standing United States Golf Association position: that all square-grooved clubs except Ping Eye 2's were acceptable. When the USGA, which had done additional testing of square-grooved clubs at Beman's request, reaffirmed its position and refused to outlaw any clubs but Ping Eye 2's, Beman and his policy board broke with the rest of the golf world. Beman announced in March of 1989 that *all* square-grooved clubs would be banned on the American tour, not just the Ping clubs. Beman's single-mindedness was expected to create havoc at a time when golf was truly becoming a sport with international competitiveness for the first time. Unless the rest of the world bends to Beman's ruling, which is unlikely, it is anticipated that international players will play one set of clubs on the PGA Tour, and another set everywhere else—including the U.S. majors, which are not part of the PGA Tour.

Karsten Manufacturing Corporation, whose Ping Eye 2 clubs were banned by the USGA, filed a one-hundred-million-dollar lawsuit against the USGA during the summer of 1989. Karsten Manufacturing charged the USGA with violation of antitrust laws and slander. The Royal and Ancient Golf Club—and later the PGA Tour—were also included in the suit.

Wayne Grady, the Australian golfer who finished tied for twenty-fifth at the 1988 Westchester tournament, defeated Greg Norman in a playoff to win the Australian PGA tournament in late 1988. He retained his hot hand into 1989, and captured his first American victory at the 1989 Westchester tournament, before going on to finish second in the 1989 British Open.

Ken Green, the Connecticut native who wanted to win the 1988 Westchester tournament in front of his neighbors, willed a win in the 1989 Greensboro tournament, a match he had lost in a playoff the previous year, to avenge that defeat.

Seve Ballesteros, the winner of the 1988 Westchester tournament, held the lead in the 1989 Masters with nine holes to play, before contributing a ball to the waters of Augusta National in the closing holes to finish in fifth place. Ballesteros also finished tied for third at the 1989 Houston tournament, the only other time he was in contention in the States while playing the reduced schedule of a nonmember of the PGA Tour.

The Westchester tournament was known as the Manufacturers Hanover Westchester Classic for the last time in 1989. The financial institution whose name was in the title withdrew its sponsorship, and was replaced by an automobile manufacturer, which renamed the tournament the "Buick Classic."

During 1988, U.S. Open champion Curtis Strange routinely either won the tournaments he entered or he was not in contention. Outside of his four 1988 victories, Strange finished in the top ten in only two of his twenty-four PGA Tour events. Strange was a changed man in early 1989. He finished third in three tournaments, and fifth in one, while significantly lowering his average number of strokes per round. Strange became a better golfer during the first half of 1989, but he did not wear his red shirt on Sunday, and he did not win a tournament. Then, in June of 1989, Strange was in the hunt going into the final round of the U.S. Open, he put on his red shirt, and he became the first man since Ben Hogan in 1951 to win back-to-back U.S. Opens. The victory earned Strange the cover of *Sports Illustrated*, with the tag line, "Move over Ben." A delighted Strange said in the aftermath of his win that, while his 1988 victory had been for his father, this one was for him.

Among the bounty Strange reaped from his new status in golf was a lucrative, long-term contract with MacGregor Golf Company, whose golf clubs Strange had used since 1984. As part of his MacGregor contract, Strange appeared in magazine advertisements saying, "No one pays me to play MacGregors." In an amazing bit of advertising wizardry, Strange was paid handsomely not for using the company's clubs, but for saying he wasn't paid for using them.

The managers of Sandy Lyle and Nick Faldo asked Deane Beman to meet with their players during the 1989 U.S. Open. Beman granted the request, only to learn later that Seve Ballesteros, other overseas players, and the executive director of the European PGA Tour would be present at the gathering. The contingent of international golfers Beman found at the meeting on Tuesday of Open week told Beman they wanted the fifteen-tournament requirement reduced, with the implied threat that they might stop playing in the States if it weren't. Beman, the master strategist, told the boys he would talk to his policy board and get back to them.

Two weeks later, Beman announced that the tour would consider amending the fifteen-tournament rule in a manner that was quintessential Beman. At the end of the 1989 season, Beman said the tour would vote on whether to reduce the requirement for overseas players to twelve U.S. tournaments—*but*—only nine of those tournaments could be ones of the players' own choosing. If a player decided to play only twelve tournaments, he would select nine tournaments, and Deane Beman would specify the other three tournaments in which he would be required to participate. It was presumed that the assigned tournaments would be chosen from among those that traditionally have relatively low purses and poor attendance by top players. If a player decided to play thirteen tournaments, he would select eleven tournaments and Beman would assign two. If a player decided to play fourteen tournaments, he could select thirteen tournaments and Beman would assign one. And, under the proposal, if a player decided to play fifteen or more tournaments, he would be free to pick and choose among the entire schedule, just as he was before the proposed rules change.

None of the contenders in the 1988 tournament in Curtis Strange's hometown of Williamsburg fared especially well during 1989. Peter Jacobsen improved on history slightly. Jacobsen was not in contention during early 1989, then finished in sixth place at the 1989 U.S. Open, as opposed to twenty-first place in 1988. Two weeks after the 1989 Open, Jacobsen returned to the Western Open in Chicago, where he had lost the 1988 tournament by double-bogeying the seventy-second hole. Jacobsen held on to a tie for the lead through the conclusion of regulation play in the 1989 Western Open, before losing the tournament in the first hole of a playoff. A rock band of PGA Tour members that performs take-offs on popular songs with golf lyrics added, of which Jacobsen is the lead singer, cut a record album at the end of 1988.

Tom Sieckmann, the winner of the 1988 Virginia tournament, finished tied for ninth the week after his victory, but was not in contention again through 1989, despite his assiduous work on his game. Mark Wiebe, who lost in a playoff at the 1988 match, did not win during 1988 or 1989.

Jeff Sluman, the winner of the 1988 PGA Championship, finished eighteenth on the 1988 money list at $503,321, with two top-ten finishes after his win in Oklahoma. Sluman injured his shoulder early in the 1989 season, and then developed appendicitis and had to undergo surgery, keeping him out of contention on the tour during the first half of the year. Willie Wood, the golfer with whom Sluman stayed during the 1988 PGA, lost his wife to cancer during 1989. She was twenty-six.

Ian Baker-Finch, the Australian golfer who was in contention at the 1988 World Series, played in two more U.S. events in the fall of 1988, finishing at 133 on the money list, and earning stand-by status near the bottom of the exemption list for 1989. Based on that standing, Baker-Finch, his wife and new baby moved to Florida in early 1989 and applied for resident alien status with the U.S. Immigration and Naturalization Service. Baker-Finch finished no higher than twenty-fourth, and missed two cuts, during his first five 1989 tournaments, before winning a tournament in Texas in May. The win earned Baker-Finch his tour card and a two-year exemption on the PGA Tour.

Mike Reid, the winner of the 1988 World Series, found some of his beloved adversity during the final round of the 1989 Masters tournament, which was played in a steady rainfall. Reid came out of nowhere on Sunday—as though he were back fantasizing about winning the Masters during a rainy round of golf as a kid—running off a string of four birdies and grabbing the lead in the tournament on the 12th hole, before bogeying the 14th and double-bogeying the 15th by drowning his ball in a pond. Reid finished the 1989 Masters in sixth place.

Tom Watson, the runner-up at the 1988 World Series, came very close to winning his sixth British Open during 1989. Watson led an unusually large contingent of forty-eight Americans—due, some speculated, to a reawakened desire among U.S. golfers to defend their honor in the international game—at the tournament staged at Royal Troon in Scotland. Royal Troon is a course in the British Open rotation of courses on which Americans have traditionally done well, and the weather at the 1989 Open was very un-British: dry, warm, and sunny. But, with an American not having won the British championship since 1983—when Watson had last won there—British bookmakers, in addition to accepting bets on any specific golfers winning the match, were also offering odds against *any* American winning it.

Watson remained in contention until the final holes, when he dropped to fourth place. Greg Norman made yet another final-round charge in a major on Sunday, shooting a course-record 64, and finishing in a tie with fellow Australian Wayne Grady and American Mark Calcavecchia. Six of the top ten spots in the tournament were occupied by Americans—including Fred Couples—at the conclusion of regulation play.

Mark Calcavecchia was a rising young star on the American tour, having won once annually from 1986–88—he finished second to Sandy Lyle at the 1988 Masters—and twice in early 1989. He is a tenacious, colorful and long-hitting twenty-nine-year-old, whom Jack Nicklaus, perhaps hedging his bets on Greg Norman, has said reminds him of the Jack Nicklaus that Nicklaus used to know.

The British Open employs a unique playoff format in which the contestants play four holes, total their scores, and move on to sudden death if there is no winner. Greg Norman stormed into the playoff, birdieing the first two holes, before creating disaster yet again. Norman dropped a stroke on the third hole, and came to the fourth hole tied with Calcavecchia and two shots ahead of Wayne Grady. With a remarkable come-back victory still within reach, Norman put his final drive into a fairway bunker, his second shot into a greenside bunker and, to eliminate any possibility that he might win, he hit his third shot off the course and out of bounds.

Calcavecchia sliced his drive on the final hole into the rough, where the ball hit a spectator and stopped dead, over two hundred yards from the green. Calcavecchia hit a brilliant five-iron out of the rough, under the tremendous pressure, to within six feet of the pin. Calcavecchia then dropped the putt for a birdie to record his first win in a major.

There was considerable irony in Calcavecchia being the man to reclaim honor for the PGA Tour in the British Open. Calcavecchia, who turned professional in 1981, lost his exempt status on the tour during part of 1986, and he occupied himself during the 1986 Honda Classic by serving as a caddie for his friend Ken Green. Calcavecchia regained his exempt status in 1987 and proceeded to win the 1987 Honda Classic—using clubs with square grooves. Having a man who had caddied in a tournament one year win it the next year was all the proof veteran tour players needed to convince them that square grooves had to be outlawed in the States. "Only high-tech, unsporting equipment could allow something like this to happen," they screamed. At the 1989 British Open, Mark Calcavecchia demonstrated that the man who swings the clubs will always overshadow his equipment.

It rained sporadically throughout the 1989 PGA Championship, and Mike Reid responded in character. Reid led the tournament from the first round until the 16th hole of the final round, when he sliced his drive into a lake and fell into a tie. Reid double-bogeyed the 17th to lose the tournament to Payne Stewart. Joining Reid in second place was Curtis Strange who, despite wearing his red shirt, missed the opportunity to win two majors in a single season by one stroke. Strange was assaulted by camera noise during a swing on the closing holes, and he shouted profanity at the photographers on the sidelines after the shot. Strange's curses were picked up by the television microphones and he was later deluged with letters of complaint from TV viewers. Strange issued an apology and paid a fine to the tour office as a result of the incident.

The International tournament in Colorado modified its unorthodox format slightly during 1989, and Greg Norman reversed his 1988 opinion about the event and opted to attend. After suffering repeatedly from poor early-round performances, Norman responded to the International format, in which all the golfers who survive the cuts start even on Sunday morning, by claiming his first 1989 U.S. victory.

Jamie Hutton, the young leukemia victim who visited Norman at the 1988 Hilton Head tournament, continued to make progress in his struggle against his illness. Hutton accompanied Norman at three 1989 tournaments. Hutton's presence didn't assist Norman during the first two tournaments, but at the third, a late-season event in Milwaukee, Norman secured his second 1989 victory in the States. The two U.S. victories, combined with two Australian victories, returned Norman to the top of the Sony World Rankings.

Akron, Ohio, received two bits of good news during 1989. The city learned that it would retain its PGA Tour event—the World Series—in 1990. And the Tokyo-based Bridgestone company, the new owners of Firestone Tire & Rubber, announced that it would return the Firestone headquarters to Akron.

Curtis Strange came to the 1989 World Series with the lowest scoring average on the tour—69.44—and in good position to win the Vardon Trophy that is awarded to the year's low scorer. The Vardon Trophy would have been another prestigious accolade for Strange, but the crown slipped from his fingers while he was in Akron. Strange pulled a muscle in his neck while stretching in bed to hang up a telephone. The injury forced Strange to withdraw from the tournament in midround, which disqualified him from the Vardon Trophy race. The rules for the award require that a golfer have no incomplete rounds during the year.

The 1989 Ryder Cup match was played in Sutton Coldfield, England, in late September. The match, pitting American and European golfers in a three-day tournament in which none of the twenty-four participants earned a cent, was much anticipated. The American team longed to avenge their 1985 and 1987 losses to the Europeans, and the golfing public looked to the competition to establish definitively where the world's best golfers resided. Rather than providing these resolutions, however, the match demonstrated that there is no longer any correlation between golfing ability and nationality. The teams played to a deadlock, with most of the competitors from both teams alternately distinguishing and embarrassing themselves at some point during the proceedings. The tie allowed the Europeans to retain possession of the Ryder Cup until 1991, but few observers took this proprietorship to denote superiority.

RJR Nabisco, which did not sell off massive parts of the corporation in the first year after its ownership changed, continued its lavish sponsorship of the PGA Tour. The Nabisco Championship again concluded the season, with the 1989 tournament purse being increased to $2.5 million. When the million-dollar Nabisco bonus pool was factored in, the money bestowed upon the tournament's thirty competitors was stupefying. Tom Kite, who lost the 1988 Nabisco to Curtis Strange in the playoff, won the 1989 tournament, which was also decided in a playoff. Kite's take for the week was $625,000. When Kite's Nabisco bounty was combined with his winnings from the prior months of the season—during which he won two other tournaments—he became the tour's newest million-dollar man with 1989 earnings of $1,395,278. Kite, who has won thirteen tournaments—none of them majors—during his eighteen years of the tour, surpassed Jack Nicklaus and Tom

Watson to become the new leader of the tour's career list at $5,600,691.

Deane Beman's proposal to reduce the number of U.S. tournaments overseas players would have to play—if the golfers would submit to playing in assigned tournaments—managed to offend the sensibilities of everyone affected. Overseas players recoiled at the prospect of being assigned to tournaments, tournament sponsors blanched at the thought of having golfers conscripted into their events, and Beman's rank and file—but not his stars—denounced the idea of giving foreign players any special considerations. As a result, Beman's proposal was resoundingly defeated by the tour's policy board, leaving the fifteen-tournament rule standing.

Although Beman professed surprise about the reversal, he didn't ascribe the outcome to any inherent flaws in his proposal, or to protectionism on the part of his members. Instead, Beman told reporters at the Nabisco Championship that his board had simply seen through the nefarious intentions of the overseas players— such as Seve Ballesteros—who had pushed for a rules change. "They tried to improve their leverage position," Beman, golf's master strategist, said, "and it just didn't work."

Index